DISRUPTING DEPORTABILITY

DISRUPTING DEPORTABILITY: TRANSNATIONAL WORKERS ORGANIZE

Leah F. Vosko

ILR PRESS

AN IMPRINT OF CORNELL UNIVERSITY PRESS   ITHACA AND LONDON

First published 2019 by Cornell University Press

Library of Congress Cataloging-in-Publication Data

Librarians: A CIP catalog record for this book is available from the Library of Congress.

ISBN 9781501742132 (cloth)
ISBN 9781501742149 (pbk)
ISBN 9781501742156 (pdf)
ISBN 9781501742163 (epub/mobi)

For Sydney & for Gerald

Contents

Acknowledgments

When I embarked on the research culminating in this work, I did not anticipate that my investigation would result in a book. However, as I came to understand the nature and depth of the challenges facing workers laboring transnationally, especially those seeking to organize to minimize threats and acts of removal, I realized that what follows is a story that needs to be told.

Several institutions and organizations provided me with the opportunity, time, and space to write this book, and a number of individuals supported me along the way. Institutionally, I owe a great debt to the United Food and Commercial Workers (UFCW) Canada for granting me access to their archive of materials surrounding the legal cases examined herein and to staff members of Local 1518 in British Columbia (BC), as well as Hastings Law, Vancouver, for helping me navigate their immensity. Although I do not list their names here because many staff members also served as research participants, I extend my sincere thanks to these individuals whose abiding commitment to improving the situation of migrant workers made a lasting impression on me. One individual, however, a nonparticipant who helped pave the way for my research, deserves acknowledgment: Naveen Mehta, UFCW Canada's General Counsel and Director of Diversity & Inclusion. For their financial support, I am likewise grateful to the Canada Research Chairs Program and to York University, especially its Office of the Vice-President Research & Innovation and Faculty of Liberal Arts & Professional Studies, which serves as my institutional home. The idea for this book first took shape at Cornell University, where during a sabbatical I had the pleasure of participating in a yearlong weekly research seminar, "Immigration: Settlement, Integration, and Membership," attended by Cornell faculty across the social sciences and several scholars from elsewhere. I am grateful to all of the participants in this seminar and especially to Michael Jones-Correa, its convener, and to coparticipant Maria Cook, who, along with Lance Compa, also offered me helpful feedback at an early stage, and invited and welcomed me to Cornell.

I initially undertook research for *Disrupting Deportability* in parallel with another project, a collaborative initiative resulting in the coedited volume *Liberating Temporariness: Migration, Work, and Citizenship in an Age of Insecurity* (2014). In connection with this project, I had countless helpful conversations with my coeditors and close York-based colleagues Valerie Preston and Robert

Latham, as well as the contributors to *Liberating Temporariness* and an allied seminar on this theme. Along the way, I also benefited from many exchanges with, and input from, another wonderful York-based colleague, Eric Tucker: Eric's advice was always spot on, and his challenging yet consistently encouraging comments made a huge difference to me. Outside York, I am similarly grateful to William Walters, who read segments of the manuscript and offered instructive input and critique at an important moment in the writing process, and to Katherine Lippel for her ongoing interest and polite prodding about the progress of the project.

Many colleagues, both within and beyond the academy, invited me to present research related to *Disrupting Deportability* and/or attended presentations and offered critical feedback: I thank, in particular, Adelle Blackett, Barbara Cameron, Christina Gabriel, Amanda Glasbeek, Luin Goldring, Jennifer Hyndman, Barbara Neis, Chris Ramsaroop, and Deirdre Walsh. I also benefited—and learned a great deal—from interacting with the graduate research assistants who tenaciously helped me locate, organize, and navigate the large volume of documentation on which the analysis in this book relies. Nicole Bernhardt, Tyler Chartrand, Olena Lyubchenko, Corey Ranford, and Cynthia Spring each assisted me at vital stages—and I thank them for their diligence and commitment. Additionally, as I wrote *Disrupting Deportability*, I had the pleasure of working with four outstanding administrators—Kim McIntyre, Alice Romo, Heather Steel, and Aparna Sundar—whose support for allied projects gave me the space to complete the manuscript. And after submitting the manuscript, I received insightful anonymous reviews from external referees and members of the ILR's external editorial board, as well as valuable editorial support from Fran Benson. Subsequently, I was delighted to discover the wonderful photographic work of BC-based Cheryl Wiens, which appears on the front cover. As Cheryl explained to me, this image depicts a temporary migrant worker in a BC raspberry field at the end of the season. By capturing the jacket at the end of the row together with the worker who is visible but at a distance from it, the image conveys the transnational realities of workers' employment situations, the loneliness and isolation flowing from them, and the deportability upon which they rest. I am grateful to Cheryl for permitting me to use her photograph in this work.

Fortunately, I have an incredibly supportive network of family and friends and, in the case of this project, a welcoming BC family. I thank my sister, Judith Vosko, and her family for supporting me as I pursued the fieldwork for this project and, more generally, for their love and support. I am also eternally grateful to my mother, Phyllis Vosko, for her unending love and encouragement and for putting up with the lengthy absences of her grandson, and to my father-in-law, Morry Kernerman, for his consistent enthusiasm for my research and for always engaging me in stimulating conversations on related subjects. This project would never have come to pass were it not for my dear friend Kathy McGrenera (aka Auntie Kathy) and her community (especially my Elise McGrenera and Nancy Marion), who embraced much of my extended family, summer after summer, as I conducted fieldwork. In Vancouver, my fantastic friends Jacky Coates, Marjorie Cohen, Sylvia Fuller, Brenda Kilpatrick, and Michelle Dodds, never ceased being interested in my research. Likewise, back East, several of my friends, especially Deborah Clipperton, May and Dan Friedman, Mary Gellatly, Deena Ladd, Stacey Mayhall, Kiran Mirchandani, Laurell Ritchie, Lisa Roy, Renuka Satchithananthan, Peter Unwin, and Marion Werner, never failed to listen attentively to the story I seek to tell in this book.

I began the research for *Disrupting Deportability* when my dear son, Sydney Lev Vosko-Kernerman, was an infant. Sydney and his loving Aba, my life partner Gerald Kernerman, enthusiastically encouraged me at each and every stage of the research and writing process. They even joined me in the field—where they gave their all to the (fruit and vegetable) picking, eating, and processing that my research generated. I dedicate the book to them in the hope that the world in which Sydney grows up becomes kinder, gentler, and infinitely more open and welcoming to those among us compelled and/or motivated to move across borders.

Tables

Figures

Abbreviations

BCAC	British Columbia Agricultural Council
BCCA	BC Court of Appeal
BC SC	British Columbia Supreme Court
CA	collective agreement
CFU	Canadian Farmworkers Union
CIC	Citizenship and Immigration Canada
ESA	Employment Standards Act (British Columbia)
ESDC	Employment and Social Development Canada
FARMS	Foreign Agricultural Resource Management Services (FERME in Quebec)
HRSDC	Human Resources Development Canada
ILO	International Labour Organization
IOM	International Organization for Migration
IRCC	Immigration, Refugees, and Canadian Citizenship Canada
LMIA	Labour Market Impact Assessment
LRB	Labour Relations Board (British Columbia)
LRC	Labour Relations Code (British Columbia)
MOL	Ministry of Labor and Social Provision (Mexico)
MOU	memoranda of understanding
NGO	nongovernmental organization
OECD	Organisation for Economic Co-Operation and Development
SAWP	Seasonal Agricultural Worker Program
SCC	Supreme Court of Canada
STPS	Mexican Secretariat of Labor and Social Welfare
TFWP	Temporary Foreign Worker Program
TMWP	temporary migrant work program
UFCW	United Food and Commercial Workers Union
UNESCO	United Nations Educational, Scientific, and Cultural Organization
WALI	Western Agricultural Labour Initiative

DISRUPTING DEPORTABILITY

Introduction

In the age of migration management, temporary migrant work is a significant phenomenon in many OECD countries where relative labor shortages fuel demands for temporary migrant work programs (TMWPs) that provide comparatively low labor standards and wage levels. In this context, workers laboring transnationally in such programs are turning to unions for assistance in attempt to realize and retain access to rights. Yet even those engaged in highly regulated TMWPs permitting circularity—or repeated migration experiences involving one or more instances of emigration and return (Wickramasekara 2011)—confront significant obstacles tied to their deportability.

Rising to dominance at the turn of the twenty-first century, migration management is a global policy paradigm fostering such ordered transnational movements of workers presumed to be achievable with coordination between the sending and host states of migrants, often with the involvement of intergovernmental organizations. Its goal is to channel (legally authorized) migration flows through multiple arrangements (Piché 2012). To reconcile increasing emigration pressures in lower-income countries with dwindling opportunities for the legal entry of workers perceived to be "low skilled" (Ghosh 2012, 26) in higher-income countries, this paradigm promotes TMWPs. Accordingly, the overall ranks of temporary migrant workers grew significantly in the OECD after 2003, dropped briefly around the 2008–2009 recession, and regained buoyancy shortly thereafter, rebounding quite strongly in Australia, Canada, New Zealand, and the United States (appendix 1, table A.1; OECD 2010, 31; OECD 2012, 35; OECD 2014, 24–25).[1]

With migration management in ascendancy, the conditions of work and employment of many workers laboring transnationally are governed by intergovernmental agreements, policies, and guidelines overseen by empowered actors such as sending- and host-state officials (e.g., consular employees and staff of ministries of labor and immigration) as well as often representatives of intergovernmental organizations and employer associations. The Canadian context insofar as it is characteristic of analogous high-income countries in the OECD that rely on such (typically bilateral) arrangements to regularize temporary migration for employment has maintained a high proportion of temporary migrant workers throughout their existence. The Canadian experience illustrates how, despite an apparent commitment to a "triple win" for workers, sending states, and host states, this paradigm benefits powerful host states disproportionately, and particularly employers therein. Though migration management does not prescribe overt and highly punitive forms of discipline, in operation it safeguards host-state employers' access to low-waged labor while limiting unregulated (or "illegal" or "irregular") migration and ensuring that temporary migrant workers remain deportable. In the face of this heightened vulnerability, in contexts in which unionization is permissible such as in British Columbia (BC), Canada, some temporary migrant workers are managing to organize and bargain collectively, partly in an attempt to limit the possibility of removal.

This book tells the story of one such group: Mexican nationals participating in a subnational variant of Canada's model of migration management program, the Seasonal Agricultural Worker Program (SAWP). It explores how these workers organized to circumvent deportability, but despite achieving union certification, securing a collective agreement (CA), and sustaining a bargaining unit, ultimately remained vulnerable to threats and acts of removal. To summarize the case: in 2008, temporary migrant workers engaged by Sidhu & Sons Nursery Ltd. in BC sought to unionize with the support of Local 1518 of the United Food and Commercial Workers Union (UFCW).[2] Two years later, BC's Labour Relations Board (LRB), the independent administrative tribunal enforcing provisions of its Labour Relations Code (LRC), certified Local 1518 as the representative bargaining agent for a unit composed exclusively of this group of temporary migrant workers. Subsequently, the parties reached a first CA through arbitration. Although restrictive in many ways, this CA—motivated by union members' concerns to prevent both unjust termination, which typically prompts immediate repatriation, and contract nonrenewal—introduced timely grievance and arbitration procedures and novel terms that extended season-to-season seniority to circular migrant workers.

In the season after this CA came into force, however, the future of the bargaining unit was called into question, and some union members were prevented from returning to Canada. Meanwhile, a few senior SAWP employees made a dubious application for decertification. In response, Local 1518 filed an unfair labor practices complaint with the LRB in 2010. In its complaint, the union asserted, first, that three parties—the employer, "certain employees" (all SAWP participants who applied for decertification), and Mexican officials—interfered with the bargaining unit complement by blocking the visa reapplications of union members otherwise eligible for recall under the CA.[3] Second, Local 1518 contended that these parties inappropriately intervened in a decertification application by threatening and then engaging in the blacklisting of union supporters. In a move noteworthy for its potential to draw attention to practices of the multiple actors involved in the design, administration, and day-to-day oversight of TMWPs, the union attempted to call to account not only the employer in the host state and certain employees but also Mexican officials. In response, the state of Mexico argued successfully to the provincially based LRB that, as a sovereign state, it was immune from the proceedings of this tribunal (BC LRB 2012a). The sending state was, however, unsuccessful in having factual evidence related to this action suppressed in the adjudication of Local 1518's complaint against the two remaining parties.[4] In hearing the union's complaints, adjudicators considered the conduct of Mexican officials in establishing the facts, and after a protracted set of hearings, they concluded that the decertification vote was unlikely to have disclosed employees' true wishes. Although the LRB did not find sufficient evidence that either the employer or certain employees had committed unfair labor practices, in an unprecedented acknowledgment of SAWP employees' deportability and how it can impinge on the exercise of collective bargaining rights, suggesting that Mexican officials had likely threatened and participated in blacklisting of assumedly pro-union employees, based on information likely obtained from the employer or certain employees, the LRB refused to count the decertification vote (BC LRB 2015, para. 80). Its ruling thereby left the bargaining unit intact, but, as future developments would show, highly vulnerable as well.

In subsequent years, bargaining unit members confronted the mounting problem of attrition, resulting in a decrease in membership numbers and thus raising the threat of the unit's dissolution. It is the employer's prerogative under the SAWP to adjust the size and composition of its temporary migrant workforce at any time for virtually any reason. In this instance, both overt and more subtle efforts to reduce the size of its workforce by another BC employer (Floralia Plant Growers Ltd.), where Local 1518 also represented a bargaining unit encompassing SAWP employees, highlighted the various forms attrition may take.[5]

Looking through the rare window into deportability offered by this case, in these pages, I chronicle the effects of this social condition, characterized by the possibility of removal, on the exercise of labor rights by temporary migrant workers with the prospect of return. The experiences of the SAWP employees of Sidhu, together with those of Floralia, highlight the means through which sending- and host-state officials, together with host-state employers, can thwart access to labor rights participants among TMWPs that permit circularity where unionization is technically possible. Collectively, they show that, as it applies to TMWP participants with the prospect of return, deportability is an essential condition of possibility for migration management, despite its stated commitments to human, social, and civil rights. In practice, because of the paradoxical nature of human rights, the principles to which migration management aspires do not—and indeed could never—apply fully to noncitizens in an interstate system characterized by sovereignty. Thus, TMWPs, such as the SAWP, which are perceived to represent "best practices," simultaneously sustain this approach to governing migration and represent its limit.

Giving substance to this argument, the following chapters highlight the utility of disaggregating practices frequently subsumed under the banner of deportability, focusing on those inhibiting meaningful collective representation among temporary migrant workers with the prospect of return. The unique empirics surfacing in the case of SAWP employees at Sidhu—alongside those emerging in the related case of SAWP employees at Floralia—make it possible to bring into view how deportability operates among participants in a TMWP cast as a model of migration management. They open space for examining its "modalities" or the "particular mode[s] in which . . . [it] . . . exists or is experienced or expressed" and reveal the significance of three modalities (*Oxford Dictionary of English* 2010).[6] The first is the prospect of termination without just cause, prompting repatriation during a preestablished seasonal employment contract and/or the denial of future participation on the receipt of a negative employer evaluation. A second modality, the possibility of blacklisting, involves the application of a cluster of overlapping administrative practices that can contribute to expulsion from a TMWP that permits circularity: this modality can confront employees perceived to be pro-union before or during an organizing drive or union members who have successfully organized and whose union is either negotiating or has reached a CA with the respective employer. The third modality of attrition, made possible by employers' prerogative to alter the size and composition of their temporary migrant workforces, is particularly threatening to participants who manage to unionize, including those with CAs containing provisions relating to recall based on season-to-season seniority.

While these modalities surface in chronicling workers' efforts to limit threats and acts of removal through unionization, such efforts, which take bold expression in the case examined here but are by no means unique to it, also point to possibilities for forging change not only in the BC and Canadian contexts but also elsewhere. Indeed, the investigation of these modalities illustrates the importance of providing concrete means to attain more secure employment and residence status: in the here and now, having greater routes to permanent residency and, at a minimum, open work permits and other means of fostering labor mobility on a stable basis (i.e., predictable ongoing opportunities for seasonal employment characterized by decent working conditions) and on protected grounds (e.g., by enabling unions to apply for work permits to assist in matching workers with suitable eligible employers, and ensuring that decent terms and conditions of employment are enforced). With regard to rights to organize and bargain collectively specifically, charting employees' experience of deportability before, during, and after a unionization drive underscores the need not only for formal certification of bargaining units encompassing TMWP participants (e.g., SAWP employees) but also for the adoption of grievance and arbitration procedures, and of processes for the acquisition of seniority and eligibility for recall, suitable to and enforceable among workers laboring transnationally. It also highlights the potential of scaling up provisions of CAs, created with temporary migrant workers in mind, to the level of intergovernmental agreements, policies, and guidelines governing TMWPs such as the SAWP. More broadly, discerning the *how* of deportability underscores the importance of upholding labor rights in the design and administration of TMWPs in a manner that reduces rather than reinforces dissonances between immigration and labor laws, policies, and practices shaping modalities of deportability, dissonances that are by no means unique to the experience of the temporary migrant workers chronicled here.[7]

Structure of the Book

By exploring the legal struggle engaged in by seasonal migrant agricultural workers who labor transnationally to obtain and maintain meaningful access to collective representation, this book traces processes and practices, normally hidden from view, that foster deportability and struggles against it. The examination of deportability, and the modalities through which it operates and is thereby lived, unfolds in four chapters that offer a critique of migration management as it takes shape in relatively high-income host states and relatively low-income sending states. A conclusion, identifying alternative policy directions to bring about improved working conditions for migrant workers, follows.[8]

Initiating this exploration, chapter 1, "Deportability among Temporary Migrant Workers: An Essential Condition of Possibility for Migration Management," develops this argument: as it applies to participants in a TMWP permitting circularity, deportability is a fundamental condition of possibility for, rather than an anathema to, migration management. The chapter provides both a critical review of the global policy discourse on migration management and a survey of the multiplying forms of temporary migration for employment in the OECD to which it gives rise; it then locates Canada's SAWP within this paradigm and identifies the workers' rights it suppresses. Through these avenues, the chapter illustrates how deportability is a means of (direct and indirect) control fundamental to this TMWP. Subtle processes and practices contributing to TMWP participants' deportability are nevertheless difficult to identify and document. In response, this book draws on "feminist objectivity," a methodological approach delineated in chapter 1 that aims to expand and transform "ways of seeing" by attending to fragmentary and contextualized forms of knowledge that enable a greater understanding of social phenomena (Haraway 1988). Informed thus by feminist objectivity and laying the groundwork for the exploration of challenges faced by SAWP employees at Sidhu in their legal struggle to realize and retain their access to rights, chapter 1 concludes by elaborating the foremost modalities of deportability operating in this case.

To re-create a narrative highlighting processes and practices not otherwise traceable (i.e., the *how* of deportability), chapters 2 to 4 address three main stages in the struggle of SAWP employees at Sidhu to exercise their rights to organize and bargain collectively in response to the three modalities of deportability made visible through the legal challenges leveled by their union. Chapter 2, "Getting Organized: Countering Termination without Just Cause through Certification," documents the attempts of the union representing SAWP employees at Sidhu to organize, gain certification, and secure a first CA for a bargaining unit encompassing participants in a TMWP permitting circularity. Through an analysis of the legal proceedings surrounding UFCW Local 1518's bid for certification, it explores SAWP employees' two important motivations for organizing: namely, to preempt termination without just cause prompting premature repatriation and to secure mechanisms for recall suitable to workers laboring transnationally. The chapter focuses on how, in the context of the employer's hostility to agricultural workers' organizing and obstacles to organizing domestic agricultural workers at the same workplace, the LRB came to certify a bargaining unit comprised exclusively of SAWP participants at Sidhu.

Chapter 2 demonstrates that Local 1518, in seeking to represent SAWP employees, faced challenges stemming both from outmoded assumptions underpinning the framework for labor relations in the LRC and from in-built features of the SAWP that confound central tenets of this legislation. On the one hand, as is typical of other jurisdictions in Canada and elsewhere in North America, a central aim of BC's LRC—and one that is often underscored by its associated tribunal—is to foster industrial stability, albeit alongside its twin goal of facilitating access to collective bargaining. This aim contributes to the LRB's preference for all-employee or "wall-to-wall" bargaining units. It is reinforced by the norm upon which the operation of the LRC pivots—a native-born male in industry, engaged typically in a full-time ongoing employment relationship with one employer, who resides permanently in one geographic location in a single country in which he normally holds national citizenship. However, this preference does not align well with the transnational realities (Fleras 2014) faced by temporary migrant workers engaged habitually in seasonal employment and holding only temporary residency status and rights to work in their place of employment. This is especially true for those issued work permits that tie their rights to be in a host state to specific employers. Yet, as an (im)migration program, the SAWP is premised on meeting employers' demands for a consistent yet flexible supply of low-waged workers in sectors characterized by persistent labor shortages (i.e., where Canadian workers are deemed to be unavailable), partly by providing them with the unconstrained right to terminate (and hence repatriate) TMWP participants.

In its attempt to obtain certification for a unit of SAWP employees, Local 1518 thus came up against tensions arising both from the LRB's understanding of its role of facilitating access to collective bargaining under the LRC, which was tied to its approach to determining an appropriate bargaining unit, and from limits posed by the parameters of the TMWP in play. Consequently, the unit obtained certification, but only on a restricted basis: certain monetary items and items governing the transnational flow of labor were the main subjects of collective bargaining, and the first CA between Sidhu and Local 1518 did not cover the full range of areas addressed typically in such agreements. At the same time, it introduced mechanisms aiming to limit termination without just cause prompting premature repatriation and offered novel provisions on recall and seniority. Reflecting the logic—and indeed the limit—of migration management, in the final analysis, the SAWP nevertheless was able to override CA provisions secured for TMWP participants by their union. These SAWP employees' experience of seeking and securing collective representation thus illustrates how agreements between states facilitating international migration for employment on temporary yet repeated bases depend on temporary migrant workers' deportability, so that unions' efforts to mitigate its foremost modalities—in this first instance, to limit threats and acts of termination without just cause—are impeded from the start.

After SAWP employees at Sidhu gained certification, union members returned to Mexico at the completion of their seasonal employment contract, having been notified that Canada had approved their visas and feeling confident that their right to continue their employment with this employer had been secured under the CA.

Yet several were denied the possibility of return. Chapter 3, "Maintaining a Bargaining Unit of SAWP Employees: The Challenge of Blacklisting," probes the *how* of this second modality of deportability. It explores the challenges faced by those SAWP employees at Sidhu who were perceived to be pro-union by sending-state officials, based presumably on information gleaned from their employers, in being able to return to the host state for successive seasonal employment contracts, despite their eligibility for recall under their first CA.

The chapter chronicles complaints of unfair labor practices, coercion, and intimidation that were pursued by Local 1518, which challenged the blacklisting directly and indirectly; the union's efforts revealed the climate of fear at the workplace (i.e., the threat of dismissal from future employment) and documented practices of blacklisting. The chapter also explores how the union exposed interference by Mexican officials, such as consular employees, who were effectively compelled to prioritize securing remittances over fulfilling their responsibility to foster the smooth functioning of the SAWP for the mutual benefit of workers and employers. This hard evidence of improper interference allowed Local 1518 to successfully dispute a decertification application, which had been pursued by certain SAWP employees selected for readmission for a subsequent season in the wake of the blacklisting affair. The analysis underscores how, while the LRB only considered Mexican officials' conduct in establishing the facts of the case after dismissing the union's complaints against this sovereign sending state, blacklisting can function among temporary migrant workers with the prospect of return; it identifies possibilities—in this instance, provided under the SAWP and representing a fundamental limit of CAs—for sending states, seeking to appease host-state employers, to cultivate a climate of fear and/or prevent repeat temporary emigration through various blocking practices. In the face of such sending-state action, chapter 3 also illustrates that, through the delegation of key roles and responsibilities and, hence, authority (e.g., those related to the oversight of readmission processes and aspects of documentation) normally undertaken by host-state officials to actors outside their purview, even a sympathetic labor relations tribunal can be prevented from implementing host-state labor laws within its purview, despite indubitable evidence of their evasion on the part of a sending state. In this case, the LRB could do little to address unprincipled (and otherwise presumably unlawful) actions tied to blacklisting and their effects on temporary migrant workers with the prospect of return.

Chapter 4, "Sustaining Bargaining Unit Strength: The Specter of Attrition," considers challenges to maintaining strong bargaining units posed by threats of attrition, either through formal decertification or by other means producing similar outcomes. The chapter first documents trends in numerical attrition at Sidhu, in the context of Canada's introduction of other more highly deregulated

TMWPs operating in agriculture and those programs' subsequent growth. The size of the bargaining unit at Sidhu, comprised of SAWP employees exclusively, shrank after certain employees' attempt to decertify it, despite the fact that the LRB had refused to cancel its certification. Given the absence of an active attempt to decertify the bargaining unit, it is nevertheless difficult to determine how attrition continued at Sidhu. To demonstrate the *how* of this often subtle modality of deportability, the chapter chronicles strategies fostering attrition in the bargaining unit encompassing SAWP employees at Floralia, which, as chapter 3 demonstrates, the union originally tried to draw into the foregoing complaint of unfair labor practices and coercion and intimidation directed at Sidhu.

This examination of developments at Floralia helps uncover the various forms this modality can take. It demonstrates that strategies directed at attrition can range from undue interference in a decertification vote and the manipulation of seniority-based recall processes codified in CAs but managed, in practice, by officials of sending and host states, to engage non-unionized employees via another entity (e.g., direct employers of other seasonal agricultural workers who may or may not themselves be SAWP participants). In the case of Floralia, in 2015, a disputed attempt at decertification was ultimately unsuccessful because the LRB ruled that a group of recently arrived SAWP employees did not have the ability to exercise genuine "choice" (i.e., of representation) in casting their votes. The decision suggested that there had been undue interference on the part of the employer and that, if these bargaining unit members had been able to vote freely, they would not have voted to decertify. Still, even though the LRB forestalled this formal attempt at decertification, evidence surfacing in a subsequent unfair labor practice complaint launched by Local 1518 after its certification was restored shows that this employer engaged in other, more deceptive tactics aimed at diluting bargaining unit strength, which were more difficult to document.

Such tactics included actions that the LRB deemed to be unlawful under BC's LRC. One such tactic was the manipulation of the recall process, facilitated by institutional mechanisms of the SAWP that can operate at cross-purposes with labor relations tribunals' typical approach to the restoration of bargaining units (i.e., elements of program design and operation governed by an agreement between the sending and host state that provide employers flexibility in adjusting the size and composition of their temporary migrant workforces). In addition, non-unionized employees of a separate entity were hired to perform the work of the employees in the bargaining unit. The analysis in chapter 4, which assesses the state of the bargaining unit at Floralia as a means of investigating the dynamics of attrition in a context akin to that at Sidhu, where the employer seemingly sought to replace SAWP employee bargaining unit members with temporary migrant workers participating in another highly deregulated stream of Canada's

TFWP that technically fell outside the circumscribed bargaining unit, thus highlights the multiple strategies available to employers in pursuit of attrition. It thereby underscores the significance of this modality of deportability for temporary migrant workers with the prospect of return, including unionized SAWP employees with unique seniority-based CA rights to recall. While attrition is of a different order than termination without just cause and explicit threats and acts of blacklisting, as a modality of deportability it can be decisive in achieving similar and potentially more far-reaching ends. Attrition can lead to dismissal from future employment for sizable groups of SAWP employees with the prospect of return and can constrain access to rights among temporary migrant workers more broadly.

Having investigated the struggle of SAWP employees at Sidhu to exercise their rights to organize and bargain collectively in confronting threats and acts of termination without just cause, blacklisting, and attrition, the book concludes by reflecting on the significance of their legal case for expanding understandings of the meaning of deportability and its applicability to TMWP participants laboring not only in Canada but also in other relatively high-income host states embracing migration management and the measures it prescribes. Emphasizing that deportability is a fundamental feature of migration management, the conclusion contends that if temporary migrant workers emigrating from low-income countries that rely on remittances gained from wealthier countries are to have the genuine possibility of realizing their rights, there is a need both to envision alternatives based on an understanding of deportability's modalities and to begin to implement changes viable within the horizon of possibility. While acknowledging that obstacles to limiting deportability writ large will inevitably remain as long as migration management prevails, given its prioritization of the interests of substantive socioeconomic beneficiaries (Mundlak 2009), the conclusion calls for labor policies that hold such beneficiaries more accountable. It advocates scaling up innovative features of CAs and other forward-looking practices that enable temporary migrant workers' collective representation for inclusion in intergovernmental agreements and calls for their implementation via policy design and administration at the inter-, host-, and sending-state levels. Making interventions aimed at curbing—and thereby disrupting—deportability among temporary migrant workers, the book puts forward promising avenues for transcending dissonances between immigration and labor laws, policies, and practices shaping modalities of deportability addressed to the here and now.

1

DEPORTABILITY AMONG TEMPORARY MIGRANT WORKERS

An Essential Condition of Possibility
for Migration Management

In 2010, with the support of UFCW Local 1518, SAWP employees of the BC-based Sidhu & Sons unionized successfully after a lengthy and contentious series of engagements. Though not the first in the province to encompass temporary migrant workers, the resulting bargaining unit was unique in covering a group of SAWP employees exclusively. So too was the unit's first CA, which sought to address key challenges stemming from the deportability faced by union members laboring under a TMWP in which repeated seasonal employment contracts, and hence migration experiences, are allowable. And yet after surviving for nearly a decade and with its employer continuing ostensibly to rely heavily on temporary migrant workers, this bargaining unit faced an uncertain future due to threats and acts of removal deployed by a wide array of institutions and actors against its members on an ongoing basis.

This chapter develops the contention at the heart of this book—surfacing in the close empirical analysis of this case examined in subsequent chapters—that deportability, as it applies to participants in a TMWP permitting circularity, is an essential condition of possibility for migration management. Under this paradigm, TMWPs, such as the SAWP, which are perceived to represent "best practices" by, for example, offering participants the prospect of return, simultaneously sustain this approach to governing migration and represent its limit, including in contexts in which unionization is permissible. The legal struggle of SAWP employees of Sidhu to unionize, secure a first CA, and maintain bargaining unit strength gives substance to these claims. It reveals how deportability is lived among temporary migrant workers and the central modalities through which it functions. As such, these SAWP employees' experience provides rich empirical evidence for a grounded critique of migration management revealing that, despite its call for "regulated openness," this global policy paradigm introduces new modes of control.

Preparing the ground for the investigation of the legal struggle of SAWP employees of Sidhu to follow, the ensuing investigation proceeds in four parts. In the first section, it describes and critiques the embrace of migration management in global policy discourses. By endorsing greater authority for new actors and institutions in the absence of accountability mechanisms and by supporting policies and practices stemming from technical considerations, the analysis suggests that migration management introduces more indirect or subtle modes of control, rather than advancing its stated goal of providing for greater openness.

In classical immigration countries of the OECD, the expansion of temporary migration for employment is central to the widespread embrace of migration management and bears significant responsibility for the construction of immigration as a "net positive" for all parties involved. The second section sketches the dynamics of this phenomenon in several such countries, considering the forms temporary migration for employment takes with a focus on the circular variety; it then probes how these forms take shape in Canada, placing an accent on the evolution of the country's flagship TMWP in agriculture and describing its design and operation. This portrait of temporary migration for employment to Canada also assesses the limits and possibilities afforded by labor and employment laws and policies applicable to SAWP employees in light of dissonances between this body of labor law and policy and immigration law and policy. On this basis, section two then questions whether the SAWP is indeed an example of best practices from the perspective of workers' rights, highlighting the TMWP's reliance on the new modes of control integral to migration management outlined in the first section.

Having identified such modes of control and begun to chart their effects on SAWP employees, section three explores deportability's import in an era in which migration management dominates paradigmatically, particularly the significance of this notion in describing the social condition not only of undocumented migrant workers but also of legally authorized temporary migrant workers with the prospect of return and thereby in understanding impediments that they face in gaining meaningful collective representation. A related goal of this section is to delineate and rationalize the methodological approach and methods adopted in chapters 2–4 by locating the inquiry vis-à-vis three bodies of literature on which the book builds: theoretically oriented scholarship on deportability; critical analyses of TMWPs, especially those pertinent to the SAWP, including sociological and legal/policy analyses; and inquiries into the political economy of labor migration to Canada.

In its focus on how deportability functions in practice, the following chapters' exploration of the legal struggle of SAWP employees at Sidhu nevertheless departs from the procedures for inquiry and empirical emphases of the forgoing three complementary bodies of literature. Deportability, as it affects temporary migrant workers with the prospect of return, such as SAWP employees, often operates through subtle processes and practices that are difficult to document by using standard methodological approaches and singular research methods. In response, this inquiry adopts a methodological approach often labeled as "feminist objectivity." Committed to reflexivity and open to contestation, feminist objectivity pursues critical knowledge that is context sensitive and necessarily partial: it offers a window into greater understanding, rather than achieving a panoramic perspective, with the larger goal of transforming "ways of seeing" (Haraway 1988, 584–585). In building a case study based on this approach, chapters 2–4, which comprise the body of the book, draw on mixed methods to make visible practices and processes that are normally hidden from view, but nevertheless foster deportability and struggles against it. In this way, they seek to illuminate deportability's inner workings. Together, these methods offer a window into how the institutional design and administration of this TMWP, shaped by both immigration and labor laws and policies, as well as the interpretation and implementation of its central provisions and especially the practices to which they give rise, structure participants' field of action.

Finally, section four delineates three central modalities—termination without just cause; blacklisting of union supporters normally prompting dismissal from future employment in the host state (i.e., expulsion); and attrition within migrant workforces, including those with formal rights to organize and bargain collectively that have achieved unionization—through which deportability is experienced by participants in TMWPs permitting circularity. It thereby sets the stage for chapters 2–4, which analyze each modality through an investigation of the legal struggle of the SAWP employees at Sidhu and the related struggle of SAWP employees at Floralia.

Migration Management: Discourses, Actors, Practices, and "New" Modes of Control

The early twenty-first century has been marked by the ascendancy of an approach characterized in the global policy discourse as "migration management." For Bimal Ghosh (2000), the first to give the notion analytical precision, migration management is meant to entail, and convey, managing for more orderly, predictable, and humane migration objectives that are only possible through global coordination. Efforts to manage migration are not new (Torpey 2000; Salter 2003).[1] What is new is the attempt to generalize a global, orderly (i.e., legally authorized) migration model through arrangements (Piché 2012) designed to reconcile two conflicting tendencies: increasing emigration pressures confronting workers in relatively low-income sending countries and dwindling opportunities for the legal entry of "low-skilled" workers into relatively high-income destination countries (Ghosh 2012, 26). As a solution, Ghosh (27) proposes "regulated openness," whereby sending and host states of migrants, often working in conjunction with intergovernmental organizations, develop shared policy objectives and harmonized norms and priorities, and advance these aims through forging partnerships geared toward shaping and channeling migration flows.

The idea of migration *management* has been subject to increasing scholarly scrutiny (e.g., Andrijasevic and Walters 2010; Geiger and Pécoud 2010; Guild 2009; Pécoud 2013). A central overarching critique, well articulated by Geiger and Pécoud (2010, 2–3, 6), is that this notion serves, at worst, as an "empty shell" and, at best, refers to at least three trends, which may or may not overlap: first, the reliance on a group of new *discourses* or narratives about "what migration is and how it should be addressed," casting migration as a normal and ideally a positive and open process that should take into account the interests not only of countries and regions but also of humankind (and therefore human security, development, and rights); second, the increasing involvement of new *actors*, beyond sending and receiving states, in migration policy development inside and across states and also in on-the-ground processes related to mobility; and, third, the emergence of a range of *practices* to foster new priorities (e.g., anti-trafficking) as well as long-standing aims (e.g., controlling unsanctioned migration) that may take on new guises (e.g., the creation of TMWPs, training public servants in border patrol, public information campaigns on irregular migration, etc.).

In turn, these scholars—along with others probing the meaning of migration management (e.g., Walters 2010a) and questioning its inherent assumption that TMWPs appreciably improve standards of living among participants and their families and communities—have drawn attention to the dynamics underlying each of its associated trends, exposing their omissions, limitations, and internal contradictions and emphasizing their contribution to "new" modes of control. For example, they show that, even though new policy discourses suggest that the closing of borders is not necessarily in the interest of states and emphasize global human rights, these discourses fail to problematize the role of capital: for Geiger and Pécoud (2010, 14), migration management ignores "the role of the corporate sector—in creating conditions for both the emigration of workers and their exploitation in destination states."[2] In response to migration management's granting of more authority to new actors in activities ranging from overseeing education initiatives to administering TMWPs, these analysts emphasize intergovernmental organizations' heterogeneity and frequent lack of accountability.[3] While Geiger and Pécoud (4; see also Pécoud 2010), for instance, acknowledge that such organizations' fragmentation may be functional, there are inherent risks in offering organizations with different (often nonpublic) mandates the opportunity to steer policy development and oversee migration-related activities; these potential dangers are revealed by Andrijasevic and Walters (2010) in their study of migration management and the International Organization for Migration (IOM). A final critique of practices identified with migration management relates to their technocratic character—that is, despite their diversity, practices associated with migration management stem typically from technical considerations rather than policy choices—and their depoliticizing effects. With regard to the expansion of TMWPs, this critique contrasts sharply with the language and assumptions underlying the notion of the "triple win" that such programs promise to generate for sending and host states and for migrants themselves. Indeed, the "triple win" notion is widely criticized for ignoring power asymmetries among such states, as well as between migrant workers and their sending- (and host-) state governments; neglecting the role of capital (and obscuring the overwhelming benefits of TMWPs for many employers); and masking the reality lived by many migrants that international migration for employment, and the national border crossings it involves, is a "site . . . of social struggle and politics" (Andrijasevic and Walters 2010, 997; Castles and Ozkul 2014).

In each of the foregoing ways, migration management introduces a diffuse range of practices which may, on the surface, "seem to disconnect from control and are commonly (and misleadingly) opposed to control" (Geiger and Pécoud 2013, 2). As a global policy paradigm, migration management is thereby distinct from its precursor under which individual nation-states authorized and regulated cross-border movements of people.[4] In practice, however, migration management actively retains and reconfigures control. On the ground, the reconfiguration of control under migration management in the OECD takes expression in the emergence of a two-tier system of migration for employment, aimed (albeit not always explicitly) at filling "high"- and "low"-skilled positions, respectively, with the former tier tending toward permanency and the latter associated with temporariness in terms of citizenship/residency status (on the OECD context, see especially contributions to Vosko et al. 2014; on the Canadian case, see Alboim and Cohl 2012; Hennebry 2012; Rajkumar et al. 2012). At the same time, this formalization is imperfect, and arguably intentionally so. Given the technocratic character of migration management, its ascendance has been accompanied, for practical purposes, by the multiplication of forms of temporary migration for employment and by the growing porosity of the permanent–temporary distinction, which enable host states in particular to respond to quickly changing demands for labor (on the EU, see Geddes 2015; on Canada, see contributions to Lenard and Straehle 2012; Vosko et al. 2014; on the United States, see Ness 2011).[5]

Migration Management in Practice: Canada and Other Classical Immigration Countries of the OECD

The embrace of migration management by classical immigration countries of the OECD coincides with a movement away from the post–World War II orientation to permanent immigration, directed at male "heads of household" of European heritage and leading to long-term settlement, family unification, and eventually citizenship and its associated rights, entitlements, and obligations.[6] Accompanying this shift, as noted in the introduction, is an overall trend, reinforced in policy discourses and by the range of actors (new and old) involved in the migration process, toward temporary migration for employment to the benefit of, in particular, host states and especially employers within them.

Indeed, as Sassen-Koob (1981) observed formatively, temporary migrant workers' (intergenerational) reproduction occurs in the sending state, and (daily) maintenance takes place only partly in the host state. Thus, the shift to temporary migration for employment allows host states, and employers within them, to externalize the costs of labor supply renewal in various ways that result in short- and long-term savings (e.g., limiting costs associated with unemployment and labor protection; Burawoy 1976; Sassen-Koob 1978). As in the previous permanent immigration model, programs emblematic of migration management can also take a gendered form; this is true typically of those in agriculture (e.g., under the Canada–Mexico SAWP), in which men predominate, and these participants' intergenerational reproduction, along with elements of their daily maintenance, as well as that of their dependents, is undertaken by their partners and relatives who typically reside permanently in the sending state.[7]

Defined broadly, temporary migration for employment "involves migration for a specific motivation and/or purpose with the intention that, afterwards, there will be a return to the country of origin or onward movement" (European Migration Network 2011, 14). Technically time limited, although not necessarily limited to a single migration and return, it can take many forms, one of which is circular migration, where migrants are allowed to move between their countries of origin and destination country on a recurrent basis (Wickramasekara 2011). Although forms of temporary migration for employment are multiple and varied, the OECD divides temporary migrant workers into four descriptive group-ings, each of which may involve migration under various entry categories.[8] One such grouping is seasonal temporary migrant workers, who may migrate on such bases under varied, long-running arrangements and whose numbers may be capped or subject to other controls (OECD 2014, 161).[9] The OECD's measure of seasonal temporary migrant workers is both a good indicator of trends in agri-culture and a reasonable indicator of the magnitude of circular temporary migra-tion for employment, since many such work experiences reflect annual seasonal cycles.[10] As with other forms of temporary migration for employment, the number of seasonal temporary migrant workers declined across the OECD after 2008 as a result of the global recession and the subsequent elimination of mobility restrictions among the EU countries.[11] In non-EU OECD host states, such as Australia, Canada, New Zealand, and the United States, the number of seasonal temporary migrant workers also declined during the 2008–2009 financial crisis and gradually rebounded thereafter, such that it became a significant feature of each of their labor markets (appendix 1, table A.2). Indeed, in the Canadian case, considering forms of temporary migration for employment, numbers of seasonal temporary migrant workers were the most resilient in Canada as they rebounded to approximately 2008 levels by 2010.

Behind such trends in classical immigration countries lies a shift, consistent with the new forms of control characteristic of migration management, from somewhat unsystematic "first-era" to "second-generation" TMWPs aimed at fostering deliberately "ordered movements" (Castles and Miller 2003; see also Plewa and Miller 2005). Initiated in the mid-twentieth century, first-era TMWPs proceeded on the assumption that the "need" for temporary migrant workers would be short-lived, as it was assumedly generated by specific, presumably time-limited, gaps in labor markets; in this era, only one TMWP typically operated per country. The shape of second-generation programs reflects economic devel-opments in the 1980s and 1990s associated with neoliberalism and its imperative to tailor such programs to the needs of particular employers and sectors. The re-sult is often the proliferation of many different TMWPs and, hence, entry cate-gories per country. To fulfill demands for labor, such programs are characterized by country-specific rules governing recruitment, employment, and returns, as well as by greater employer power (Martin 2007).

Amongst such varied TMWPs, despite harsh criticisms of certain early variants, such as European guest worker programs (Castles 2006), formalized circular TMWPs have become increasingly popular with governments and with inter-governmental organizations (e.g., the Global Commission on International Migration and the ILO). Part of this popularity stems from the bi- or multilateral agreements between sending and host states on which such TMWPs are based:

under these agreements, both states normally have influence over determining program parameters and oversight, and host-state employers and employer associations often do as well. As many scholars observe, in spite of TMWPs' stated orientation to human rights, "co-development goals," and "triple wins for migrants, countries of origin and destination" (Boucher 2008, 1469; Castles and Ozkul 2014), support for those fostering circularity as a means of migration management also comes more narrowly from an interest in maintaining low wages (on Canada, see, e.g., Bauder 2006, 4; Faraday 2012) while curbing "illegal" or irregular migration from low-income countries participating in these often deeply racialized programs (Gabriel and Macdonald 2012; Piché 2012; Preibisch 2012; see also Hennebry and Preibisch 2010). It is therefore not surprising that proponents of TMWPs fostering circularity, including those in Canada, advocate those that are geared to filling low-skilled positions.

Trends in Temporary Migration for Employment in Canada and the Case of Agriculture

In recent decades, Canada has become an exemplar of migration management in the form of temporary migration for employment, which has grown steadily alongside the expansion of particular forms geared to recruiting workers for low-skilled positions (Simmons 2010; see also Kelley and Trebilcock 2010). In Canada, temporary migration for employment is larger numerically than permanent migration under economic categories (i.e., defined as a category inclusive of all immigrants admitted as permanent residents for economic reasons), which typically constitute over 50 percent of all permanent residents annually (a broader group that includes not only those migrating for economic reasons but for the sake, for example, of family reunification) (IRCC 2016a, 2018b).[12] Considering entries, whereas 302,821 temporary migrant workers entered Canada in 2017 (a dramatic increase from 116,540 in 2000), Canada received just 159,262 permanent (economic class) immigrants that year (up from 136,287 in 2000); considering permanent economic immigrants and temporary migrant workers (i.e., work permit holders) in percentage terms, temporary entries increased from 46 percent to 66 percent of total entries between 2000 and 2017, a period in which the percentage of SAWP participants remained relatively stable (hovering between 12–17 percent of all entries of temporary migrant workers) (figure 1.1; see also appendix 1, table A.3).

Temporary migration for employment to Canada is most easily quantified by the type of work permit issued, which is based on the (im)migration program in question. Work permits are divided between those that require a labor market test and those that do not.[13] The major types of work permits requiring a labor market

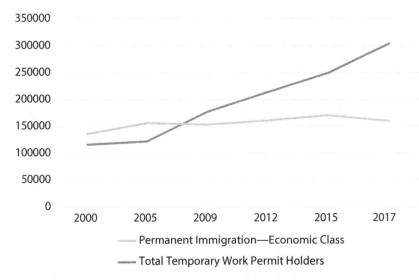

FIGURE 1.1. Entries of Temporary Work Permit Holders and Permanent Residents (Economic Class) to Canada, by Selected Year, 2000–2017

Sources: CIC 2010, 6 and 66; CIC 2012, 6 and 66; IRCC 2015b, tables 3.1 and 3.2; IRCC 2015a, 4; IRCC 2018a, 13 and 29.

test involve Agricultural Work in Occupations and Activities Related to Primary Agriculture, select higher and lower-skilled positions on a government-defined list, and, until Spring 2019, the In-Home Caregiver Program (formerly the Live-in Caregiver Program). In contrast, the major types of work permit not requiring a labor market test are those involving international agreements, the International Experience Program (tailored to students), intracompany transferees, and spouses of eligible migrants. Temporary Foreign Agricultural Workers in Occupations and Activities Related to Primary Agriculture represent a sizable segment of work-permit holders requiring a labor market test. Between 2004 and 2017, their total number grew at a faster pace than the overall growth in temporary migrant work flows: from 19,880 to 48,095 (appendix 1, table A.4).

In Canada, temporary migrant work in agriculture cuts across four program streams: the agricultural stream (introduced in 2011), the stream for high-wage agricultural positions, the stream for low-waged agricultural positions, and the SAWP. The SAWP is the only one of these streams, and the TMWPs with which they are associated, that encourages circularity; it has also long served as Canada's preeminent "low-skill" TMWP, despite the shift in the formal programmatic emphasis from skill to wage level in the labeling of the various TMWPs. Furthermore, in contrast to programs of its type in agriculture operating elsewhere in the OECD, the SAWP is the only one that has operated without interruption since

TABLE 1.1. Number of Agricultural Positions Granted a Positive Labour Market Impact Assessment (LMIA), by Selected Jurisdiction and Canadian Total, 2005–2017

AGRICULTURAL POSITIONS WITH A POSITIVE LMIA	JURISDICTIONS	2005	2006	2007	2008	2009	2010	2011	2012	2013	2014	2015	2016	2017
Seasonal Agricultural Workers Program	BC	855	1,600	2,890	3,795	3,695	3,530	3,980	4,985	5,140	5,585	6,981	7,550	7,159
	AB	475	570	705	1,045	1,005	935	965	1,065	1,165	1,371	1,251	1,331	1,376
	ON	6,575	20,420	17,660	18,340	18,170	18,195	18,700	18,500	20,845	22,639	24,223	19,386	26,163
	CAN.—Total	11,825	26,610	25,340	27,845	28,780	27,685	2,8835	29,020	34,045	36,718	41,702	40,238	44,742
Agricultural Stream	BC	—	—	—	—	—	—	385	880	1,095	943	1,650	2,104	3,610
	AB	—	—	—	—	—	—	220	815	610	665	788	866	888
	ON	—	—	—	—	—	—	870	1,340	1,260	1,506	2,155	2,656	3,496
	CAN.—Total	—	—	—	—	—	—	2,160	7,680	8,485	8,106	9,977	13,004	14,608
Higher-skilled Positions (in agriculture)	BC	25	45	135	120	50	65	70	80	60	52	32	36	21
	AB	140	225	310	405	360	495	425	650	425	428	241	82	21
	ON	75	275	335	310	170	270	240	180	150	103	55	33	15
	CAN.—Total	425	780	1,270	1,190	950	1,130	930	1,190	935	858	485	200	156
Lower-skilled Positions (in agriculture)	BC	10	105	395	1,030	430	445	285	105	80	111	20	2	38
	AB	140	410	885	900	690	790	840	550	360	289	159	70	146
	ON	490	985	1,695	1,715	1,785	1,915	1,275	1,110	930	812	510	194	303
	CAN.—Total	1,340	2,930	4,370	6,145	7,475	7,045	6,030	2,385	1,905	1,795	1,139	835	1,072

Sources: ESDC 2014a; ESDC 2014b; ESDC 2016b; ESDC 2017; ESDC 2018.

*Jurisdictions include: British Columbia (BC), Alberta (AB), Ontario (ON), and Canada (CAN).

1966, suggesting that even in the "first era" some groups of racialized migrants were not considered candidates for permanent immigration and that the interest in maintaining low wages in sectors such as agriculture is long-standing (on BC, see, e.g., Jensen 2013, chap. 3; on elsewhere in Canada, see, e.g., Satzewich 1991; Basok 2002). In line with Canada's growing emphasis on TMWPs, the SAWP expanded at the turn of the twenty-first century to encompass jurisdictions beyond those involved at its inception (Ontario and Quebec): for example, the province of BC joined the SAWP in 2004. Accordingly, the number of participants admitted annually grew appreciably. Considering yearly entries across Canada, SAWP participants grew from 16,710 in 2000 to 35,175 in 2017 (appendix 1, table A.3). SAWP participants migrating to BC constitute a significant subset of this increase; between 2005 and 2017, the number of positive labor market opinions (since labeled "impact assessments" or LMIAs) granted to SAWP participants in this province, a measure that approximates growth in employer demand for migrant workers under the agricultural program, grew from 855 to 7,159, an eightfold increase over the period (table 1.1).[14]

The SAWP Model

On account of its longevity and its "success," often attributed to the bilateral governmental agreements through which it operates and its circular character, in the global policy discourse the SAWP is often touted as a "model" TMWP whose "best practices" exemplify the advantages of migration management (Basok 2007; Vertovec 2008; Hugo 2009; Hennebry and Preibisch 2010).[15]

From the host-state perspective and that of its employers, who are permitted to specify the individual employees they want and to access their labor power year after year, the SAWP's overarching advantage is assumed to be that it fills a genuine labor shortage: employers are expected to hire Canadians first, before resorting to temporary migrant workers. At the same time, labor shortages in agriculture are understood to persist seasonally. From the perspective of workers, the prospect of unlimited seasonal return and the existence of minimum terms of engagement (described shortly) are presumed to be desirable. Finally, from the perspective of sending states, the program is lauded for providing predictable channels of migration for employment for emigrants, who are required to return to their country of origin after engaging in employment in the host state; there they are encouraged to invest their remittances, which are perceived as a tool of sustainable development. The SAWP is also said to reduce "illegal migration" and, given its much-touted advantages, to exemplify, in the words of Mexico's former vice consul to Toronto, "how migration can work in an ordered legal way" (Obrador as cited by Gabriel and Macdonald 2012, 104).[16]

ORIGINS

The SAWP's roots date to the Caribbean Seasonal Workers Programs, which emerged in 1966 in Ontario to provide employers with a supply of relatively low-wage English-speaking seasonal workers; the 1960s was a time of labor shortages, and agricultural employers lobbied for such a program (Satzewich 1991; on the origins of the SAWP, see also Basok 2002; Sharma 2006). However, the program came to function as a means to limit undocumented migration while maintaining exploitive conditions in agriculture with the addition of Mexico as a sending state. As Satzewich (2007) shows, the presence of undocumented Mexican migrant workers on Canadian farms swelled in the 1970s when employers lobbying for the expansion of the Caribbean SAWP to include Mexico, because Mexican workers were then presumed to be less inclined to voice their grievances, were met by resistance on the part of Canadian officials in the Department of Manpower and Immigration. At the time, despite the protestations of employers, who openly expressed preferences for particular types of employees and who objected to the government-sanctioned annual wage increases provided to program participants, these Canadian officials were keen to maintain sufficiently high wage levels among Caribbean SAWP employees to avoid undercutting Canadian nationals. This strategy backfired, however, when some employers looked beyond this state-sanctioned TMWP in agriculture to recruit and engage undocumented Mexican workers, as well as marginalized workers holding Canadian citizenship, and employed them under exploitive conditions.[17]

It was the growing presence of undocumented Mexican migrant agricultural workers that led Canada to invite Mexico, much in need of remittances because of the oil crisis in the early 1970s, to join the SAWP in 1974 (Satzewich 2007, 271–272). The effect was the lowering of the bottom of the labor market for temporary migrant workers engaged in agriculture, resulting in the "disciplin[ing] [of] Caribbean workers' and their government representatives' demands about wages and working conditions" to the benefit of employers (273). Underscoring how TMWPs characteristic of migration management can contribute to exacerbating exploitive conditions of work in host states (Geiger and Pécoud 2010, 14), the number of SAWP employees from Mexico, a source of low-cost labor, soon came to exceed those from Caribbean countries. This development, which entailed recruiting workers from new sending countries as a means to maintain low wages, both reflected Canada's historical approach and foretold its future direction in managing flows of temporary migrant workers, especially in agriculture. Beginning in the early 2000s, with the deregulation of TMWPs in agriculture through the introduction of new streams, countries such as Guatemala, the Philippines, and Thailand, became source countries. That is, they were compelled by the dynamics of global racialized capitalism to participate in a system that structurally embeds the underdevelopment and dependence of low-income countries and regions, through what Harvey (2003) has labeled "accumulation by dispossession"— whose forms have varied from direct colonial confiscations to more recent expropriation through debt and discipline (McNally 2011)—and what Fraser (2018) describes as the racialized subjugation of expropriated populations. Further institutionalizing Canada's recruitment of a racialized, largely male agricultural workforce migrating under highly restrictive conditions, this approach has contributed to reproducing and sustaining structural patterns of dependency, poverty, and underemployment in low-income sending states while reinforcing the economic dominance of higher-income countries (on the institutionalization of a racialized migrant agricultural workforce in Canada and its connection to global inequality, see especially Satzewich 1991; Hennebry and McLaughlin 2012; Choudry and Smith 2016; and Thomas 2016; see also Budworth, Rose, and Mann 2017; Wells et al. 2014).

OVERSIGHT

Currently, the SAWP operates on the basis of extensive involvement, especially in the oversight of participants' movements and performance in employment, of both Canada—a host state in which immigration is a "concurrent power" of the federal government and the provinces, but over which the federal government has paramountcy—and sending states. It is governed by bilateral agreements between Canada (or a provincial government, in the case of BC) and sending states, expressed in memoranda of understanding (MOUs) outlining the responsibilities and obligations of employees, employers, and governments.[18] These MOUs are then translated into standard employment agreements, agreements that coexist at the federal and, in the case of BC, provincial levels, because immigration policy making is shared between the federal government and the provinces and there is variation in provincial labor laws.[19] These agreements set out terms negotiated annually by the Canadian government, sending states, and employer representatives drawn from three industry associations: the Fondation des Entreprises en Recrutement de la Main-d'oeuvre agricole Étrangère or FERME, the Foreign Agricultural Resource Management Services originating in Ontario or FARMS, and the BC Agricultural Council (BCAC). Operational guidelines for the program are set forth as annexes to the MOUs and are reviewed annually.

Under the SAWP, agreements between Canada's federal and provincial governments (BC in this case) and participating sending states, including, of central interest in this book, Mexico, contain a range of terms. They include provisions on accommodation, which must be provided by the employer, be "suitable" and be "affordably available"; travel, which the employer must pay for in BC; wage levels; and repatriation (ESDC 2016a). Reflecting the SAWP's seasonal orientation, employment contracts are of limited duration, lasting between a minimum of 240 hours (over a period of six weeks or shorter) and a maximum of eight months, and only permit work between January 1 and December 15 (see, e.g., HRSDC 2013, s. I, para. 2a). They result in the issuance of a closed work permit, meaning that workers are required to work for a specified employer. However, as noted earlier, the SAWP does not limit the tenure of workers' participation in the TMWP, allowing them to return year after year.

OPERATION

Since 1988, the SAWP has been administered by industry associations (such as FERME, FARMS, and the BCAC, formerly the Western Agriculture Labor Initiative or WALI) in Quebec, Ontario, and BC, respectively, backed by Canadian employers from across the provinces, with the support of host-state government officials, principally Canadian immigration (and labor) officials at the federal level and likewise by sending state officials (Rolland 2017, 19). Representatives of employer associations oversee employer applications, a process involving fulfilling employer requests for labor.

Sending-state officials, in turn, are responsible for initial worker recruitment, selection, documentation (e.g., the provision of passports and visas in conjunction with Canadian officials), and aspects of readmission, undertaken in the Mexican case by its Ministry of Labor and Social Provision (MOL) in the interior. They also post government agents (consular officials in the case of Mexico) in Canada to assist in the day-to-day operation of the program (e.g., in carrying out placement and mediating on-farm disputes). Given that the SAWP encourages circular migration, sending-state officials—in Mexico's case, both those in the interior and consular officials—also play a significant role in readmission (Hennebry 2010; Preibisch 2012).

Finally, host-state officials determine labor market needs; in this instance, as with most other TMWPs operated by Canada and geared to filling "low-skill" positions, the process involves Labour Market Impact Assessments (LMIAs), completed by Employment and Social Development Canada (ESDC), Canada's federal labor department, and Service Canada, the federal government agency that provides a single point of access to a wide range of government services and benefits. If such an assessment confirms labor shortages, closed work permits (i.e., tied to a specific employer) are provided to migrant workers seeking seasonal agriculture work.[20] Through Canadian consulates abroad, Canadian officials (normally federal immigration officials) also provide migrant workers with access to visas to Canada. However, such documentation is provided indirectly via Mexican authorities, who dispense the visas to migrant workers whom they have selected for admission and readmission once these workers have completed processes and documentation mandated by the sending state. In certain instances, federal labor officials in Canada may also assist employees who are seeking to change employers, but such requests are not granted uniformly. Since the regulation of labor in Canada largely takes place at the provincial level, provincial host-state officials are principally responsible for ensuring that the conditions of work and employment of temporary migrant workers laboring under the SAWP meet applicable minimum employment standards.[21] In jurisdictions where unionization of agricultural workers is permitted, provincial government officials are also responsible for ensuring that these TMWP participants have the right to organize and bargain collectively; concomitantly, courts and tribunals are required to facilitate their access to collective bargaining.

BC LABOR AND EMPLOYMENT LAWS APPLICABLE TO SAWP EMPLOYEES

In BC, the most important vehicles through which temporary migrant workers may access their labor rights and protections are the provincial Employment Standards Act (ESA) and the LRC. The BC ESA sets out minimum standards applicable to non-unionized employees with respect to wages, hours of work, holidays, and other workplace rights. Agricultural employees, including TMWP participants, fall within its scope, although SAWP employees must be paid in keeping with the contract tied to the TMWP. Coverage for agricultural employees' under the ESA is nevertheless only partial; they are, for example, not entitled to overtime pay and are protected only against excessive hours of work detrimental to health and safety. Agricultural employees paid piece rates also typically receive a lower minimum wage.[22] And those paid on an hourly basis are excluded from statutory holiday and, effectively, annual vacation entitlements.[23] For SAWP employees, this exclusion translates into virtually no holidays with pay during their terms of employment, a general standard under BC's ESA, as well as no vacations with pay or pay in lieu, resulting in a lower set of social minima than most other employees covered by the ESA in the province.

Such limited coverage, and the labor market insecurities it perpetuates, makes resort to the LRC, which notably extends the right to organize and bargain collectively to agricultural workers, desirable among many subgroups, including TMWP participants such as SAWP employees. Agricultural workers' inclusion in the LRC is nevertheless of recent origin, and access to collective bargaining among temporary migrant workers is tenuous (as shown in chapter 2). BC only began to formally include agricultural workers in labor relations legislation in 1975, at which point a sizable subset were immigrants.[24] The province did so after a labor-friendly government repealed the agricultural exclusion from the LRC.[25]

Furthermore, on their inclusion, agricultural workers were covered by an LRC that was incompatible with their employment situation. Indeed, consistent with Tucker's (2014) helpful threefold heuristic, BC's LRC was modeled initially and remains styled after the U.S. Wagner Act: its defining elements with respect to trade union formation are majority rule and bargaining unit exclusivity, achieved through certification by majority vote (although card check has prevailed in certain periods), and government officials' determination of certification units. The LRC also empowers government officials to establish appropriate bargaining units.[26] It takes as the norm highly decentralized collective bargaining, premised on the assumption that bargaining will typically be organized by industry and occur at the enterprise level.[27] Additionally, the BC LRC's overall aim is to promote industrial stability while enabling access to collective bargaining, much like the Wagner Act model prevalent elsewhere in Canada (BC MOL 1996). Such elements complement its formalist orientation, which effectively means that employers can refuse to recognize unions unable to maneuver seamlessly through legal channels.

Historically, by fostering unionization among blue-collar, white male citizen workers in mass production and resource industries, and thereby contributing to the establishment of industrial unionism, this Wagnerian orientation impeded unionization among workers in secondary industries and small firms, as well as among workers who are recent immigrants or who otherwise hold tenuous residency status, have limited power, and may only be permitted to engage in employment seasonally. That is, in BC as elsewhere in Canada, it has worked against organizing among SAWP employees—not only as temporary and seasonal agricultural workers but also as racialized largely male migrants with tenuous residency status (explored further in chapter 2).

Nevertheless, after agricultural workers' exclusion was lifted, unions did use the LRC's formal legal channels to represent them, achieving a few certifications in the mid-1970s. Then, in the 1980s, the Canadian Farmworkers Union (CFU) became involved in several organizing drives; however, after confronting significant challenges flowing partly from the limits of the Wagner Act model, it shifted from organizing directed at unionization toward community development, such that the former effort faded in the late twentieth century.[28]

In the early 2000s, there was, once again, interest in organizing in agriculture in BC, this time on the part of the UFCW, which had gradually achieved a foothold in this sector in other Canadian provinces and was prompted to extend its organizing efforts geographically as well as test the confines of two Supreme Court of Canada (SCC) decisions.[29] Initially, marking its first effective bid to the LRB to represent a group of workers encompassing SAWP employees, the UFCW Local 1518 successfully secured certification of a bargaining unit at Greenway Farms Ltd. The statutory means through which a labor relations board establishes that a majority of employees want to be represented by a union (in BC, by written evidence in the form of signing a card, followed by a vote) and constitute an "appropriate bargaining unit" as well as compels the employer to recognize and bargain with the union, securing certification is challenging for those with limited power and resources. For TMWP participants in BC, as elsewhere, this already contentious process is complicated by workers' tenuous residency status and the authority granted to employers to ultimately determine their presence in Canada. Therefore, on the one hand, Greenway Farms was a watershed in BC because, despite the Wagnerian-style LRC, the LRB affirmed Local 1518's certification in the face of a challenge levelled by the grower, which the agricultural industry supported, thereby concretizing temporary migrant workers' rights to collective bargaining in the province.[30] On the other hand, because of the contentiousness of the certification shaped by Mexican workers' temporary residency status—which does not align with the norm of the native-born citizen-worker underpinning BC's Wagnerian-style LRC—and the power of employers to determine their presence in Canada (because of the issuance of closed work permits), certain employees at Greenway filed an application to decertify just one season after the initial certification. This decertification application, moreover, was successful due to the employer's decision, demonstrating the real threat of attrition explored in chapter 4 and permissible under the SAWP, to recall just one-third of the SAWP employees involved in the initial unionization drive in the season prior.

An Example of "Best Practice"? Workers' Rights under the SAWP

Notwithstanding its apparent success in promoting TMWPs as a form of legal and orderly migration, and despite the formal rights to organize and bargain collectively accorded to workers in provinces such as BC, where the LRC applies to employees in agriculture, the SAWP gives considerable power—and control—to employer associations in defining terms and conditions of employment. It also grants host- and sending-state officials significant authority in recruitment, selection, and placement processes. In these ways, the SAWP fails to live up to its characterization as a model of "best practice" with regard to workers' rights. As prevailing research demonstrates, this failure flows partly from built-in limitations of provincially based minimum employment standards that are applicable to SAWP employees. Yet it flows primarily from obstacles to organizing and bargaining collectively, stemming from the territorial basis of labor law and policy in a globalized context in which capital is increasingly deterritorialized (see, e.g., Basok 1999; Binford 2009, 10; Hennebry and Preibisch 2010; Hennebry and McLaughlin 2012; Preibisch 2012; on deterritorialized capitalism, see, e.g.,

Mundlak 2009). In Hennebry and Preibisch's (2010) evaluation of the SAWP according to internationally recognized rights-based approaches to labor migration, drawing on those taken by UNESCO, the ILO, and the IOM, SAWP fares poorly in recognizing migrant workers' qualifications, offering opportunities for skills transfer, avoiding the imposition of forced savings schemes, and providing pathways to permanency. Echoing the work of Basok (1999; see also Binford 2009), these authors also emphasize the consequences of the primary modes of control that are most at odds with SAWP employees' rights: the provision of closed work permits, limiting participants' mobility in the labor market and augmenting power imbalances between SAWP employees and their employers (see also Preibisch 2010, 104); the lack of transparency of (re)admissions processes (see also Binford 2013); and the de facto ability of employers to select workers on the bases of nationality, gender, and health status (see also Gabriel and Macdonald 2012; Preibisch 2012). Studies suggest that, even when evaluated against rights-based measures of a "successful" TMWP, itself arguably a contradiction in terms so long as rights to work, settlement, and security of presence are tied to permanent residence and/or citizenship in a nation-state (Latham et al. 2014), the SAWP does not perform well.

Such contentions prompt Gabriel and Macdonald (2012) to conclude that the SAWP's "best practices" are better understood as "governing strategies" and also to reject comparing the SAWP's parameters to its equally poorly performing U.S. counterpart, the H2-A program, as a means of measuring success. At the same time, these and other critics acknowledge that, compared to other TMWPs, the SAWP remains relatively more desirable among migrants who have few options. The scheme permits circularity and is based on a formal intergovernmental arrangement functioning under the oversight of both Canada and participating sending states. In these ways, the SAWP offers benefits that are superior to many provided by Canada's other TMWPs, including those targeting agriculture. In provinces where agricultural workers have the right to organize and bargain collectively, such as BC, its parameters also leave open the possibility for unionization among TMWP participants with the prospect of return. It is in this context that the ensuing chapters examine how deportability is not anathema to, but rather sustains migration management, especially the "new" modes of control on which this global policy paradigm relies, despite the espousal of "regulated openness."

Deportability and Migration Management

Alongside the expansion of TMWPs in high-income host states such as Canada, there is a continued and, in some instances, increasing resort to deportation or "the removal of aliens by state power from the territory of that state, either voluntary, under threat of force, or forcibly" (Walters 2010b, 68; see De Genova 2010; Collyer 2012).[31] This "deportation turn" (Gibney 2008) has taken center stage in studies of undocumented migrants, such that a large body of scholarship is devoted to historicizing and denaturalizing deportation as a form of expulsion (see, e.g., Walters 2010b). On its face, involving the reassignment of individuals to states to which they are considered to belong (Hindess 2000, 1495), this deportation turn is seemingly antithetical to migration management with its focus on managing to achieve more orderly and predictable human objectives (i.e., its concerns with human rights, the dignity of migrants, human security, and the like) through the generalization of a global orderly (i.e., legally authorized) migration model achievable through multilateral arrangements (Piché 2012). Yet, arguably, migration management depends on the capacity for removal and/or repatriation. In classical immigration countries expanding formal channels of temporary migration for employment, deportation, and especially its possibility, is vital to achieving control. That is, threats and acts of removal are key to reconciling conflicting forces, shaped by geopolitical economic power dynamics, of increasing emigration pressures concentrated, in particular, in relatively low-income countries versus dwindling opportunities for the legal entry of workers to fill jobs characterized as low skilled in, especially, relatively high-income countries. Deportability thereby plays a role in the governance of TMWP participants by sending and host states, as well as by employers.

Deportability: The Concept and Its Origins

Dissecting classical immigration countries' use of TMWPs to help tighten border controls for the most vulnerable migrants as part of the shift to migration management calls for an expansive conceptual toolkit. Key to this analysis is the understanding that deportability, a notion distinct from de facto deportation but reflecting its logic, encompasses the threat of removal. As a concept conceived as "the possibility of being removed from the nation-state," deportability is powerful because it seeks to capture a social condition and an accompanying set of social practices that include but also extend beyond externalities or hard limits, such as formal protocols on repatriation (De Genova 2002, 438–439).[32] De Genova initially deployed this term to depict the situation of undocumented or "illegal" Mexican migrant workers in the United States, whose labor power is rendered as disposable and ultimately temporary (i.e., deportable) through administrative practices that he associates with the spectacle of immigration enforcement; he subsequently emphasized the racist character of this low regard for migrants from non-European countries as illustrated by repeated mass expulsions from the United States of migrants (and indeed citizens) of Mexican heritage (De Genova

2007).[33] With regard to undocumented migrant workers, for De Genova (2002, 439, citing Cockcroft 1986; Calavita 1993, and Kearney 1998, emphasis added), "what makes deportability so decisive . . . is that some are deported *in order that most may remain*;" it reveals the operation of the border as a revolving door, whose openings and closings are "implicated in *importation as much as deportation*."[34]

To date, most scholarly explorations of deportability, following De Genova, are theoretical in their emphasis. To the extent that they explore real-world examples, they focus on undocumented migrant workers' experiences within host states, which are shaped primarily by employers therein. They theorize, for example, inclusion through illegalization or the transposition of physical borders into undocumented workers' everyday lives (see, e.g., Talavera et al. 2005). Some authors, such as Mezzadra and Neilson (2013, 146, see also 143), helpfully point out that "the 'illegal' migrant" is "a deportable subject, whose position in both the polity and the labor market is marked by and negotiated through the condition of deportability, even if actual removal is a distant possibility or a threat that has become the background to a whole series of lifetime activities." Even for such authors, however, the undocumented migrant worker inside the host state is the prevailing focus.[35] Yet this focus risks overlooking situations confronting temporary migrant workers, including those who are legally authorized, who, given their residency status occupy a more liminal space shaped both by the separation of the border from the wall (Brown 2010)—in the case of SAWP employees, the expansion and re-location, or "de-location" of the border to the farm—and the temporalization of the border and its associated zones of "waiting, holding, and interruption" (Mezzadra and Neilson 2014, 143).

Deportability among Temporary Migrant Workers: An Expanded Conception

Partly because of the theoretical orientation of much scholarship on deportability and partly because of the focus on undocumented workers in applying the concept, few studies explore how deportability relates to the experiences of temporary migrant workers with the prospect of return and to the spaces and places they inhabit (for exceptions addressing SAWP employees, see, e.g., Binford 2013; Basok et al. 2014). Yet this group, including participants in TMWPs permitting circularity, face a unique form of deportability stemming from the uncertainty institutionalized into agreements between sending and host states; that is, their deportability is a feature of their legal status.

In response to TMWP participants' growing numbers in classical immigration countries such as Canada, especially in sectors with long-standing demands for labor such as agriculture, inquiries are emerging to address the dynamics behind those workers' supposed acquiescence to dirty, dangerous, and demeaning work, especially those who have the prospect of return (see, for example, Basok 1999, 2002; Preibisch 2010; Hennebry 2012). Critical sociological analyses of TMWPs by Binford (2009, 2013) and Basok et al. (2014), centering largely on the experiences of SAWP employees migrating from Mexico, represent noteworthy examples. They advance the study of the prospect of deportation and its effects on this seeming docility among SAWP employees in Canada. Particularly illuminating is Binford's (2013) suggestion that two complementary understandings of deportability apply to this group: one narrow and the other expansive. Departing from De Genova's (2005) insight that "illegality" is experienced by undocumented Mexican migrants through a tangible sense of deportability, Binford (2013) argues that, although SAWP employees enter Canada legally, and in this way differ from undocumented Mexican migrants in the United States, they must meet employers' demands in order to remain. Put bluntly, "when a worker is fired, the contract becomes voided and the right to remain in Canada is immediately suspended"; accordingly, the worker shifts from "a legal temporary worker into an 'illegal' who must be 'deported'" (50). A second understanding of deportability experienced by this group entails dismissal from future employment in the host state (i.e., permanent expulsion), resulting, for example, from negative evaluations completed by employers and reviewed by Mexico's MOL in the interior. For Binford (2009, 508), for instance, the nonrenewal of SAWP employees who have returned to Mexico "has the same effect as deportation, even though it comes *after* as opposed to *during* the contract period." Binford's (2013, 62) mix of theoretical and empirical work is also instructive in applying and extending De Genova's arguments about the significance of deportability for the racialized extraction of value (see also Fraser 2018)—specifically, his demonstration of how deportability "binds" production in Canadian agriculture to the neoliberal constructions of surplus labor in rural Mexico and the consequences that it has for Mexican workers' present and future economic circumstances.

Basok et al.'s (2014) analysis of the reproduction of deportability among TMWP participants engaged in agriculture, including in the flagship SAWP, also highlights employer power. By focusing on how disciplinary power (Foucault 1977) serves employers' interest, however, they make two further interventions to explore dynamics operating at what Cornelisse (2010) characterizes as the "internal level": first, whereas host-state actions contribute significantly to undocumented workers' vulnerability, other actors also heighten temporary migrant workers' insecurity, including employers, international organizations, recruiters, and sending states; second, with the reproduction of the deportation regime by multiple actors, many migrants "disciplin[e] themselves and other migrants to comport themselves in a particular way," thereby "co-constructing" the regime's disciplinary power (Basok et al. 2014, 1394). These authors' qualitative research reveals how uneven power relations—which Satzewich (2007) describes elsewhere as amounting to "extra-economic coercion"—are made more salient by employers, who, in the presence of vague state-sanctioned employment contracts that make arbitrary dismissal permissible, use the threat of deportation as a fear tactic to encourage high productivity at low wages. Their research also shows how such power relations are perpetuated by Mexican MOL and consular officials, who wield the deportation threat in advance of TMWP participants' departure and/ or placement on farms to encourage employees' docility, and by the IOM, which warns employees to avoid communicating any concerns to activists and threatens to suspend relatives of employees from TMWP participation who defect from the program (Basok et al. 2014: 1401–1402). Furthermore, through their analysis of TMWP participants' narratives, Basok et al. (1406–1407) show that workers often respond to the possibility of removal through self-regulation. Such practices identified by these authors include working quickly, getting along with employees holding different citizenship/residency statuses, and always being on their best behavior, which may involve avoiding going offsite during their time off and even "making others deportable" by engaging in what they call "snitching" (e.g., reporting undocumented workers to authorities)(1406–1407).

Deportability in a Model TMWP: Insights of Prevailing Scholarship

By revealing the depth of SAWP employees' fear and its real and multiple sources, as well as how it can affect TMWP participants' actions, such critical sociological studies of the SAWP and TMWPs more broadly offer evidence that deportability extends beyond undocumented workers to temporary migrant workers with the prospect of return. Their rich qualitative analyses also underscore that, as TMWP participants, SAWP employees' fear is palpable even in the absence of quantitative evidence of large numbers of deportations, which would, of course, be at cross-purposes with host-state economies' demands for inexpensive and compliant labor (on the U.S. case, see Gomberg-Muñoz and Nussbaum-Barberena 2011; see also Ness 2005). This body of scholarship opens space for examining the operation of deportability in TMWPs characteristic of migration management under which participants are accorded formal rights to organize and bargain collectively. At the same time, the methodological approaches adopted by some sociological scholarship on the SAWP centering on participants' experiences—even though these studies seek to give voice to "vantage points of the subjugated" on the basis that "vision is better from below the brilliant space platforms of the powerful"—stop short of attending fully to the manifestations of deportability and how the range of potential actors involved in migration management can contribute to perpetuating this mode of control and its associated institutions and structures and their respective constraints (Haraway 1988, 583). They leave unaddressed the lacuna surrounding legal and administrative processes and practices—often obscured from view—that give rise to deportability, including those affecting TMWP participants seeking to access their rights to organize and bargain collectively, and the underlying political and economic exigencies affecting their shape.[36] No doubt, studies chronicling SAWP participants' experiences proceed on the bases of sound and responsible rationales. Yet, there is scant attention to *"how to see from below* is [itself] a problem" requiring scholarly consideration (Haraway 1988, 583, 548, emphasis added).

To illuminate central mechanisms of deportability, it is critical to discern how the institutional design of TMWPs such as the SAWP, which is framed jointly by both immigration and labor law and policy, entrenches the dissonances between those bodies of law and policy and also to apprehend how various actors interpret and implement their foremost provisions and how associated struggles over their meaning and enactment play out. In pursuit of this twofold objective, two other strands of literature, informed by distinct methodological approaches and methods, offer further insights: critical legal and policy analyses of TMWPs operating in Canada, including the SAWP, and scholarship on the political economy of labor migration to Canada. The former body of scholarship encompasses an extensive literature examining, via documentary and legal analysis, variations in TMWPs and the parameters of the laws and policies that bring them into being. Contributions of this literature, which come principally from law, political science, and sociolegal studies, include distillations of how various rights and protections are accorded to TMWP participants with respect to work, security, and settlement (see, e.g., contributions to Lenard and Straehle 2012; Rajkumar et al. 2012); detailed investigations of the legal regulation of entry and exit of TMWP participants, such as those in programs geared to filling "low-skilled" occupations (see, e.g., Fudge and McPhail 2009); and explorations of the extent to which rights and protections extended to particular groups "on paper" translate into practice (see, e.g., McLaughlin et al. 2014; Marsden 2014).

Within this body of scholarship, a subset of studies explores how and to what extent collective and protective labor laws and policies apply to specific groups, devoting attention to the situation of TWMP participants, including SAWP employees. Some such studies trace agricultural workers' longstanding exclusion from provincial collective bargaining legislation (on Canada as a whole, see especially, Tucker 2012; see also contributions to Faraday et al. 2012; on the BC case specifically, see especially Jensen 2014) and the impacts of subsequent gradual and often-qualified inclusion for groups of workers including TMWP participants

(Russo 2011, 2012; Jensen 2013). This group of studies highlights contemporary challenges SAWP employees confront in seeking to realize their rights to organize and engage in collective bargaining (e.g., in successfully claiming a community of interest, gaining certification, securing a collective agreement, and staying unionized) and isolates the origins of such obstacles in immigration and/or labour law and policy (e.g., in the bargaining unit determination process intrinsic to labor relations laws, policies, and practices or, under the SAWP, in provisions that permit employers to terminate SAWP employees with limited rationale, prompting premature repatriation).

Operating at a different level of analysis, still other legal analyses explore how immigration laws and policies interact with labor laws and human rights instruments at various scales. Such analyses probe, for example, the relationship between precarious migration status and precarious employment that these distinct bodies of law and policy—with differing jurisdictional boundaries—reflect and engender (see especially Fudge 2012b; Marsden 2012, 2014; see also Vosko 2010, chap. 2; Vosko 2011; Goldring and Landolt 2013a; Marsden 2014). Through a normative commitment to laying bare the material interests benefiting from and the power relations served by TMWP participants' deportability, this current of legal analysis overlaps with scholarship on the political economy of temporary migration to Canada.

Literature on the political economy of labor migration to Canada examines TMWPs, such as SAWP, in the context of larger global trends of regional integration, transnationality, neoliberalism, the globalization of care, and global labor mobility (see especially, Gabriel 2008, 2011; for a review of trends outside but encompassing Canada, see also Plewa and Miller 2005; Castles 2006).[37] This literature is particularly concerned with answering important "why" questions; by addressing the relationship between political and economic dynamics and tendencies, it aims to illustrate the nature and extent to which employers (and capital interests more broadly) benefit from TMWPs. Writers in this vein also devote sustained attention to the case of agriculture, especially given the longevity of the SAWP, a TMWP that the Canadian government has long justified on the basis of labor shortages so extensive as to merit a program for promoting "permanent temporariness" (Rajkumar et al. 2012; on the allied notion of permanently temporary, see also Hennebry 2012), obscuring a major factor beyond these so-called shortages' origins, that is, persistent employer demands for low labor costs presumably achieved by the provision of low wages, limited job security, and the like.

This inquiry into how deportability operates among SAWP employees and affects their exercise of the rights to organize and bargain collectively takes, as its point of departure, answers to these "why" questions, focusing on whose interests are served, as posited in scholarship on the political economy of labor migration to Canada. Yet, rather than examining the design of immigration and labor laws and policies and their impacts (e.g., on the expression of voice among TMWP participants) in line with legal and policy analyses, this book focuses on certain "how" questions to discern the means through which deportability is produced and reproduced, often in ways that benefit elite and capital interests and power. This approach to analysis thus assumes that, on their own, sociological studies of participants' experiences in programs such as the SAWP, critical legal and policy analyses of TMWPs, and scholarship on the political economy of labor migration can each only go so far in revealing how laws, policies, and programmatic guidelines are interpreted by different institutions and actors in the migration process and in showing the effects of these interpretations and contestation over their application. In an era of migration management, filling remaining knowledge gaps necessitates studying what is often hidden from view; namely, the actions (and interactions) of actors and institutions, including consular officials, officials inside sending states responsible for implementing labor and emigration law and policy, and adjudicative bodies in host states in various domains at multiple levels (e.g., provincial labor relations tribunals, provincial and federal courts and courts of appeal) and how they structure TMWP participants' field of action.[38] Only through such investigation does it become possible to reveal how the SAWP both contributes to and relies on deportability and, particularly, how this model of migration management—especially the contestation over threats and acts of removal that it mitigates and engenders simultaneously—affects union organizing and collective bargaining as a means of realizing and retaining access to labor rights and protections.

Studying Deportability among SAWP Employees Exercising Their Rights to Organize and Bargain Collectively

In examining deportability's social and material construction, this inquiry into the efforts of a group of male temporary migrant workers seeking to organize and bargain collectively and, subsequently, to maintain bargaining unit strength is grounded in a methodological approach often labeled "feminist objectivity."[39] Theorized cogently by Haraway (1988, 584), feminist objectivity seeks "partial, locatable, critical knowledge" that rejects the attempt by social science to develop an all-encompassing view grounded nowhere; it is reflexive because "it grounds or warrants empirical claims by relating them neither to a mind-independent world nor to a set of cultural values," partly by acknowledging the mutually constitutive relationship between the knower and the known, the analyst and the object(s) of analysis, and instead to scholarly knowledge production practices themselves (Jackson 2011, 157).[40] Feminist objectivity thus responds to criticisms leveled by social constructivism and postmodernism by seeking to transcend "totalization" and "relativism," terms adopted by Haraway (1988, 584), or what scholars such as Bourdieu (1990) term "objectivism" and "subjectivism." As a methodological approach, it "privileges contestation" (Haraway 1988, 584–5). It also values what Haraway (584) calls, following Kuhn (1982), "passionate detachment" or normative commitments to find ways to "see from below" without "romanticizing and/or appropriating the vision of the less powerful" to foster transformation in knowledge production systems.[41]

Informed by this methodological approach and its normative commitments, particularly its recognition that "the experience of meaning is part of the total meaning of experience" (Bourdieu and Whiteside 1996, 3), this book studies modalities of deportability—or ways in which it exists, is experienced, and is expressed—prominent among temporary migrant workers with the prospect of return. The book identifies these modalities through an analysis of the documented attempts of UFCW Local 1518, working on behalf of SAWP employees at Sidhu, as well as another bargaining unit encompassing SAWP employees (at Floralia) confronting similar problems, to use legal channels to help TMWP participants realize and retain formal labor rights in the host state. The chapters to follow probe such attempts, which offer an unprecedented window into the processes and practices shaping deportability and the campaigns against it—that is, into how deportability is resisted and reproduced symbiotically and thus lived.

Among temporary migrant workers as a whole, deportability is notoriously difficult to document because of the dearth of empirics typically available. Yet those materials surfacing through and surrounding legal proceedings pertinent to this case are diverse and extensive. This material might also be characterized as "messy," in the sense that it is out of sync with dominant methodological approaches that seek "to make the world clean and neat" (Law 2007, 595). Consequently, consistent with the commitments to being conscious of "*how* we see" and hence the interpenetration of theory and research (Bourdieu and Wacquant 1992, 43), to avoid both totalization and relativism, and to implement a research design aimed at transformation, the ensuing chapters engage mixed methods in a context-sensitive study of the case of SAWP employees of Sidhu. Taking an "active" approach that aims to "maintain the integrity of a single study, compared to inadvertently permitting the study to decompose into two or more parallel studies," the chapters undertake an *analysis of laws and policies* on the books and of case law available publicly while also engaging in a *documentary analysis* of supporting materials provided as evidence by the parties at multiple stages in the proceedings of the BC LRB, BC SC, and BC CA and integral to these courts' and tribunals' renderings, and of accompanying submissions (written and oral) emerging through hearings at various levels (Yin 2006, 41; see also Mirchandani et al. 2018; Hesse-Biber 2007).

To supplement and further contextualize this legal, policy, and documentary analysis, it is very important to hear the voices of various actors and agents involved in the case and to understand how institutional processes and practices played out. Therefore the following chapters also draw on qualitative *in-depth interviews*.[42] These key informant interviews were conducted annually over the seven-year period during which the most important aspects of the legal case study unfolded. Those interviewed include lawyers involved in the case and individuals from diverse backgrounds giving formal testimony (e.g., consular officials, union personnel based in Canada and Mexico at the national and subnational levels, and political representatives): their reflections reveal the "stories" behind "the official story" or public narratives surrounding the case (Maynes et al. 2008), offering unique "vantage points" from which to apprehend "knowledges of the subjugated" (Haraway 1988, 581, 590).[43] Key informants did not include individual employees involved directly in the legal struggle, although employee testimony features centrally in the analysis alongside the reflections and assessments of their advocates. The exclusion of this group was a deliberate choice. It was guided by the risk of participation posed to employees known or perceived to be pro-union, or engaged in union organizing at the farm in question, or to have experienced blacklisting, as revealed by the extensive qualitative research documenting SAWP employees' experience of deportability on which this book builds. The choice also flowed logically from the decision to focus on different routes to understanding deportability.[44]

The analysis of these diverse empirics through multiple methods allows for delineating processes and practices that produce deportability—as a means of (direct and indirect) control fundamental to migration management—among temporary migrant workers with the prospect of return who are exercising their rights to organize and bargain collectively. Critical mixed-methods help uncover particular "truths" surrounding what deportability *does* and therefore what it *is*, which neither legal nor qualitative analyses can expose independently. Through their application, this book aims to re-create a narrative highlighting the realities of how deportability operates, realities that are evident to its subjects but are often otherwise concealed by the very administrative and legal processes in place to ensure the smooth functioning of a given TMWP. Underscoring the power relations that inform knowledge creation and authorization, the engagement of critical mixed-methods thus seeks to disrupt dominant understandings and make space for alternative perspectives (Aradau and Huysmans 2013).

Modalities of Deportability

Studying the case of SAWP employees of Sidhu through multiple methods makes it possible to unearth the inner workings of deportability among SAWP employees with the prospect of return who are opting to exercise their rights to organize and bargain collectively. Among this group, processes and practices augmenting deportability and thwarting the exercise of labor rights are multiple and varied. Yet, as this case shows, three prominent modalities heighten the possibility of removal either immediately or in the form of expulsion from future employment in the host state: termination without just cause, blacklisting, and attrition.

TERMINATION

The most clear-cut possibility of removal—the prospect of immediate termination triggering repatriation—entails premature cessation of the seasonal employment contract by the employer. That the employer has the power to terminate the worker is indicative of how, typical of migration management, TMWPs often delegate state control partly to private actors (e.g., employers, intermediaries, and other actors) who are unaccountable to the principles of democratic governance.[45] The parameters of termination are set out in the Canada–Mexico standard employment agreement, which dictates that an employer may cease employment contracts for any reason at any time without allowing for the possibility of employee appeal. The only caveat is that the employer must consult with a Mexican government agent in advance of issuing a notice of termination. After doing so, the employer is entitled to prematurely terminate "the WORKER'S employment for non-compliance, refusal to work, or *any other sufficient reason*" (ESDC 2016a, X.1, emphasis added). Indicative of the threat of deportation, and encouraging disciplinary forms of subjectification absent is any requirement for termination with just cause.

Even though an identical provision permitting premature termination does not exist in the BC–Mexico agreement, the termination of employment leading to repatriation still occurs in BC, given the deference paid to the Canada–Mexico agreement in practice.[46] In this context, acceptable "official" reasons for premature termination cited commonly by employers include bad weather conditions leading to declining yields and/or demands for products, although there is considerable evidence that employers most often exercise this possibility with employees known to have associations with or positive views of unions (see, e.g., UFCW 1518 2009d). In instances in which premature (i.e., immediate) termination is not a practical option for employers, those who hire Mexican SAWP employees in BC, as elsewhere (e.g., in Ontario and Quebec), also have historically had the mechanism of the employee evaluation at their disposal, a highly opaque process overseen by Mexico's MOL. At the conclusion of the seasonal employment contract, employers have long been required to evaluate Mexican SAWP employees. Indeed, except in cases where a CA is in place and seeks to regulate recall, these evaluations play a central role—arguably the most important role—in guiding Mexican officials engaged in selection and placement processes. These evaluations exert particular influence in determining whether or not the former SAWP employee is to be recalled to work at a given farm in Canada for the subsequent season (STPS 2011; STPS n.d.; UFCW 1518, staff representative, interview, July 19, 2017). Given the availability of mechanisms enabling the employer to terminate employees mid-contract or to fail to offer (often long-serving) employees future employment, securing a CA that would regulate termination and the recall process was a key factor motivating the bid to organize by SAWP employees of Sidhu, as explored in chapter 2.

In the behind-the-scenes relationships between host-state employers and sending-state officials, upon which it relies, but is often obscured by formal governmental agreements, the evaluation process also shares similarities with the second modality explored herein, namely, blacklisting.

BLACKLISTING

As applied to TMWP participants with the prospect of return, blacklisting includes threats and acts that can (and often do) occur in the presence of otherwise positive signals that recall is likely: independently or cumulatively, these actions have the effect of limiting the ability of employees to return to their former employer in the host state or to the host state more generally, often because they are or are perceived to be pro-union, are engaged in unionization efforts, or are bargaining unit members. Reflecting blacklisting's commonplace association with trade union activity (see, e.g., Segal 2009; Van den Broek 2003), in practice, it is carried out frequently by employers, or at their behest (explicit or assumed), in response to employees' attempts to exercise their labor rights or is otherwise used as a means of discouraging this exercise.[47] Under migration management, as a mode of control, blacklisting can involve a variety of new actors: intermediaries, employer associations, NGOs, and officials in sending and receiving states. However, the actions of these players typically reinforce, rather than undermine, national sovereignty and thereby approaches to governing migration predating the migration management paradigm.

In Canada, as a means of dismissal from future employment, blacklisting of SAWP employees with the prospect of return has been documented as occurring under several circumstances, although a common means is employers' provision of negative evaluations to "troublemaking" employees described earlier (Binford 2009; STPS 2011; STPS n.d.). More covertly, and the focus of chapter 3 given the experience of SAWP employees of Sidhu, sending-state officials stationed abroad (e.g., consular employees) and intermediaries (e.g., private recruiters or international organizations) brokering migration arrangements can also contribute to blacklisting by flagging habitual "complainers," especially union supporters, for officials in sending states (Basok et al. 2014). As a threat, the blacklisting of a single TMWP participant or a group of participants by these and other actors can cultivate a climate of fear, discouraging their counterparts' interaction with unions. As an act, it can also entail the doctoring of official records tied to program administration to obstruct the return of otherwise eligible unionized circular TMWP participants covered by CAs designed explicitly to preempt repatriation from future employment.

ATTRITION

The third modality of deportability, the risk of attrition, is of a different order from termination prompting repatriation and blacklisting. Attrition is often subtle and gradual, rather than direct and immediate. While it can be directed at specific employees, employers' reduced resort to temporary migrant workers through the SAWP is not necessarily aimed at preventing the return of particular individuals or groups. Nor does it entail formal removal per se (i.e., either in the form of termination prompting repatriation during the term of an employment contract or in nonrenewal or the denial of future participation in the SAWP). In not requiring immigration authorities' explicit removal of unwanted persons, as has been common historically (Walters 2010b), attrition reflects how, under schemes consistent with the migration management paradigm, practices of expulsion can appear to reflect straightforward and therefore benign decisions taken by employers in response to developments in markets (e.g., fluctuations in demand for agricultural products). Such practices can nevertheless involve both subtle and overt forms of coercion. Facilitated symbolically by a "Canadians first" approach to hiring in the elaboration of the operational parameters of the SAWP and other TMWPs, attrition can involve employers' decision not to recruit through TMWPs altogether and/or to use various means available to reduce their numbers. It can also involve recruitment through particular TMWPs, growing since the early 2000s, discouraging unionization or hindering viable collective bargaining.[48] Where unions are absent and/or unionization is infeasible, under the SAWP employers can exercise their prerogative by failing to invite back participants without providing any rationale. In contrast, in the presence of unionization, CAs may obligate employers to fulfill certain criteria for renewal if they wish to continue to engage SAWP employees and/or other TMWP participants—depending on whether the bargaining unit includes all employees or, in the case of Sidhu, SAWP employees exclusively. The prospect of renewal is also entirely dependent, as chapter 4 shows in its investigation of employer attempts to reduce the bargaining unit at Floralia, on whether or not unions are able to effectively enforce CA provisions and bar formal decertification.

Initiating the investigation into the legal struggle of SAWP employees of Sidhu, chapter 2 probes openings for termination without just cause. It explores Local 1518's disputed attempts to gain certification of a bargaining unit covering TMWP participants and subsequently to secure a CA, partly as a means of preempting such actions that often lead to repatriation or contract nonrenewal, resulting in dismissal from future employment (i.e., expulsion). In so doing, the chapter begins to reveal both how the SAWP, often characterized as a model TMWP, reproduces deportability and how its modalities are difficult to thwart even through unionization.

2

GETTING ORGANIZED

Countering Termination without Just Cause
through Certification

> "The distinctions between the SAWP and domestic workers are
> marked and real. Simply because they arise from differing terms and
> conditions of employment and employment status, rather than job
> duties, does not make them any less meaningful from a collective
> bargaining standpoint. These distinctions lead to concerns and
> interests particular to the SAWP employees. This is a real consideration
> that needs to be acknowledged when determining the appropriateness
> of the proposed unit."
>
> —BC Labour Relations Board, 2009 Reconsideration Decision permitting the
> establishment of a bargaining unit of SAWP employees

In 2008, against the backdrop of renewed support for organizing by the national
union, which was beginning to respond to calls for assistance by temporary migrant workers engaged in TMWPs that permit circularity, UFCW Local 1518 initiated a bid to represent agricultural employees at Sidhu in 2008. Through this
undertaking, it sought to test the limits of BC's Wagner Act–styled LRC, which
fostered industrial unionism and thereby unionization among male blue-collar
worker-citizens in mass production and resource industries, by applying to represent a bargaining unit encompassing employees participating in the BC–Mexico
SAWP. Reflecting the core concerns of members of the proposed bargaining unit,
and challenging impediments built into the LRC to unionization among workers in secondary industries and small firms, as well as among seasonal migrant
workers holding tenuous residency status, the union was motivated to curb deportability among SAWP employees. Specifically, it sought to limit threats and acts
of termination without just cause, prompting premature repatriation, during the
term of the seasonal employment contract, as well as to secure mechanisms for
the acquisition of seniority season to season suitable to workers laboring transnationally via a TMWP permitting circularity.

Early on in the unionization drive, obstacles to the certification of a wall-to-wall bargaining unit encompassing both domestic and SAWP employees precluded the organization of Sidhu's entire agricultural workforce.[1] However, SAWP employees' resolve to unionize remained strong—as did their union's willingness to pursue certification for a bargaining unit comprised of SAWP employees exclusively. In this context, as TMWP participants, SAWP employees' unique reasons for seeking collective representation took central stage. Ultimately, they also provided BC's LRB with the rationale it needed to certify a bargaining unit. Still, despite adjudicators' modernized interpretation of what constitutes a community of interest under the province's LRC, the LRB limited the scope of collective bargaining applicable to a unit comprised of SAWP employees in the interest of industrial stability. The resulting CA thus included only a narrow set of terms. Among those terms, nevertheless, were provisions aimed at blunting the potential negative consequences of certain aspects of SAWP agreements, such as the permissibility of termination without just cause during the term of an employment contract, and novel terms, such as those providing workers laboring transnationally seniority season to season and recall on this basis.

Such measures were, however, circumscribed by the preamble to the CA, which affirmed that its contents were not to conflict with intergovernmental agreements governing the SAWP and that, in instances of potential conflict, the terms of the Canada–Mexico SAWP were to govern. The preamble also characterized the SAWP as an agreement between Canada and sending states for the purpose of "hiring of temporary support" on a seasonal basis "when Canadians or permanent residents are not available" (Sidhu & Sons Nursery Ltd. and UFCW 1518 2010, para. a-d, art. 4.03). The struggle of SAWP employees of Sidhu to get organized and bargain collectively thereby illustrates how deportability is integral to the framework regulating the recruitment, hiring, oversight, and dismissal of workers under this TMWP. While the SAWP's parameters are often cast as "best practices" of migration management, modalities, such as termination without just cause, are embedded within the TMWP and thereby difficult to transcend by a CA.

This chapter chronicles the legal struggle of Local 1518 in pursuit of certification of a bargaining unit at BC's LRB, illustrating the centrality of termination without just cause to the operation of a TMWP emblematic of migration management. Revealing the "new" modes of control that the TMWP delegates to employers, the first section delineates a practice permissible under the Canada–Mexico SAWP: "cessation of employment" during a fixed-term (i.e., seasonal) contract prompting premature repatriation. It identifies how this practice, which was a key motivator for SAWP employees of Sidhu to unionize, conflicts with the fundamental tenets of protective and collective labor and employment laws, policies, and practices in Canada. Turning to the struggle at the LRB and focusing on its interpretations of what constitutes a "community of interest" and the traditionally difficult-to-organize doctrine, the second section charts the three stages in Local 1518's disputed application to represent a bargaining unit of SAWP employees at Sidhu. While the LRB initially declined to certify a unit of SAWP employees because of its interest in ensuring industrial stability across Sidhu's entire agricultural workforce, the union made a successful request for reconsideration, building on the notion of the traditionally difficult to organize, in which it argued that an equally central rationale of the LRC is to provide access to collective bargaining. In response, the LRB stopped short of characterizing SAWP employees as traditionally difficult to organize, but concluded that industrial stability could be maintained by limiting the topics that could be addressed by the CA; specifically, the LRB excluded those provisions related to work jurisdiction from the scope of collective bargaining, by which it meant matters related to control over the work process common to workers inside and outside the bargaining unit (e.g., the assignment of work). At the same time, the LRB affirmed that collective bargaining need not follow a strict work jurisdiction model. CAs governing the terms and conditions of employees participating in TMWPs could thus reasonably include provisions addressing transnational aspects of workers' employment situations. The chapter concludes, in section three, with an analysis of the CA, focusing on its provisions for timely grievance and arbitration processes in instances of alleged unjust termination, as well as recall on the basis of seniority. This section also evaluates the strength of these provisions in light of the inclusion of statements in the CA's preamble giving paramountcy to the SAWP, a framing that, as future developments would show, contributed ultimately to reducing the potency of such provisions. In assessing such CA provisions' potential to mitigate SAWP employees' deportability, this discussion prepares the ground for explorations of their efficacy in practice in chapters 3 and 4, as well as reflections in the conclusion on how those provisions with the most promise could be scaled up to the level of intergovernmental agreements.

Termination without a Requirement for Just Cause under the SAWP: A Mode of Employer Control

Under the SAWP, host-state employers, the direct economic beneficiaries of TMWPs, are granted significant authority in managing the flows of participants: their entry (i.e., hiring and placement), exit, and recall (i.e., temporary or permanent return to the sending state). This delegation of authority, under the SAWP, enables nonstate actors unaccountable to the principles of democratic governance to exercise "new" modes of control. One such mode of control granted to employers is the ability to terminate, with relative ease, SAWP employees during the term of their seasonal employment contracts. As noted in chapter 1, the Canada–Mexico standard employment agreement dictates that an employer may cease seasonal employment contracts for any reason at any time, without allowing for the possibility of employee appeal, so long as there is consultation with a Mexican government agent in advance. While a SAWP employee is placed with a specific employer (and bound to that employer via a closed work permit), the grower in question is entitled to terminate "employment for non-compliance, refusal to work, or *any other sufficient reason*" (ESDC 2016a, X.1, emphasis added).

By making termination without just cause permissible, this provision of the standard employment agreement runs counter to employment standards legislation in several jurisdictions in Canada and the tenor of laws and policies governing collective bargaining, which promote procedural fairness and acknowledge power imbalances inherent in the employment relationship. In Quebec and Nova Scotia, as well as in the federal jurisdiction, which covers workers across Canada in federally regulated industries (e.g., airlines, telecommunications, and the like), where the SCC mandated it for non-unionized employees covered by the Canada Labour Code in 2016, employment standards legislation protects employees against unjust dismissal in some measure. Even in the absence of such protection, in supporting the rights of employees to be members of trade unions and to participate in unions' lawful activities (and employers to likewise be members of and to participate in employer associations' lawful activities), and in promoting procedural fairness in the provision of these individual and collective rights, labor relations legislation throughout Canada enables CAs to provide or supplement such protection through provisions governing hiring, promotion, and termination procedures, as well as recall in instances of layoffs (see, e.g., BC LRC 1996, S. 4(1) and (2)). In practice, therefore, CAs seek to curb arbitrary behavior. They are particularly important in regulating practices surrounding termination in industries, such as agriculture, that are characterized by seasonal hiring and layoff cycles, especially those in which temporary migrant workers, for whom termination and seasonal layoffs result typically in repatriation, form a sizable component of the labor force.

Under the Canada–Mexico SAWP and its BC variant, reasons for termination cited by employers often relate to diminishing demands for products that contribute to reduced labor needs or to poor weather conditions leading to declining crop yields. These "official reasons" are questionable on their own terms; given the short duration of all seasonal employment contracts under the SAWP, employers accrue minimal labor cost savings by terminating employees early. Yet, there is evidence that employers may exercise their ability to terminate without just cause for other reasons, notably, as a means of eliminating SAWP employees known or believed to be pro-union. Although a CA was not yet in place, the termination of a group of SAWP employees by Abbotsford, BC-based Floralia—whose experience with attrition is documented in chapter 4—offers a vivid example. In the legal proceedings surrounding SAWP employees' bid to unionize at Sidhu, it came to light that Floralia successfully terminated, and promptly repatriated, a group of SAWP employees, citing poor weather conditions, on the same day that the grower received an application for certification.[2] In another BC example, also surfacing and playing out during the LRB hearings in the Sidhu case, a grower (Village Farms Inc.) in close proximity to Sidhu told eight of its SAWP employees that they were being terminated and would be repatriated, among other reasons, because "they had contacted the union" (UFCW 1518 2009c).[3]

In instances in which immediate termination is not a practical option but in which employers want to preempt SAWP employees' return to Canada in a subsequent season, growers in BC, as in other provinces party to the Canada–Mexico SAWP, have other mechanisms at their disposal. Through a process overseen by Mexico's MOL, Mexican SAWP employees are typically evaluated by their employers at the conclusion of their seasonal employment contracts. To ensure reassignment (or not) of SAWP employees by a certain date to a farm where they have worked previously, employers must submit an assessment to Mexico's MOL for each SAWP worker (STPS n.d., 2011). Before 2010, employers were required to fill out a written assessment, which was to be submitted to MOL by the SAWP participant immediately on the worker's return to Mexico; this assessment indicated the length of time and number of hours worked during the foregoing season, the reason for the worker's return to the sending state, who was paying the worker's return airfare to Mexico, and the employer's opinion of the worker's performance. In 2010, this evaluative process was integrated into the new SIMOL system (Sistema de Movilidad Laboral: "labor movement system") or the electronic log that Mexican officials have since used to track SAWP employees, segments of which are accessible not only to sending- and host-state officials but also to employers, to prevent employee manipulation of the process when delivering the evaluation from the employer to Mexico's MOL (UFCW 1518 representative, interview, July 19, 2017). The post-2010 online evaluation process, overseen by Mexico's MOL, and in operation at the time of writing, requires less information than the earlier written assessment. In this online process, the mandatory "general assessment" segment asks the employer to provide an assessment of worker performance, whether the worker will return the following season, and, if so, the probable date of return; details on seniority, the number of hours worked, and reason for return are to be included in an optional extended assessment form (STPS 2011).

In practice, under both the pre- and post-2010 variants, a positive evaluation leads typically to an invitation to return to the same farm, assuming that the grower justifies the need for temporary migrant workers to Canadian government officials and also requests (or "nominates") the worker in question, whereas a negative evaluation typically leads Mexico to cut off the former SAWP employee from future participation. More broadly, as Basok (2002, 120) demonstrates, a negative evaluation is a means of flagging troublemakers to the Mexican officials: "if the farmer reports that the worker in question is lazy, does not get along with others, drinks too much, or is slow or rebellious, he or she will have a hard time getting approved from the program in the following season." True to migration management's ostensible commitments to ensuring triple wins for migrant workers, host-state employers, and sending states, the evaluation process outlined in the pre-2010 form (STPS n.d.) is self-described as a means to improve "the selection process of the seasonal agricultural workers program." Yet, by emphasizing the asymmetrical power relations between the lower-income sending and the higher-income host state, and the reliance of the former on remittances, in reality it allows the sending state to fulfill the preferences of host-state employers by design. This mechanism is therefore integral to termination as a modality of deportability: insofar as SAWP participants with the prospect of return are subject to recall provisions of CAs where they exist, when they return to the sending state in between fixed-term employment contracts, the evaluation process offers an alternative means by which employers can thwart their return. In addition, as chapter 3 shows, this administrative mechanism can enable blacklisting. More broadly, the evaluation process serves to discipline temporary migrant workers to tolerate (and avoid making grievances about) labor practices they view as unfair in order to reduce the possibility of removal from future participation in the SAWP and thus access to the relatively higher wages available in the host state.[4]

Local 1518's bid to unionize agricultural employees at Sidhu aimed to limit deportability among SAWP employees, but the threat of removal, exemplified by the permissibility of termination without just cause, continued to be enshrined in intergovernmental agreements; this threat was strengthened by the absence of clear mechanisms for governing recall, despite the SAWP's promotion of circularity and the evaluation process overseen by Mexico's MOL. Among the domestic and SAWP employees comprising the wall-to-wall unit that the union sought to organize initially, preventing termination without just cause and limiting the discretion accorded to private actors, such as employers, in deciding which SAWP participants were given the opportunity to return were thus priorities.

Even after the union's failure to organize a wall-to-wall unit, and after witnessing arbitrary acts of termination against SAWP employees prompting their premature repatriation by BC growers such as Floralia and Village Farms, SAWP employees of Sidhu remained determined to secure certification and a first CA. Their resolve was strengthened by the 2009 decision regarding Greenway Farms in which the LRB affirmed that the LRC applies to participants in a TMWP administered federally and does not conflict with the SAWP, since the latter mandates only minimum terms that CAs may supplement or exceed (BC LRB 2009b, 28). Still, in seeking to represent a bargaining unit comprised of SAWP employees, Local 1518 faced formidable obstacles. It first had to convince the LRB that this segment of Sidhu's agricultural workforce, on the basis of their common migration status, constituted a community of interest appropriate for the purposes of collective bargaining. It also had to demonstrate that the certification of a bargaining unit comprised exclusively of TMWP participants need not undermine industrial stability.[5]

The Struggle at the LRB: Local 1518's Disputed Application for Certification of a Bargaining Unit of SAWP Employees

Local 1518's disputed application to the LRB to represent a bargaining unit of SAWP employees (i.e., for certification) pivoted first on illustrating that a unit comprised of temporary migrant workers was appropriate under the Wagner Act–styled LRC and aligned with the LRB's policies on bargaining unit formation.

Bargaining Unit Determination: The Need to Establish a Community of Interest

After receiving an application for certification, it is the BC LRB's responsibility to decide whether the group identified in the application is a suitable one for collective bargaining purposes. Four factors, which have been refined over time to align with the labor relations model, inform adjudicators' decisions. These factors are known as similarity in skills, interests, working conditions, and duties; the structure (physical and administrative) of the employer; functional integration; and, geography. Additionally, the LRB considers the practice and history of the current collective bargaining relationship and of collective bargaining in the industry or sector (BC MOL 2003, 15). Together, these components help establish whether or not a particular group of workers represents what is known as a "community of interest" (BC LRB 2008, para. 28).

Responding to the changing nature of employment and the disconnect between the composition of BC's workforce and the Wagnerian orientation of its LRC, in

1993 the LRB consolidated and modernized community-of-interest factors in its decision regarding *Island Medical Laboratories* (*IML*) (BC LRB 1993). In this ruling, which influenced its approach to bargaining unit appropriateness, the LRB affirmed the factors of geography and administrative and physical structure of the employer. Yet adjudicators recognized that the factor of similarity in skills, interests, duties, and working conditions could effectively divide white- from blue-collar workers and, particularly relevant to the drive to organize SAWP employees at Sidhu, could contribute to the tendency to establish distinct bargaining units on the basis of workers' form of employment (i.e., part-time versus full-time, temporary versus permanent) or to exclude temporary and part-time workers entirely from bargaining units. The decision also suggested that the LRB's application of this factor was not always neutral, but was often founded on unprincipled grounds such as "gender, skills, or sometimes an unstated division based upon class," examples to which immigration status could be added; the *IML* decision thereby indicated that the LRB was no longer required to grant this factor the priority it had previously (28). The adjudicators also reinterpreted functional integration: concurring with prior interpretations that this factor dampened the potential establishment of bargaining units cutting across classification lines, but indicating that such certifications are permissible, the decision noted that "the preference for an all-employee unit is . . . not an 'invariable' rule'" (23). Moreover, it proposed that "if a group of employees seeking certification have a fairly coherent community of interest, the fact that there may be others outside the group who may share other similar skills or interests or duties, *would not be sufficient to defeat a favorable community of interest determination*" (33, emphasis added).

    The *IML* decision also recognized that in BC, as elsewhere, securing certification is challenging for those with limited power and resources. In instances where workers are uniquely vulnerable, the LRB may choose to emphasize its role in facilitating access to collective bargaining. Here the decision referred to the "traditionally difficult to organize" doctrine, first established in a 1974 case involving unit of employees of the Insurance Corporation of BC that was seeking certification. In this case, the LRB indicated that "there are certain types of employees who are traditionally difficult to organize and there are some employers who are willing to exploit that fact"; in such instances, the LRB affirmed its discretion to "not stick rigidly to a conception of the best bargaining unit in the long run" (BC LRB 1974, 5). Subsequent to this case, it judged a group of employees to be traditionally difficult to organize by "evidence of a relationship between low union density in a particular industry and the structural or systemic aspects of the workforce which have made it difficult to organize" (BC LRB 1999, 33). In a few further cases involving the retail and insurance industries, the LRB then required a union seeking the traditionally difficult-to-organize designation for a group of employees not only to provide evidence of the low level of union density in an identified industry or sector but also to show how certain characteristics of that industry or sector contributed to this trend and, in fact, constrained organizing efforts; the union also had to provide evidence concerning any other relevant considerations (34).[6]

Still, the LRB's overarching approach to bargaining unit determination, which remained largely unchanged, together with unions' scarce resources, significantly limited efforts to pursue this designation of behalf of the difficult to organize. In the *IML* decision, the LRB nevertheless did acknowledge the traditionally difficult-to-organize doctrine, suggesting that, among those workers, the standard of appropriateness may be "'relaxed' to assist in the establishment of collective bargaining," specifically, to foster initial certifications based on an appropriate, but not necessarily *the* most appropriate, unit (BC LRB 1993, 17). This endorsement of the doctrine, as well as the modernized community-of-interest factors delineated in *IML*, shaped Local 1518's strategy in its application to represent a bargaining unit comprised of SAWP employees at Sidhu.

A Bargaining Unit of SAWP Employees: Local 1518's Application

Local 1518's application drew extensively on mechanisms for enabling access to collective bargaining. As the legal proceedings unfolded, the union's arguments for greater inclusivity relied on the modernized factors established in the *IML* decision and engaged the traditionally difficult-to-organize doctrine as a secondary argument. However, the union confronted substantial challenges, resulting in a lengthy three-stage proceeding at the LRB. Given the Wagnerian orientation of the LRC—which assumes a male worker in industry, engaged in a full-time ongoing employment relationship with one employer, who holds national citizenship, and who resides permanently in a single location in the country of employment as the norm—disputes over the union's application revolved principally around whether workers' common migration status (i.e., their presence in Canada as TMWP participants) could form the basis for designating a bargaining unit appropriate.

THE FIRST APPLICATION

In its first application in August 2008, Local 1518's arguments were structured to align with the role of the LRC in providing access to collective bargaining (UFCW Local 1518 2008c, para. 1.1).[7] The union then advanced a twofold argument regarding the factors considered by the LRB in determining whether a group shares a community of interest: it made the case, first, for rendering that SAWP employees' labor under terms and conditions of employment distinguished from domestic employees as a result of participating in a TMWP. The union described the different legal regimes in play in the oversight of temporary migrant and domestic agricultural workers' employment situations, indicating how the SAWP operates on the basis of standard employment contracts addressing such issues as term/duration of employment, hours of work, medical insurance, air travel, lodging, meals, termination of employment, and repatriation. It also stressed that such contracts ultimately expire (paras. 9(o), 11).

In pursuit of this primary argument, the union centered its assertion of SAWP employees' community of interest on the first and third *IML* factors.[8] It described how the most important factor of similarity in skills, interests, duties, and working conditions strongly favored the union's application for certification since SAWP employees, as foreign nationals, and Canadian workers, as citizens or permanent residents, have distinct interests as a result of their differing employment status and working conditions (UFCW 1518 2008c). Accordingly, "although much domestic labour legislation applies to the workers (save for those based on citizenship) . . . SAWP employees do not work under the common law employment regime that Canadian workers work under" (para. 3.8). Underlining their deportability, SAWP employees' presence in Canada is also entirely dependent on employers' effort yet ultimate failure to recruit workers domestically; additionally, unlike Canadian workers who are free to work continuously year-round, SAWP employees are denied the right to uninterrupted employment or, for that matter, recall. Regarding the third factor of functional integration, Local 1518 contended further that "there is no employee interchange between individuals inside and outside of the proposed unit on a day-to-day basis" since SAWP employees are prevented by immigration policy from becoming non-SAWP employees and thus "there is a clearly identifiable [dividing] line" (paras. 4.1, 4.2, 5.2).

In case the LRB was not convinced by the primary argument that the SAWP employees shared a community of interest as set out in the *IML* decision, the union put forward a secondary contention that SAWP employees are traditionally difficult to organize. To substantiate this argument, Local 1518 suggested that agricultural workers have historically had, and continue to have, low union density. Here, it cited *Dunmore*, a 2001 case in which the SCC recognized agricultural workers' vulnerability and governments' positive obligation to protect this group's right to form and participate in unions. Local 1518 then noted that these workers are poorly paid, perform work under onerous conditions, and often have low levels of education and societally recognized skills, in addition to limited employment mobility. The union argued that these disadvantages, in addition to the fact that they are both temporary migrant workers and seasonal (i.e., temporary) employees, "make it more difficult for agricultural workers in general [to obtain union representation], *and SAWP employees in particular*," because of the provisions of agreements governing selection, placement, stay (e.g., the provision of closed work permits), and working conditions affecting their employment situation and their application (UFCW 1518 2008c, para. 22, emphasis added; see also para. 2.23).[9]

In response to the union's application for certification, the employer questioned the appropriateness of a SAWP employee-only bargaining unit by identifying key similarities between domestic and SAWP employees: it contended that SAWP employees were not sufficiently distinct for rational lines to be drawn around them as a bargaining unit (Sidhu 2008a, para. 53). Specifically, Sidhu rejected interpreting functional integration in line with immigration status, preferring, instead, to consider employees' job duties (Sidhu 2008a, paras. 42–52). It argued that the *IML* decision discourages certifying a unit that cuts across job classifications, because doing so could, by potentially exacerbating conflicting interests not conducive to the resolution of disputes through collective bargaining, compromise industrial stability (submission C, para. 5). For the grower, bargaining units must be "conducive to the orderly resolution of . . . disputes by the parties" (Sidhu 2008b, paras. 28–29). Furthermore, historically, decisions of the LRB had not allowed for units of this sort, and such a certification would not reflect recent trends in certifications involving agricultural workers, which typically encompassed "appropriate unit[s] of *all* farm workers" (para. 46, emphasis added).

The employer also boldly refuted Local 1518's secondary argument: it claimed that the lack of evidence of a relationship between low union density in agriculture and structural or systemic aspects of the workforce impeding organizing made it impossible to demonstrate conclusively that SAWP employees are traditionally difficult to organize. Even if the traditionally difficult-to-organize doctrine were to apply, the employer argued, this designation does not offer a basis for certifying a unit cutting across job classifications since the *IML* decision recognized that, despite its provision for relaxed standards of appropriateness, the LRB is still empowered to draw "rational" and "defensible" boundaries around units (Sidhu 2008b, para. 27).

THE LRB'S FIRST DECISION

On October 14, 2008, in response to Local 1518's highly disputed application to represent SAWP employees at Sidhu (UFCW 1518 2008d, 1), the LRB relayed its decision. Based on its examination of the essential facts of the case, the LRB characterized the employer and the union as in agreement: these parties concurred that domestic and SAWP employees of Sidhu perform the same job, but labor under different terms and conditions of employment (BC LRB 2008, para. 17). Therefore, determining whether the proposed bargaining unit of SAWP employees was appropriate, given the community-of-interest factors set out in *IML*, and, if not, taking into account the relaxed standards of appropriateness applied to workers deemed to be traditionally difficult to organize, was the task at hand (para. 17).

In outlining its decision, the LRB reiterated "a preference for all-employee units," but indicated a willingness to "certify a less than all-employee unit provided the unit is appropriate" (BC LRB 2008, para. 25). It further noted that it was "assum[ing] *without deciding* that agricultural workers are traditionally difficult to organize," given the SCC's decision in *Dunmore*; it opted not to make a definitive statement that would so characterize the employees concerned (para. 103). Addressing the union's primary argument, the LRB's first question was as follows: as participants in a TMWP that restricts their residency in Canada and sets out specific terms and conditions of employment (i.e., as temporary migrant workers), did SAWP employees at Sidhu represent a distinct community of interest?

Applying *IML*'s test of appropriateness, the LRB first considered all four factors to address this question. In its view, if SAWP employees and domestic agricultural workers' interests diverged, this divergence arose from the temporary nature of migrant workers' employment relationships and unique terms and conditions of employment *as shaped by immigration policy* (BC LRB 2008, para. 33). Although it recognized SAWP employees' distinct interests insofar as their workplace concerns were intertwined with their tenuous residency status and, as a group, they were governed by two separate legal regimes (i.e., federal immigration policy and BC labor law), the LRB did find a number of significant administrative aspects to be widespread among the entire workforce (paras. 38–42).

On the basis of physical and administrative structure, the LRB found limited grounds for differentiating between foreign and domestic workers (BC LRB 2008, para. 42). In its evaluation of functional integration, it concluded that this factor did not allow a "rational" or "defensible" line to be drawn around a bargaining unit of SAWP employees (para. 47). Finally, with regard to geography, the LRB ruled that all of the employer's locations constituted a single bargaining unit spatially.

In response to the union's secondary argument—that SAWP employees are traditionally difficult to organize—the LRB was unconvinced that there was sufficient justification for separating a job classification at a single given worksite; that is, to effectively divide the workforce based on workers' immigration status (BC LRB 2008, para. 81).[10] Though sympathetic to the union's argument that the agricultural industry, comprising many temporary migrant workers confronting adversities related to transnational aspects of their employment situation, is traditionally difficult to organize, the LRB ruled that SAWP employees were not distinct to a degree that would "substantially mitigate . . . or eliminate . . . the labor relations concerns that inevitably arise when a classification is divided" (BC LRB

2008, paras. 82, 86–87). As a result, it gave the organization of the employer's affairs priority over carving out a bargaining unit of temporary migrant agricultural workers unified by their common migration status (para. 86). In explaining its position, the LRB emphasized that, because the LRC assumes that bargaining work and nonbargaining work are easily distinguished, it "places few limits on the scope of what can be negotiated" in CAs (paras. 86, 87). As a result, the employer could face certain challenges if the farm worker classification were subdivided. For example, the LRB anticipated problems arising from whether and how to allocate "additional work . . . to domestic farm workers (outside the bargaining unit) or to foreign farm workers (within the bargaining unit)" and problems surrounding how to approach layoffs due to these groups' 'functionally integrated work'" (para. 87; see also paras. 92, 103). Notably, the LRB made this statement even though Canada's bilateral agreements with sending states indicate unequivocally that SAWP employees are to be laid off first. Concerned that the preceding issues could undermine industrial stability, the LRB rejected Local 1518's first application for certification of a unit comprised of SAWP employees.

THE REQUEST FOR RECONSIDERATION

In response to the LRB's rejection of Local 1518's first application for certification, the union appealed to the board to review its decision (i.e., applied for "leave for reconsideration"), taking the position that the adjudicators had not fulfilled the LRB's duty to foster access to collective bargaining. The union argued that the original decision "deprived a marginalized and traditionally difficult to organize group access to collective bargaining" and that, although the decision "purported to assume that the sector was difficult to organize," it did not relax the LRB's appropriateness criteria accordingly (UFCW 1518 2008e, para. 5).

In response to the LRB's policy of discouraging cross-classification bargaining units, the union asserted that because employment status and terms and conditions of employment are integral to workers' community of interest, the LRB should find that SAWP employees constitute a single classification (UFCW 1518 2008e, para. 65). However, if the LRB was genuinely convinced that SAWP employees belong to a broader farm worker classification, Local 1518 provided a secondary argument: the LRB should adhere to the *IML* test of "whether the unit applied for has a sufficient community of interest *despite being part of a broader classification*" (para. 66, emphasis added).

Citing the reasoning provided in the original legal proceedings, the employer disagreed with the union's two-pronged argument. But in spring 2009, the LRB's reconsideration panel ruled that a "fresh determination" was required; that June, the Reconsideration Decision affirmed that issues extending beyond those that are explicitly work related can be considered when determining whether a community of interest exists. It thereby implied that terms and conditions of employment and employment status fall within the "'interests' criterion" (BC LRB 2009a, para. 74). The panel, however, did not provide any direct statements in response to the union's traditionally difficult-to-organize argument. It also maintained that, if SAWP employees were "found to be part of a single classification," the LRB had the license to "make an exception to the . . . 'restriction' against certifying units that cut across job classifications" (para. 74; see also para. 75). Indicating that collective bargaining need not follow a strict work jurisdiction model, the panel concluded as well that the Original Decision adopted too narrow a view of what constitutes a CA (para. 81). Given the LRB's general inclination to avoid cross-classification units in the interest of industrial stability, its view of SAWP employee-only bargaining units was tepid; nevertheless, the Reconsideration Decision made it possible to introduce novel CA provisions addressing transnational aspects of workers' employment situations.

THE SECOND APPLICATION

Shortly after receiving the Reconsideration Decision, Local 1518 made a second application to represent a unit of SAWP employees, vigorously pursuing the claim that such a unit is appropriate for collective bargaining because its members share a community of interest. Well aware of SAWP and domestic agricultural employees' similar duties and functional integration, the union prefaced its argument by noting that "it doesn't matter that the SAWP workers may also share a community of interest with other farm workers . . . [what matters is] whether members share a community of interest which is likely to further harmonious organization and facilitate collective bargaining" (UFCW 1518 2009a, para. 3.6). It then stressed that because the four-factor test is meant solely to provide guidance to the LRB, some factors may be given precedence over others (para. 3.13). In the case of SAWP employees, it was the union's view that the most relevant factors related to their shared interests as temporary migrant workers:

> The SAWP workers are employed temporarily, where others are employed permanently. They live on the Employer's property, where others are entitled to find accommodation elsewhere. They depend entirely on the Employer to provide them with clean drinking water and sanitation, while others, clearly, do not.

The union also noted that because SAWP employees "work under contract negotiated by sovereign nations," they differ from domestic employees because they are not "free to negotiate their own terms and conditions of employment," a limitation exacerbated by the deportability they experience as temporary migrant workers with the prospect, but by no means guarantee, of return (para. 3.14). Furthermore, it contended that SAWP employees are traditionally difficult to organize (para. 3.25).[11] Mindful of the LRB's concerns about potential labor relations problems resulting from the certification of a unit cutting across classification lines, Local 1518 suggested further that it would not necessarily represent SAWP employees solely "with regard to the work they are presently performing" (para. 3.38). Implying that it was motivated to negotiate a CA limiting TMWP participants' deportability, and true to its commitment to move beyond bread-and-butter issues, the union would emphasize "dignity and respect" concerns: reflecting its debt to the worker center operated by the Agricultural Workers' Alliance (AWA), a cross-sectoral alliance of groups, including unions and non-governmental organizations supporting agricultural workers across Canada, particularly concerned with the human and labor rights challenges facing those that are migrants, which the union credited for preparing the ground for certification, Local 1518 would emphasize "dignity and respect" in collective bargaining. To reduce the likelihood of SAWP employees being returned to sending states without cause, for instance, it would pursue an effective grievance procedure (para. 3.39).

In responding to the union's second application, Sidhu continued to underscore the potential labor relations difficulties arising from a cross-classification unit (Sidhu 2009b, para. 135). Although the employer acknowledged SAWP employees' distinct interests as outlined in the Reconsideration Decision, it held the view that such differences "do not form the basis for a rational and defensible line to be drawn around the SAWP workers to the exclusion of the other farm workers" (para. 17; see also paras. 85–89). Sidhu also indicated that the functional integration of all agricultural workers would make a separate classification comprised of SAWP employees inappropriate (para. 19). Additionally, it refuted the application of the traditionally difficult-to-organize doctrine, claiming once again that the union had neither "established any difficulty organizing employees hired pursuant to the SAWP" nor identified "structural or systemic" issues causing low union density among foreign workers or the nursery sector (para. 20).[12] If the LRB deemed SAWP employees traditionally difficult to organize, however, the grower argued that certifying the unit in question was unwarranted since the facts failed to justify dividing agricultural workers (para. 128). As evidence for its stand against an SAWP employee-only bargaining unit, Sidhu also offered a list detailing other certifications to illustrate the predominance of all-employee units provincially in BC and elsewhere. However, Local 1518 later poked holes in this list, demonstrating that most of the examples involved manufacturing or processing employees instead of traditional agricultural workers and that at least four units listed by the employer were voluntary recognition agreements (schedule E, para. 18v; UFCW 1518 2009b, paras. 2.19, 2.20).

As the disputed application unfolded, the parties developed and sharpened their arguments such that the disputes came to center not only on whether there was justification for a bargaining unit comprised exclusively of SAWP employees but also on the related issue of whether temporary migrant agricultural workers are traditionally difficult to organize. Indeed, toward the end of the process, in response to the Original Decision's "presum[ption] . . . that agricultural workers are traditionally difficult to organize," which the Reconsideration Decision did not refute, Sidhu pointed to the protective nature of SAWP's provisions to argue that SAWP employees specifically are "not difficult to organize." It noted that, under the auspices of the SAWP, temporary migrant workers "have agents who assist them within the country and are not without representation" (Sidhu 2009b, para. 50) and that the TMWP provides participants with essentially the same right of job mobility as domestic workers by enabling them to transfer to other participating farms (para. 63), two aspects of the SAWP that can have the paradoxical consequence of heightening temporary migrant workers' vulnerability. This is because, as explored in chapter 3, SAWP employees' requests for transfers are rarely completed, and "agents" or employees of the Mexican consulate responsible for assisting SAWP employees are often compelled to prioritize host-state employers' interests and discourage unionization through various strategies, including by threats and acts of blacklisting (see also Binford 2009; Hennebry and McLaughlin 2012). Sidhu also noted that because more than half of foreign workers have worked with their employer for two or more years, SAWP employees can reasonably expect to return to their employer in subsequent seasons (para. 22).

Further disputing the union's view that SAWP employees are traditionally difficult to organize, Sidhu enlisted two nonstate actors as interveners: the Western Agricultural Labour Initiative (WALI) and the BC Agricultural Council (BCAC). These interveners supported Sidhu's contention that the structure and operation of the SAWP meant that the employees were, in fact, *not* difficult to organize.[13] Pointing to weekly routines and the use of employer-provided transportation, they argued that SAWP employees were a clearly identifiable community with access to Spanish-speaking union representatives (BCAC and WALI 2009). In the face of Local 1518's references to the "'threat' of repatriation" as thwarting unionization, the interveners did not see repatriation without the consent or request of an individual worker as a practical or realistic outcome. They also pointed to a UFCW-supported AWA, which negotiated agreements with several state-level governments in Mexico enabling the alliance to represent workers with regard to health and safety, and other issues while in Canada, as evidence of workers being directed to the union before leaving Mexico (para. 3).

Local 1518 contested the interveners' testimony that SAWP employees are not traditionally difficult to organize, including their claims that workers are easy to identify and access.[14] It also clarified that the one AWA agreement with which it was familiar involved a single Mexican state, Michoachán, and covered health and safety exclusively. Furthermore, the union offered evidence that the common practice of employers accompanying SAWP employees on shopping and other outings is, in fact, a means of monitoring their off-farm movements and activities, rather than a genuine gesture of support.

The union's central objection to the interveners' arguments, however, was linked to their attempt to deemphasize SAWP employees' deportability and its role in impeding unionization. Noting some of the unique obstacles that SAWP employees face in organizing, Local 1518 referred to a then-pending unfair labor practice complaint to the LRB. Launched just days before the interveners' submission, the complaint was made against Village Farms for unlawfully terminating and attempting to repatriate eight SAWP employees after they visited the AWA office in Surrey in an attempt to connect with the union (UFCW 1518 2009c).[15] The union also pointed to examples of decertification campaigns and successful decertification votes in the nursery sector, citing one at Mayfair Farms in another western province, Manitoba, that occurred shortly after unionization. These decertification efforts often followed workers' engagement with consular officials, providing further evidence of the difficulties in sustaining bargaining unit strength for SAWP employees (UFCW 1518 2009d; means of attrition are explored further in chapter 4).

In light of such unique challenges confronting SAWP employees as TMWP participants seeking to engage in collective bargaining, the union also emphasized that, while the primary aim of the AWA is to support temporary migrant workers' dignity and respect concerns, and despite its formidable role and that of other like institutions, this alliance—and its allied worker center—held limited sway in compelling employers to demonstrate proper cause for termination where there was no CA.[16] Moreover, any efforts made by the AWA are impeded markedly when the employee concerned has left Canada (UFCW 1518 2009f, para. 10). Without a CA, there also is no guarantee that employers will rehire or request temporary migrant workers for employment in the next season (para. 10). The union thereby argued that such overarching concerns motivate the UFCW National to negotiate, through its locals across Canada and on behalf of temporary migrant workers among its membership, CAs that include terms that aim to curb SAWP employees' deportability—including provisions aimed at preventing termination without just cause, providing for the right to grieve unfair treatment, and extending seniority and recall rights (UFCW 1518 2009e, para. 12). Yet Local 1518 also attempted to demonstrate its flexibility in dealing with potential problems flowing from a cross-classification unit, the issue that it presumed would be of foremost concern to the LRB. Recognizing that "agriculture is a tough business financially," Local 1518 conceded that "wages and benefits were comparatively low on [migrant workers'] list of priorities" (UFCW 1518 2009f, paras. 14, 16) while suggesting that the union would advocate for provisions, such as layoffs in order of seniority, with the understanding that SAWP employees could be laid off first due to the primacy of bilateral agreements governing temporary migrant work (paras. 21, 28). Such interventions highlighted a strategic choice on the part of the union: reading between the lines of the LRB's comments about the potential for including novel terms in CAs, Local 1518, in its effort to secure a first certification of a SAWP-employee only unit, advocated for a fluid model of collective bargaining while also indicating its flexibility in terms of scope.

THE LRB'S SECOND DECISION

In early 2010, the LRB issued its fresh determination, which addressed three questions at the crux of the contentious application for certification. First, did the SAWP employees share a community of interest due to their migration status or under the relaxed traditionally difficult-to-organize standard? Second, if the SAWP employees were found to share a community of interest that passed the test for bargaining unit appropriateness, did their common interests take precedence over the labor relations concerns stemming from the fact that the same work was being performed by other workers at the farm in question? Third, if labor relations concerns remained at issue, what actions could the LRB take to ensure access to collective bargaining?

In its second ruling, the LRB permitted the certification of the union. Issues related to work jurisdiction, however, were excluded from the scope of collective bargaining. To justify this demarcation, the LRB cited the Original Decision, which differentiated between domestic and SAWP employees on the basis of their distinct terms, conditions of employment, and employment status (BC LRB 2010, para. 29). Referring to the parameters established in the *IML* ruling, the final decision took factors beyond work duties into consideration when determining whether a community of interest existed, making reference to additional evidence of differences between SAWP and non-SAWP employees. The LRB thereby accepted the Reconsideration Decision's contention that, in this case, "labour relations concerns [should] not [be] determinative" in establishing the appropriateness of a bargaining unit; it was not, however, persuaded that SAWP employees' community of interest was of sufficient magnitude to overshadow all other criteria of appropriateness (para. 49 citing para. 77 of the Reconsideration Decision).

Functional integration was a principal concern for the board and, as a result, held significant influence in its final decision. The ruling accepted the union's claim that SAWP employees have unique interests emanating from their quest for dignity and respect, including the need to prevent termination without just cause prompting repatriation through timely access to grievance arbitration and the regulation of recall procedures. It also affirmed that the concerns arising from these shared interests would not undermine the appropriateness of a stand-alone bargaining unit (BC LRB 2010, para. 62). Nevertheless, it found plausible Sidhu's argument that a cross-classification unit could potentially create difficulties with regard to CA negotiation and administration, considering that SAWP and non-SAWP employees perform the same work (para. 51). It thus prevented the union from pursuing bargaining unit members' interests related to access to preferred types of work; since employees would logically attempt to secure more favorable work, the permissibility of expressing work preferences through a CA could cause a significant disruption for the employer (para. 67). Were disputes to arise, they would invariably encroach upon "the Employer['s] ability to run a viable farming operation" (para. 73). Including such matters within the scope of collective bargaining could consequently undermine industrial stability.

The LRB came to the conclusion that minimizing the issues subject to collective bargaining would eliminate initial concerns about other criteria of appropriateness—for example, functional integration—and about establishing a cross-classification bargaining unit (BC LRB 2010, para. 78). Certifying the bargaining unit in this restricted way also enabled the LRB to, once again, avoid determining whether SAWP employees are traditionally difficult to organize (para. 80). For the TMWP participants concerned, the LRB's ultimate decision to certify a unit of SAWP employees both marked a departure from the Wagnerian orientation of the LRC *and* a significant gain for the temporary migrant workers concerned insofar as it acknowledged—by applying a modernized interest criterion and tepidly endorsing *IML*'s fourfold test—these bargaining unit members' migration status to be relevant to establishing their community of interest and thereby to designating an appropriate bargaining unit. At the same time, even though it relied on this modernized criterion to certify a unit of exclusively SAWP employees, the LRB limited the horizon of possibility where the negotiation of collectively agreed terms was concerned; by further reducing the union's leverage in countering the framing of the SAWP as paramount to the CA, the LRB's decision not to declare SAWP employees traditionally difficult to organize magnified this limitation.

The Collective Agreement between Sidhu and Local 1518

Approximately a year after the LRB delivered its second ruling on the disputed application and a SAWP employee-only bargaining unit was certified, Local 1518 and Sidhu successfully created a CA. The initial contract negotiations were contentious, and a CA was reached ultimately by resort to the provision for first-contract arbitration under the LRC (BC MOL 1996, div. 3, sec. 55). The parties' disagreements throughout the negotiation process were primarily based on their opposing views of the relative weight of the CA and the SAWP. Whereas the employer viewed the CA as secondary to the terms of the TMWP (Sidhu 2010), consistent with the LRB's decision in Greenway, the union argued that the SAWP solely offered minimum terms, which could be augmented by the CA under negotiation (UFCW 1518 2010). Given the limited scope of collective bargaining permitted by the LRB, job security became the most substantive issue addressed in these negotiations, which was translated into provisions mandating timely grievance and arbitration processes in instances of alleged termination without just cause and provisions providing the basis for seniority and recall season-to-season.[17]

In the final analysis, provisions of the CA provided SAWP employees with a range of rights and protections above and beyond the minimum terms specified in Canada–Mexico agreements, which prioritize host-state employers' labor needs. Rights and protections afforded by CA related to pay rates, nondiscrimination, health and safety, leaves, discipline and discharge, storage of personal property from season to season, and unpaid bereavement leave.[18] Yet the most important provisions, which used the CA as a bulwark against the threat of removal built into the SAWP, were those limiting termination prompting repatriation and facilitating the promise of circularity between the sending and host states.

To address SAWP employees' "dignity and respect" concerns, the CA made provisions for grievance and arbitration procedures that would preempt premature repatriation flowing from termination where an arbitrator deemed the employer to lack just cause. Specifically, it elaborated a three-stage complaint mechanism with rigid time limits for each step in the grievance and arbitration processes related to the termination of bargaining unit members, with attention to SAWP employees' tenuous residency status and the circumstances that could result in repatriation (Sidhu & Sons Nursery Ltd. and UFCW 1518 2010, arts. 12, 13). The CA dictated that a grievance disputing termination be filed promptly, that is, within three days of a receipt of a notice of discharge on the part of the SAWP employee (art. 12.07). It also required that, if a grievance questioned the grounds for termination of employment (i.e., whether it the employer had just cause), and the SAWP employee participant was to be repatriated, a grievance application for accelerated arbitration be processed within twenty-four hours; this expedited arbitration mandated an arbitrator to convene a hearing within five days of receiving an application, complete it within ten days of the first day of the proceedings, and issue an award within five days of concluding the hearing (art. 13.02). The CA made further provisions for ensuring that discharged SAWP employees could continue to dwell on the premises of the employer, and thus remain in Canada, until a resolution was found. Collectively, these provisions sought ideally to circumvent or, at a minimum, to blunt the effect of terms of the Canada–Mexico standard employment agreement permitting the premature cessation of employment. They aimed to reduce the risk of unjust termination, including instances whereby growers' decision to terminate (and thus threaten or trigger repatriation) is motivated by workers' or groups of workers' presumed support for or association with unions. Such provisions were reinforced by strengthened legislated protections against unfair labor practices in another part of the CA, which stated that discrimination and harassment against employees due to membership or participation in the union are intolerable and mandated that the employer to comply with the provincial Human Rights Code (art. 8.01).

With the goal of ensuring a standardized seasonal renewal of the employment contract or recall procedures, the CA also specified that "seniority of SAWP employees in prior seasons shall be maintained" (Sidhu & Sons Nursery Ltd. and UFCW Local 1518 2010, art. 7.01). Challenging the view that, under a TMWP permitting circularity, each seasonal period in which temporary migrant workers return to the sending state represents a break in employment, such provisions characterized the phase in which temporary migrant workers return to the sending state as a feature of the employment relationship. The CA thus required the employer to keep seniority lists maintaining the priority of bargaining unit members in prior seasons and specified that on "completion of the SAWP Employee's probationary period [of 5 months, effectively the duration of one season], his or her seniority shall be calculated based on accumulated hours worked, whether in the current season or prior seasons" (art. 7.01). Under such provisions, seniority could only be legitimately violated if the bargaining unit member was duly discharged and not reinstated through the grievance procedure and/or arbitration, voluntarily quit or resigned, was absent from work without prior written approval from the employer unless the employee offered a reason satisfactory to the employer, had not worked for eight months, or failed to return to work on the completion of an authorized leave without a satisfactory reason (art. 7.02). As a central plank of the CA, provisions guaranteeing season-to-season seniority aimed to create greater transparency in the recall process.

Consistent with such provisions, the CA dictated that layoffs were to be conducted "in reverse order of seniority," except in instances where there are volunteers. However, provisions on layoffs did indicate that, in accordance with MOUs, operational guidelines, and the standard employment agreement and in line with the tenor of the CA's preamble, SAWP employees could be laid off before workers holding more secure residency statuses (Sidhu & Sons Nursery Ltd. and UFCW Local 1518 2010, arts. 16.03, 16.04). With regard to recall processes for SAWP employees, the employer was to list those who had successfully completed the probationary period of five months "in order of seniority" and to copy the union on all requests for employees (arts. 16.07, 16.08). Under the same provision, the union and the employer nevertheless acknowledged that the employer did not have ultimate control over the recruitment and selection of SAWP employees because of the operation of this TMWP (i.e., Mexico retained such powers).[19]

Such novel provisions regulating recall based on workers' seniority facilitated greater season-to-season continuity in employment for TMWP participants than the circular migration permitted under the SAWP, and aimed to constrain the employer's ability to penalize union supporters through opaque practices, including the submission of negative evaluations to Mexico's MOL. In an attempt to strengthen provisions of the LRC that protect workers against unfair labor practices, such as dismissal for engaging in union activity, terms of the CA also sought to limit these SAWP employees' deportability by reducing the employer's capacity to decline to invite back, or fail to recommend for readmission at another Canadian farm, without proper justification, those recently unionized temporary migrant workers with sufficient seniority for recall.

Conclusion: Limits Posed by the SAWP's Paramountcy

Even the most novel CA provisions were nevertheless beset from the outset by limitations tied to the subsidiarity of collective bargaining to the parameters of the SAWP as an intergovernmental agreement governing working across borders. Emerging at an early stage, these limitations point to the necessity to, at a minimum, increase accountability among central socioeconomic beneficiaries of migration management and to scale up such novel provisions and innovative features of the CA to the level of intergovernmental agreements, policies, and guidelines governing the TMWP, as explored in the conclusion to this book. The CA's preamble stated that it was not "to conflict with the terms of the SAWP Agreements" and, in instances where there is conflict, "the terms of the SAWP will govern" (Sidhu & Sons Nursery Ltd. and UFCW Local 1518 2010, preamble (d)). In practice, the wide variety of permissible reasons available to growers in justifying the early cessation of employment under the Canada–Mexico standard employment agreement also undermined CA provisions for expedited grievance applications and timely arbitration hearings in cases where employees challenge termination for just cause. Furthermore, because the CA was not in and of itself able to prevent the sending state from permitting premature repatriation, in instances where a terminated unionized SAWP employee is repatriated before he or she has the opportunity to make a grievance application, the provision for expedited grievance and arbitration processes was rendered a hollow victory. Moreover, in the case of premature repatriation occurring before an arbitration hearing, the CA's ability to reinstate SAWP employees' eligibility for and access to future seasonal employment contracts was highly constrained because it could not do much (beyond offering moral suasion) to encourage Mexico to select repatriated SAWP employees for readmission into the TWMP.[20]

Provisions of the CA between Sidhu and Local 1518 providing that the seniority of bargaining unit members in prior seasons be maintained were also limited by the assumption, on which the Canada–Mexico SAWP agreement is premised, that growers must always hire citizens and permanent residents of Canada first. Such provisions governing recall were likewise weakened by the fact that under the TMWP, once the fixed-term (i.e., seasonal) employment contract is complete, the employer is under no obligation to rehire former employees, even if its labor needs persist. Therefore, despite the presence of CA provisions governing recall, Sidhu had access to a variety of means for reducing bargaining unit members' numbers, including those that do not technically violate the SAWP or its spirit. It could cease hiring SAWP employees altogether, reduce the number of SAWP employees (while still fulfilling CA requirements for recall on the basis of seniority), and resort to hiring temporary migrant workers through other streams of Canada's TFWP (e.g., the agricultural stream introduced in 2011). Indeed, the possibility of attrition under SAWP is explored in chapter 4, which probes the erosion of the all-employee bargaining unit represented by Local 1518 at Floralia as a means of contextualizing the gradual decline of the SAWP employee-only bargaining unit at Sidhu in the decade following its certification, despite its highly publicized and modestly successful challenge of blacklisting. Both the formidable obstacles to unionization and the subsequent erosion of the hard-won bargaining unit at Sidhu reveal how the SAWP agreement is premised on workers' deportability, demonstrating that the meaningful application of mechanisms for preserving bargaining unit strength supported by collective bargaining laws, such as the fair application of recall procedures in CAs, was hampered from the start.

Chapter 3 illustrates such challenges to the fair application of collectively negotiated recall provisions by exploring their circumvention during the term of the first CA through threats and acts of blacklisting.

MAINTAINING A BARGAINING UNIT OF SEASONAL AGRICULTURAL WORKER PROGRAM (SAWP) EMPLOYEES

The Challenge of Blacklisting

> "The terror that the workers go through: it's not just employers . . .
> it's everybody. . . . It's the Canadian government, the Mexican
> government, the employer. . . . [The workers,] they're relying on that
> money. They have to be here."
>
> —Former (Mexican) consular employee, interview, July 26, 2014

After a multiyear legal struggle on the part of SAWP employees of Sidhu and their union, the CA between Local 1518 and the employer came into force in 2011, promising to ensure seniority-based recall and timely grievance and arbitration processes, among other novel provisions directed at curbing deportability. That same year, however, several SAWP employees otherwise eligible for recall were denied reentry to Canada. After learning of the situation, Local 1518 launched a complaint to the LRB on behalf of bargaining unit members at Sidhu. Alleging blacklisting, the union argued that Mexican officials who oversaw the process of recruiting and selecting workers and Vancouver-based consular officials stationed to assist in the oversight of the SAWP in the sending state colluded with Sidhu to block the reentry of such TMWP participants. Their actions thereby contravened LRC provisions on unfair labor practices and coercion and intimidation.

At the same time, the union complained of improper interference in a decertification application on the part of these parties, as well as certain employees, and sought to demonstrate a pattern of interference by linking such allegations to similar claims made by bargaining unit members at Floralia. In response, the LRB agreed to hear Local 1518's suite of complaints on behalf of bargaining unit members at Sidhu, but decided to separate them from those made on behalf of bargaining unit members at Floralia. Yet, despite affirming its ability to consider the actions of Mexican officials in establishing the facts in hearing complaints against Sidhu and certain employees, the LRB ultimately dismissed all complaints against this sending state in response to Mexico's contention that, as a sovereign state, it was immune from the proceedings of Canadian courts. In the final analysis, the LRB found insufficient evidence to rule that either the employer or certain employees had violated the LRC, although it refused to count the vote, involving bargaining unit members present in the host state, conducted following the application for decertification because of improper interference by sending-state officials. The LRB viewed these officials' conduct to be tantamount to an unfair labor practice affecting workers' exercise or potential exercise of rights guaranteed under the LRC, but the only available option was to attempt to make whole what remained of the Canadian-based bargaining unit. While the LRB proceedings revealed the sending state to be a central protagonist in blocking the re-entry of TMWP participants and in the related decertification effort, national sovereignty—coupled with the operational role assigned to Mexico in worker recruitment, selection, documentation, and readmission under the SAWP—precluded adjudicators from responding squarely to threats and acts of blacklisting.

The LRB's investigation of Local 1518's complaints on behalf of bargaining unit members at Sidhu offers a rare glimpse of the operation of this modality of deportability and the potential cast of characters involved in its exercise. It exposes how blacklisting functions, both perpetuating a climate of fear and encouraging various blocking practices that heighten the threat of dismissal from future employment. Decisive evidence of blacklisting surfaced in the LRB hearings. Submissions and oral and written testimony shone a light on actions of Mexican officials aimed at circumventing provisions of the first CA between Local 1518 and Sidhu that effectively prevented a host-state employer from terminating or failing to invite back eligible unionized workers. Underlining how deportability is a condition of possibility of migration management in a TMWP permitting but by no means guaranteeing circularity, the practices and processes revealed through these legal proceedings highlight openings under the SAWP for thwarting repeat temporary emigration through various means.

This chapter investigates such openings, analyzing how threats and acts of blacklisting impeded the fair application of the CA between Local 1518 and Sidhu. The investigation takes shape in four parts. Section one describes the context for blacklisting, as well as opportunities for its exercise, in a TMWP emblematic of migration management in which sending-state government officials in the interior (i.e., MOL officials) are responsible for initial worker recruitment, selection, and documentation and also play a central role in readmission processes, and government agents posted in the host state (i.e., consular officials) are responsible for ensuring that the SAWP functions smoothly for the benefit of

TMWP participants and employers—two parties whose interests do not necessarily converge. After a review of LRC provisions that effectively prohibit blacklisting, the second section explores how, in response to a preliminary objection by Mexico that was disputed by the union, the LRB came to dismiss Local 1518's complaints against this sending state, while upholding adjudicators' ability to consider Mexican officials' conduct in establishing the facts in complaints against the employer and certain employees. This position was backed by higher courts, and it laid the groundwork for bringing into view threats and acts of blacklisting. Analyzing evidence revealing Mexican officials' conduct admissible in the LRB hearings addressing Local 1518's remaining complaints against the employer and certain employees, the third section details the cluster of overlapping administrative practices limiting the ability of bargaining unit members to return to work at their former employer (i.e., Sidhu) and in the host state more generally.[1] It documents how—by discharging their routine duties under the SAWP, together with consular officials in Vancouver who discouraged union involvement among SAWP employees through threats of blacklisting—MOL officials in Mexico successfully prevented perceived union supporters from returning to Canada without implicating the remaining parties to the union's complaint. Against this backdrop, section four describes and analyzes the LRB's tightly constrained decision. In response to Local 1518's complaints against the employer and certain employees, the LRB ruled, on the basis of insufficient evidence, that neither party engaged in unfair labor practices or coercion and intimidation. However, in a modest attempt to make whole the bargaining unit at Sidhu without treading on responsibilities delegated to the sending state under the SAWP, the LRB found improper interference into a decertification application on the basis of Mexico's actions. Thus, even this sympathetic LRB was limited in its capacity to address squarely unacceptable (and otherwise presumably unlawful) actions on the part of a sending state and their effects on temporary migrant workers with the prospect of return. Despite Mexican officials' active resistance, in the employer's interest, bargaining unit members were able to retain their first CA. Nevertheless, significant challenges to the application of CA provisions extending recall on the basis of season-to-season seniority remained. These challenges were amplified, as future developments would show, by the various forms attrition may take, to which the chapter gestures by way of conclusion.

Blacklisting under the SAWP: Sending-State Interference Impeding Access to Rights and Protections Secured in Collective Agreements

In exploring the prominence of deportability in an "age of migration" (Castles and Miller 2003), De Genova (2010, 34) detects "a decidedly inverse relationship . . . between the distinctively waning fortunes and diminishing returns of nation-state sovereignty, as such, and the exuberant attention to ever more comprehensive and draconian controls that states seek to impose upon the most humble cross-border comings and goings—and settlings—of migrants." Agreements surrounding the SAWP, as well as protocols guiding its operation, attest to this relationship and to the comprehensive controls that participating states may impose on TMWP participants as emigrants. The operational role prescribed for Mexico, as a sending state responsible for the provision of workers, and fulfilled both by its MOL in the interior and consular officials posted in the host state, is a case in point. As chapter 1 indicated, Mexican MOL officials are responsible for initial worker recruitment, selection, and documentation, as well as for readmission, whereas its consular officials assist in the day-to-day operation of the TMWP in Canada (e.g., in carrying out placement and mediating on-farm disputes).

The Mexican MOL's role in the repeat provision of temporary migrant workers under the SAWP is particularly significant to TMWP participants desiring readmission (Hennebry 2012; Preibisch 2012). Often guided by a disciplinary process described in chapter 2, whereby former SAWP employees are evaluated by their employers at the conclusion of the seasonal employment contract, MOL officials are key to determining such temporary migrant workers' future participation in the SAWP (see especially Basok 2002, 99; see also Basok et al. 2014; Binford 2009, 2013). Whereas they routinely send temporary migrant workers formally requested or "nominated"—and thus evaluated favorably—back to their former employers in the subsequent season and typically transfer to another farm those known to have performed well, for whom no work is available with their previous employer, MOL officials tend to penalize those who do not meet these criteria, often by expelling them from the TMWP, a penalty that spurred SAWP employees of Sidhu to organize.

In assisting in program oversight in Canada according to operational guidelines, consular officials are agents of Mexico appointed "for the purpose of *ensuring the smooth functioning of the program for the mutual benefit of EMPLOY-ERS and WORKERS,* and to perform duties required . . . under the employment agreement" (Canada and United Mexican States 2001, annex, 3(e), emphasis added). In this role, they are expected to serve two parties with divergent interests: TMWP participants (i.e., Mexican nationals), whose interests are assumed to align closely with those of the Mexican state, and Canadian employers. Yet, given that the government of Mexico depends on remittances, the consular officials' imperative, which they share with MOL officials in the interior, is to keep workers in line because they know that protecting the interests of the Mexican state entails promoting the smooth functioning of the SAWP for employers. The direction provided to consular officials via the Vienna Convention on Consular Relations (VCCR) (1963), ratified by Mexico in 1965, upholds this effective employer advocacy. The VCCR characterizes consular officials' functions as "protecting in the receiving State the interest of the sending State and of its nationals, both individuals and bodies corporate, within the limits permitted by international law"; it thereby perpetuates the problematic assumption that sending states (as corporate bodies) and their nationals—in this instance, those compelled to engage in temporary migrant work in their struggle against extreme poverty, who confront workplace and migration challenges within and between sending and host states—necessarily have complementary interests. However, while sending state officials may view unionization as a threat to sending state remittances, workers view it as necessary to securing decent terms and conditions of work and employment, especially as they intersect with migration (e.g., rights to recall)—bringing consular officials' roles of protecting nationals abroad into conflict with the overriding interests of the sending state (VCCR 1963, schedule 2, art. 5 (a)).

While blacklisting is prohibited under BC's LRC, and recall provisions of CAs between employers and seasonal agricultural workers encompassing SAWP employees, aim to limit this practice, it is one means available to both MOL and consular officials who are responsible for ensuring the "smooth functioning" of the SAWP, to sideline "troublemaking" workers (Binford 2009). Included in a grouping of administrative practices (introduced in chapter 1) that independently or cumulatively have the effect of limiting the ability of workers to return to their former employer in the host state or to the host state more generally, blacklisting is a modality of deportability typically affecting employees who are perceived to be pro-union during an organizing drive or who are union members, who may still be working in or are seeking to return to the host state, and whose union is either in the process of negotiating or has reached a CA with an employer. For those employees otherwise eligible for recall who have returned to the sending state and are either perceived to be pro-union or are known to have organized and secured a CA constraining their employer's capacity to decline to invite back bargaining unit members with sufficient seniority, blacklisting encompasses threats and acts involving a diversity of actors, including sending states.

Constraints on the Prohibition of Blacklisting under BC Labor Laws: Mexico's Preliminary Objection to Local 1518's Initial Complaints

Practices associated with blacklisting are arguably prohibited under BC's LRC (1996). Provisions addressing unfair labor practices by "an employer or person acting on behalf of an employer" (s. 6) bar such individuals from participating in or interfering with the formation, selection, or administration of a union (s. 6(1)). They also prohibit the discharge, discipline, or dismissal of a person because of his or her decision to become a member of a trade union and the attempt, by intimidation, dismissal, threat of dismissal or any other kind of threat, or by the imposition of a penalty, or by a promise, to compel or to induce an employee to refrain from becoming or continuing to be a member of a trade union (s. 6(3)). In turn, provisions addressing coercion and intimidation by "a person" (s. 9) prohibit their exercise where they "could reasonably have the effect of compelling or inducing a person to refrain from becoming or to continue . . . to be a member of a trade union."

Local 1518 cited these LRC provisions in its complaints to the LRB on behalf of bargaining unit members at Sidhu alleging blacklisting and improper interference in a decertification application, complaints that the union initially sought to extend to cover concurrent actions against SAWP employees at Floralia on the assumption that Mexico was a party in both cases. Regarding Mexico's actions to blacklist SAWP employees of Sidhu otherwise eligible for recall, the union contended that officials of Mexico's MOL and its Vancouver consulate, acting in the interests of and in concert with the employer, breached s. 6(1) insofar as it interfered with the administration of a trade union by not permitting workers believed to be supportive of unions to return to Canada (UFCW 1518 2011a, 7). It argued further that, in not allowing workers believed to be supportive of the union to return to Canada, Mexican MOL officials and officials of its Vancouver consulate breached s. 6(3): according to Local 1518, they engaged in "an unlawful refusal to employ . . . or to continue to employ . . . and/or unlawful discrimination in regard to employment"; "an unlawful imposition in a contract of employment a condition that seeks to restrain an employee from exercising his or her rights under the Code"; and, "unlawful intimidation and threats" (UFCW 2011a, 7). At this early stage in the proceedings, Local 1518 also argued that, when they used the threat of expulsion from the SAWP to compel a would-be returning bargaining unit member at Floralia to orchestrate a decertification campaign in addressing the sending state's concurrent actions to initiate a decertification vote at that farm, Mexican officials contravened s. 6(1) (UFCW 1518 2011b, 4). Additionally, the union claimed that these Mexican officials breached s. 9 by using coercion and intimidation; that is, they acted against bargaining unit members at Sidhu, as well as at Floralia, by not allowing several of those perceived to be union supporters to return to Canada and, similarly, by threatening a worker's future participation in the SAWP (UFCW 1518 2011a, 7; UFCW 1518, 2011b, 4).[2]

As remedies, Local 1518 sought a declaration that Mexico and its Vancouver consulate breached the LRC (as well as court orders that such breaches cease and desist) and requested compensation for damage to the union's property and workers' lost wages and benefits (to be shared between Mexico and the employer). It also called for a court order that all SAWP employees be provided with a statement, written by the union and approved by the LRB, setting out their rights to join a trade union and participate in union activities free from interference, including from foreign representatives. Additionally, the union sought dismissals of applications for decertification made both by Sidhu and Floralia. The explicit aim of such proposed remedies was to penalize Mexican officials for actions against SAWP participants known or presumed to be union supporters. Demonstrating the link between Mexico and BC employers, however, was an underlying goal for the union, which sought a ruling that sending states, when acting on behalf of employers, are subject to the LRB's jurisdiction, that simultaneously called employers to account.

Local 1518's initial complaint was met with a preliminary objection from Mexico, which sidestepped the substance of the matter: its officials' alleged involvement in blacklisting. Mexico appealed to the LRB to dismiss complaints against it, including its consular representatives, on the basis of its freedom to exercise sovereignty over its citizens at home and abroad, relying on Canada's 1985 federal State Immunity Act (SIA; Government of Canada 1985; United Mexican States-and-Consulado General de Mexico en Vancouver 2011, 3). In making this argument, through which it objected to having Canadian laws applied extraterritorially, Mexico cited the 1945 Charter of the United Nations and asserted that the LRB had no jurisdiction over sending states (United Mexican States-and-Consulado General de Mexico en Vancouver 2011, 506).[3]

In response to such contentions, Local 1518 challenged both Mexico's claims of immunity from the jurisdiction of the LRB under the SIA and its claims related to international law. It contended that Mexico waived its immunity under s. 4(2)(a) of the act by agreeing to the SAWP, which is subject to the laws of Canada and BC (UFCW 1518 2011c, para. 3.17; see also para. 3.16). If the LRB did not concur that Mexico waived its immunity through its participation in the SAWP, the union argued further that immunity did not apply since the dispute involved commercial activity in Canada (para. 2.1–2.3). In making this claim, it relied principally on the commercial activity exception under the SIA, which provides that "a foreign state is not immune from the jurisdiction of a court in any proceedings that relate to any commercial activity of the foreign state" (Government of Canada 1985, s. 5). Noting that employment contracts are commercial and given Mexico's economic interests, specifically, its receipt of significant financial benefits from contracts under the SAWP in the form of more than $80 million in remittances annually—the union argued that this commercial activity exception should apply (UFCW 1518 2011c, para. 3.37).

Responding to Mexico's contentions about international law, the union suggested that the SIA is not the only vehicle to set out exceptions to state immunity: international and common law have also developed exceptions, and furthermore, a state's ratification of a treaty can amount to a waiver of immunity.[4] The union also clarified that it was not requesting that the LRB assert extraterritorial jurisdiction, but rather that it assume jurisdiction over actions affecting labor relations in the province (UFCW 1518 2011c, para. 4.27). And it requested that adjudicators decline to entertain Mexico's objections at such a preliminary stage in the case, noting that respondents had not yet disclosed significant material documents and particulars, and that an application to dismiss is rarely granted in unfair labor practice complaints. In a move that proved highly significant when the LRB ultimately heard the case, the union suggested further that, even if the LRB were to find that the SIA prohibits it from ruling on whether or not Mexico has breached BC labor law, this would not prohibit it from ordering Mexican officials to testify or produce evidence for other purposes. Nor would it alter the LRB's authority to investigate events occurring outside of the province to ascertain whether or not breaches have occurred; specifically, the union stated that "whether or not the SIA prohibits a finding against Mexico, the facts of involving Mexico are still relevant as to whether there has been improper interference" (para. 1).

The LRB's Response to Mexico's Objection to Local 1518's Complaint

Early in 2012, the LRB dismissed Local 1518's complaints against Mexico. In casting Mexico as a nonparty to the union's complaints, it asserted that "state immunity applies" under the SIA, unless immunity has been waived or certain exceptions prevail, addressing primarily those arguments regarding the SIA's commercial exception and whether Mexico waived its immunity by participating in the SAWP (BC LRB 2012a, para. 34). It found that since Mexico garners no direct remuneration from the SAWP, the SAWP does not amount to a commercial contract.[5] The LRB also characterized the SAWP as a "diplomatic arrangement between countries" through which Mexico assists Canada in addressing domestic labor shortages (para. 38). It thereby rejected the union's arguments regarding the economic significance of remittances garnered by Mexico from its participation in the SAWP, neglecting to acknowledge how their receipt puts consular officials in a contradictory position because of the need to support Mexican nationals abroad while sustaining positive relations between the Mexican government and employers in the host state.

Furthermore, after hearing the union's subsequent application for leave and reconsideration, which questioned the LRB's interpretation of the commercial exception under the SIA, the LRB Reconsideration Panel upheld the original decision. The LRB found that Mexico's participation in the SAWP and its direct involvement in the recruitment and selection of, as well as provision of documentation to, temporary migrant agricultural workers did not amount to a waiver of immunity under the SIA. This was because the passage quoted by the UFCW— "the agreement shall be governed by the laws of Canada and British Columbia"— is not contained within the MOU between Canada and Mexico, but is rather found in the standard employment agreement, "which sets out the obligations of Mexican workers and their [BC-based] employers" (BC LRB 2012a, para. 42). Consequently, Mexico is not subject to the laws of Canada, which instead apply to host-state employers. This very interpretation illustrates clearly why employers, such as Sidhu and Floralia, presumably sought the assistance of Mexico in preventing recently unionized workers from returning to Canada in the first place: if the employers interfered with such workers' return, they would be contravening CA provisions on seniority and recall and the LRC, but provisions of the latter would be difficult to apply to a sending state.

In response to Local 1518's suggestion that international treaties to which Mexico is a signatory constitute a waiver of immunity, the LRB found that those concerned "do not establish universal jurisdiction with respect to interference with a trade union" (BC LRB 2012a, para. 43). It could also find no precedent for the notion that interference with trade union activity falls in the category of "rules of international law which have a particular status" or peremptory international norms (e.g., those prohibiting torture; para. 44). The LRB nevertheless asserted that such conclusions are "not to diminish the seriousness of such activity, which is clearly prohibited by the Code," allowing it to reach its conclusion that, even though Mexico enjoys state immunity, it "should take into account facts which take place in other jurisdictions in exercising its remedial authority within the province of British Columbia" (paras. 45, 47). Through this aspect of the ruling, the LRB conveyed that it would consider evidence related to Mexico's actions in reaching a decision on Local 1518's remaining complaints against Sidhu and certain employees, as well as against Floralia, complaints that the LRB now decisively separated (para. 49). For the LRB, the union had presented a case against these employers and certain employees "sufficient and appropriate for the purposes of the unfair labor practice provisions of the Code," and, to rule effectively, it would take Mexico's actions into account in its fact-finding, thereby upholding Mexico's immunity while preserving space for the union to pursue its other claims (para. 49). While the decision to dismiss Local 1518's complaints against Mexico reflects the limited room in which the LRB had to maneuver, its adjudicators were empowered to take account of Mexican officials' conduct in establishing the facts in complaints against the employer and certain employees with the sanction of superior BC courts, despite Mexico's best efforts to have the LRB suppress all evidence tied to its actions.[6] Subsequent proceedings of the board thereby created a foundation for bringing the blacklisting into view.

Local 1518's Complaints: Tacit Limits on SAWP Participants' Rights and Protections via Collective Agreement[7]

After the LRB dismissed Local 1518's complaint against Mexico, it proceeded to hear its complaints of unfair labor practices and coercion and intimidation on the part of the employer and certain employees, as well as of improper interference in a decertification application. In this case, the union claimed, on behalf of a bargaining unit of SAWP employees, that the employer colluded with Mexican officials, who were charged with overseeing the selection and assignment of workers, to thwart visa reapplications of union members otherwise eligible for recall. Citing improper interference, Local 1518 also pressed the LRB not to cancel its certification as the bargaining agent, arguing that workers' true desires were not reflected in the vote (BC LRB 2014).

To evaluate these remaining complaints, the LRB considered Mexican officials' conduct in determining the facts. Documentary evidence, and oral and written testimony offered voluntarily in support of Local 1518's case and admitted by the LRB, by former employees of the Vancouver Mexican consulate, UFCW employees based in Mexico, and an allegedly blacklisted SAWP employee, revealed how then-senior consular officials condemned union involvement and effectively threatened blacklisting in response. Offering an unprecedented window into acts of blacklisting, this evidence showed how consular officials overseeing the SAWP in BC worked with their MOL counterparts in Mexico to prevent TMWP participants perceived to be union supporters from returning to Canada. Subsequently, evidence presented by the union sought to demonstrate how such threats and acts of blacklisting constituted improper interference into a decertification application, calling into question the validity of an earlier vote to decertify the bargaining unit.

Complaints of Unfair Labor Practices and Coercion and Intimidation: Evidence and Counterevidence

THE THREAT OF BLACKLISTING

Under the SAWP, as the first section described, sending states are to post government agents in the host state. Under its Canada—and BC–Mexico variants, Mexico appoints consular officials as its agents in the host state to ensure the smooth functioning of the TMWP for employers and workers and to perform duties associated with its day-to-day operation. These duties typically involve carrying out placement, general oversight, and often mediating on-farm disputes, and they can, in practice, inform the readmission process. On the Mexican side, when Local 1518 alleged blacklisting, the BC SAWP was thus overseen by a government agent (the consul coordinator of SAWP). At the time, this individual worked in its Vancouver consulate alongside two other senior officials (the vice consul–health of SAWP employees and the consul general) and in conjunction with MOL officials in the interior, and this official supervised employees involved in the oversight of the SAWP locally who were responsible for transfer, mediation, and transport (Figure 3.1).

In corroborating its complaints against Sidhu and certain employees, the union asked three nonsupervisory employees, who had previously held positions at Vancouver's consulate, to share their experiences with the LRB.[8] Each of these

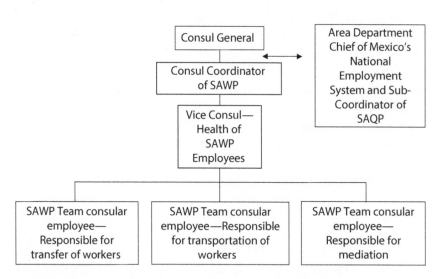

FIGURE 3.1. Mexican Consulate in Vancouver: Organization Chart

Source: Author, based on 2012-2014 field notes and interviews.

former employees testified that the area department chief of Mexico's National Employment System and subcoordinator of SAWP, who oversaw the process of selecting workers and assigning them to Canadian employers, and other senior officials regularly or openly "express[ed] strong anti-union views" (BC LRB 2014, para. 24). This anti-unionism was justified, these former employees explained, as a means of protecting the Mexican state's investment in the SAWP, on the assumption that Canadian employers would request workers from another country if they saw that Mexican SAWP employees were unionizing (BC LRB 2012b, Day 4, p. 54; Day 7, p. 4).

In this atmosphere hostile to unionism, each of these former consular employees testified that they had been directed to advise SAWP employees to eschew unions. The former employee responsible for transport, for instance, was required "to warn the agricultural workers . . . to contact no one at all, only the consulate, especially not to contact the [UFCW-backed Agricultural Workers' Alliance (AWA)] support centres" (BC LRB 2012b, Day 7, p. 8). This individual was also instructed, when overseeing manifests or lists of SAWP employees assigned to BC farms, to keep tabs on union supporters (Day 5, pp. 4, 6–7, 10, 12). This official was responsible for monitoring a radio program hosted by the AWA's local coordinator, calling senior officials' attention to all incoming questions about unionized farms and alerting employers when unions were "paying attention to . . . [their] farm" (Day 6, p. 98). Moreover, according to the former employee responsible for mediation (Day 6, p. 98), workers' fear of employers' power was such that, when dealing with disputes, former consular employees "didn't ask for [a worker's] . . . name because they [i.e., workers] never gave information to members of the Consulate because they were scared that they would be put on a blacklist if they complained about their employer[s]." Revealing techniques deployed by senior consular and MOL officials to deter SAWP employees from exercising their labor rights, such testimony showed how the consulate assumed that unionization would compromise the Mexican branch of the program, and hence workers' future employment in Canada, providing a basis for this climate of fear. Through this evidence, Local 1518 conveyed that senior Mexican officials viewed disincentivizing unionization as a means of securing BC-based employers' satisfaction, which was key to the successful operation of the SAWP—an argument that Mexico did not challenge given its desire to preserve its status as a nonparty in the case.

INSTANCES OF BLACKLISTING

Throughout the hearings, evidence that Mexican officials not only threatened but also engaged in acts of blacklisting as a means of inhibiting workers' access to Canada through the SAWP supported Local 1518's complaints about the contravention of the LRC and the circumvention of CA provisions devoted to recall on the basis of season-to-season seniority. Indeed, each of the three former consular employees recounted a February 2009 meeting where the consul coordinator of SAWP and the Mexico-based subcoordinator of SAWP trained them to guard against the return of union members otherwise eligible for recall. Convinced that unions posed threats to Mexico's continued participation in this model TMWP, the subcoordinator explained how consular employees should track pro-union workers, telling the three employees that if they "knew that a worker had been in contact with the union to let [the consulate] know" (BC LRB 2012b, Day 5, p. 27; see also Day 7, p. 19). Concomitantly, the subcoordinator showed the three consular employees how to use the SIMOL—which, as explained in chapter 2, is the electronic log used by Mexican officials to track SAWP employees since 2010—to monitor union involvement. Concerned that these data could demonstrate interference with workers' rights if held to scrutiny, the witnesses were assured by the subcoordinator of SAWP that "if you put it on the log, comment log, you can . . . change it," implying that the SIMOL could be manipulated if necessary (Day 5, p. 15). The official from the interior then further elaborated that "the [pro-union] workers would be blocked [from leaving Mexico] and, to avoid any suspicion . . . [the official] would say that the Canadian Embassy had denied them their visas" (Day 6, p. 47).

The former consular employees thus testified that the "training" in blacklisting provided by senior officials at this meeting, as well as in other instances, made them aware of the mechanics of blocking pro-union workers, who were otherwise eligible for recall, from readmission to the host state. They were therefore well positioned to describe and assess for the LRB what happened to a recently unionized SAWP employee at Sidhu whom Local 1518 claimed to have been blacklisted in 2010–2011. Using insights drawn from these former employees' evidence, the union presented a narrative outlining Mexican officials' interference, based on this former bargaining unit member's account and written documentation, which included a duplicate of his SIMOL log entries received from an anonymous source.

In the 2010 season and during the first year that a CA was in place, this particular SAWP employee had passed his probationary period and had become a member of the bargaining unit. Under the CA, he was thereby entitled to continue his employment, a right verified by Sidhu. Indeed, he received an employment contract specifying that he was expected to start, and hence to be readmitted to Canada, in February 2011. The worker then completed the predocumentation process and was notified that he had been issued a visa for travel to Canada. To obtain his passport, this visa, and his final full set of documents, next he was to report to the MOL office in Mexico City on January 27, 2011. The worker, however, received an urgent phone call, shortly after returning home from his predocumentation meeting, demanding that he present himself immediately at the MOL office in Mexico City. He did so, and as the worker recounted, a Mexican MOL official involved in coordinating the SAWP then informed him that a (presumably undocumented) person with his name had been arrested in the United States, and as a result, his visa was being withheld; little could be done to reverse the situation, he was told, because the problem was between the United States and Canada (BC LRB 2014, paras. 13–14; BC LRB 2012b, Testimony, Day 8, pp. 29–32).

The worker reported that he later traveled, for a second time, to the MOL office in Mexico City, inquiring about the status of his work visa in an attempt to rectify the situation. An MOL official consulted the records and then asked the worker what he was doing and why he was upsetting people. When the worker asked what prompted this line of questioning, he learned that the MOL was aware of his attempts to recruit people to form a union. As a result, as the union contended on the basis of a large volume of evidence gathered from the SIMOL log, the worker did not return to Sidhu in the 2011 season.[9]

On March 7, 2011, the UFCW National office received the SIMOL record for this allegedly blacklisted SAWP worker from an unknown source. The anonymous fax, labeled "first entry," in evidence and transmitted on 9:54 a.m. on January 13, 2011, included an entry prepared by the Mexico official involved in coordinating the SAWP with whom the allegedly blacklisted worker spoke in Mexico City, which, when translated, read as follows: "Call received from the Consulate in Vancouver reporting that this worker will not be able to go to Canada because he is involved in union activities. Pay attention that he does not go out" (BC LRB 2014, para. 16). With the permission of the blacklisted SAWP bargaining unit member, the UFCW National office then requested that a Mexico-based union employee inquire with the Canadian Embassy in Mexico (on April 18, 2011) about this worker's visa. The UFCW National was then given a letter from Canada indicating that the worker had been issued a visa and that there was "no record of . . . any problems in this case" (para. 20). During the hearings, the employer attempted to call into question the validity of the first SIMOL entry by bringing a different entry into evidence. By so doing, Sidhu signaled that, after it was notified of the union's complaint to the LRB, it had secured a release from the blacklisted SAWP worker permitting the Mexican government to disclose this information.

From there, Sidhu then pursued the matter with the subcoordinator of SAWP, who supposedly suggested that "the first entry was false' and offered a transcript of the true SIMOL entry, described in evidence as the "second entry." This second entry suggested that the SAWP worker had sought a change of employer. It also conveyed that, although he was granted this change, he would have to wait for another employer to make a formal request and was advised to report to the local office of Mexico's National Employment Service local office to move the process forward (BC LRB 2014, para. 18). When the union requested that the former consular employees evaluate these entries for the LRB, they each described the first entry as valid and questioned the validity of the second one. After the steps involved in determining which workers will migrate were delineated, the former consular employee that was responsible for transfer (BC LRB 2012b, Testimony, Day 5, p. 111) testified that the second entry, together with the accompanying document, indicating that the worker was to return to the MOL office for his visa did not "look right," because at this point in the process a worker who had been requested should already have been issued a visa. This former consular employee then confirmed that the SAWP worker was expected to arrive at the airport since he was listed on the manifest. In advance of the SAWP worker's expected arrival, however, the official was instructed to deviate from standard practice and not to contact this worker after indicating "inadmissible to Canada" on the SIMOL record (pp. 56–57). As this witness explained, this notation is normally used in two situations—"when the worker was denied a visa by the Canadian Embassy" and "when they wanted to block the worker and had no specific reason, no real reason"—and that, in this instance, it undoubtedly led to the blacklisting of this bargaining unit member (p. 68).

Allegations of Improper Interference: Evidence and Counterevidence

In addition to Local 1518's complaint of threats and acts of blacklisting, the union also pursued an allegation of interference with a decertification application. The union first argued that, in their campaign to decertify, certain employees used intimidation and coercion, with the support of their employer. This allegation was supported by the testimony of the former consular employee responsible for mediating disputes, who noted that, when attending a meeting with Sidhu employees curious about decertification, a worker privately stated, "What the workers have just told you, we have been told from Mexico. We had to tell someone, but we had no idea who we had to tell this to" (BC LRB 2012b, Testimony, Day 6, p. 55). On cross-examination, the former consular employee emphasized that "the worker's comment was that in Mexico they had given him the instruction to decertify" (Day 6, p. 88). In his own testimony, cited in BC LRB's decision, this particular employee, who had worked at Sidhu for seven years under the SAWP, fully acknowledged initiating the decertification campaign, but contended that he merely left decertification forms at workers' lodgings with the simple instruction, "sign or don't sign" (BC LRB 2014, para. 8).

This SAWP employee, who was instrumental in the decertification effort at Sidhu, then shared that, having been present at the 2008 certification vote, he was well aware of which employees supported the union. On this basis, he did not believe "that any [union supporters] were working for the employer at the time of the decertification vote" (BC LRB 2014, para. 8). The senior SAWP employee thereby suggested that Mexican officials thwarted the return of employees known to be pro-union and that returning bargaining unit members at Sidhu had been made aware of such interception. Hence, his testimony supported the union's second claim that "the [decertification] vote took place under a climate of fear, [where some] workers were blocked, and [others] . . . were told not to contact the union" (para. 37).

The LRB's Final Ruling: A Tightly Constrained Decision

The LRB decided there was insufficient evidence to find that either the employer or certain employees had violated the LRC. Indirectly acknowledging the clear evidence of blacklisting, which compounds temporary migrant workers' deportability, however, the board did find improper interference in a decertification vote on the part of Mexican officials. Though not in a position to inflict a penalty on sending-state actors, the LRB was empowered to adjudicate factual evidence allowable in the case. For example, in the decision, its vice chair (and chair of the panel hearing the case) evaluated the two different SIMOL entries on the allegedly blacklisted SAWP worker's file, one offered by the union and the other by the employer: ultimately it affirmed the credibility of the former, concluding that it "is the true entry which reflects the actual intentions of Mexican officials responsible for administering SAWP" and that the employer's entry "is a fabrication created after the fact . . . . completely inconsistent with the evidence I heard" (BC LRB 2014, para. 61).

Though the evidence presented during the hearings did not permit it to punish the employer for its alleged collusion with Mexican officials, the LRB did concede that the blacklisting had occurred and recognized Mexican officials as central actors. In its constrained position, the LRB took the only action available and refused to count the decertification vote. The true desires of bargaining unit members at Sidhu were unlikely to have been disclosed, the vice chair of the LRB wrote in the ruling, because of "improper interference by Mexican officials responsible for administering the SAWP" (BC LRB 2014, para. 95). As the example made of the blacklisted SAWP employee indicated, threats and acts of blacklisting, as a modality of deportability, prevented SAWP employees from casting their votes freely. In deciding not to count the vote, the board's vice chair highlighted the significance of the element of fear:

> The blocking of [the SAWP participant], who was identified by Mexican authorities as a supporter of the union, when viewed objectively, would have had a dramatic effect on the Union's members . . . more likely than not, the other employees of the Employer would be in a reasonable position to be aware of the fate of [this blacklisted individual] when they voted.

Calling the employer to account indirectly, the vice chair indicated further that "[w]hile the evidence did not point to a particular person that identified union supporters to the Consulate, it is likely this information came from someone working on the farm" (BC LRB 2014, para. 80) Yet the lack of "'smoking gun' . . . evidence establish[ing] that the employer identified [the blacklisted employee] as a supporter of the union" limited the LRB to this inference (para. 82). Accordingly, as a lawyer for the union emphasized in describing difficulties in obtaining such evidence, "unions will rarely have that kind of evidence. That's something that the employer is going to hide as much as they can, if it happened" (Lawyer for UFCW 1518, interview, July 25, 2014).

The LRB also took into account evidence of the climate of fear cultivated by Mexico's Vancouver consulate, including a statement, read by the former, allegedly blacklisted SAWP employee of Sidhu in his testimony (BC LRB 2012b Testimony, Day 8, pp. 36–37), that a Mexico-based UFCW employee made after a May 2011 press conference at the Mexican Senate denouncing the blacklisting of union activities from the SAWP:

> [t]his last year we have been confronted with serious reprisals, from the Foreign Relations Ministry . . . particularly the . . . Consulate of Mexico in Vancouver. . . . All of the workers who tried to organize themselves . . . are then blacklisted by the Consulate, this information is passed on to the [MOL] . . . , and what is told to the workers is: "you can't return to Canada . . ." a punishment that is not only unfair, but also illegal, . . . against the right of association of the Mexican workers in Canada . . . and . . . a message . . . is sent to the rest of the workers not to unionize.

The LRB also clarified its own constraints, however, when responding to evidence of improper interference by Mexican officials. Though the LRB recognized the validity of SAWP employees' fears of blacklisting, its remedial power to make whole the bargaining unit of workers concerned was limited. As its vice chair explained, "I have no power to make any orders against Mexico to cease and desist from similar activities now or in the future, nor do I have the power to make remedial orders against Mexico, a non-party to these proceedings pursuant to the State Immunity Act" (BC LRB 2014, para. 81). The LRB's early decisions to grant Mexico immunity in deference to national sovereignty, together with the higher BC courts' decisions affirming LRB adjudicators' ability to take into account the sending state's conduct for the sole purpose of establishing the facts, allowed Mexican officials to continue engaging in threats and acts of blacklisting with (near) impunity under the SAWP. The sending state was thus able to advance host-state employers' interests—in this instance, both indirectly by preserving a stable and compliant migrant agricultural workforce for BC employers and directly by working on behalf of an employer in the host state otherwise prevented from deporting or failing to invite back eligible unionized workers by the CA. More broadly, this final ruling on behalf of the tightly constrained LRB demonstrated how workers' deportability enables the sending state to ensure both host-state employer satisfaction and its own stature in this model program at the cost of its nationals' labor rights.

Conclusion: Uncovering Important Truths about Migration Management

The LRB's decision to refuse to cancel the certification of a bargaining unit of SAWP employees at Sidhu due to improper interference by Mexican officials and, especially, the documentary evidence and oral and written testimony on which it was based offer insight into the dynamics of blacklisting as a central modality of deportability affecting TMWP participants who have the prospect of return. Most accounts of the blacklisting of temporary migrant workers, including those engaged in programs permitting circularity, are necessarily partial because of the dearth of empirics available. In constructing a narrative normally obscured from view, the evidence advanced in the LRB's adjudication of Local 1518's complaints against the employer and certain employees reveals administrative practices (i.e., habits, customs, and routines) adopted by sending-state officials—both those posted in host states and responsible for local program oversight and those engaged in recruitment, selection, and documentation closer to home—in anticipating and aiming to prevent and respond to the exercise of labor rights among workers.

The detection and analysis of the blacklisting of bargaining unit members at Sidhu uncover important "truths" about the management of migration among temporary migrant workers with the prospect of return. Broadly, it demonstrates that institutionalized programs' mechanisms, promoted in the global policy discourse embracing migration management as a means of stemming the flow of "irregular migration," can impede access to and the exercise of labor rights. More narrowly, it shows that SAWP's "best practices" are by no means neutral, but are instead consistent with the dynamics of global capitalism, producing a race to the bottom in conditions of work and employment, which plays out partly on the terrain of temporary migration for employment. As the preceding analysis illustrates, this model TMWP permits sending-state officials, presumably often seeking to appease host-state employers, to behave in unprincipled ways that can involve, among other things, defying CA provisions—in this case, vital provisions on recall—by delegating key responsibilities related to readmission, such as recruitment, selection, and aspects of documentation, to those in the interior and posted abroad (i.e., by design and in practice). It also illustrates vividly how a labor relations tribunal compelled to prioritize national, and thereby sending-state, sovereignty, can be inhibited in—and even prevented from—implementing and enforcing host-state labor laws under its oversight, even after uncovering bold evidence of (sending-state) actions to circumvent them.

As chapter 4 shows, however, not all modalities of deportability are quite so bold-faced. Some operate in subtle ways, although they can be equally menacing. When the LRB ultimately rejected certain employees' disputed application to decertify the SAWP employee-only bargaining unit at Sidhu, it sought to stabilize the bargaining unit such that union members' first CA remained in force; however, not only did significant challenges to the application of its CA provisions extending recall on the basis of season-to-season seniority persist, they were likely amplified by the prospect for attrition. Going forward, Sidhu reduced the number of temporary migrant workers it requested under the SAWP, and thus the size of the bargaining unit at the farm diminished. Simultaneously, a disputed application to decertify the bargaining unit at Floralia, a related complaint of unfair labor practices launched subsequently by Local 1518, and its concomitant application for a declaration that this employer and S&G, a neighboring farm, are common employers, revealed the diverse manifestations that this modality of deportability can take. It also demonstrated the lengths to which a union had to go to prove to a host-state LRB, empowered only to address but a few overtly menacing varieties under the LRC, that anti-unionism can be at the root of attrition in otherwise viable bargaining units encompassing workers laboring transnationally, in this instance, an all-employee unit.

SUSTAINING BARGAINING UNIT STRENGTH

The Specter of Attrition

> "[Sidhu was] relying heavily on SAWP . . . but since the SAWP unit got organized . . . they are not bringing in more [SAWP] workers. The problem with Sidhu is that the unit has eroded [since] . . . the 'witch hunt' happened there. Now, everybody will talk to the union but they won't complain about things, they won't bring any details to you . . . There are no grievances at all."
>
> —UFCW Local 1518 staff representative, July 26, 2016

Despite the LRB's 2014 decision to refuse to cancel the certification of a bargaining unit of SAWP employees at Sidhu, the size of the unit contracted, continuing a pattern of erosion beginning with the first instance of union activity.[1] In 2015, the employer applied for forty-three Labour Market Impact Assessments (LMIAs) (ESDC 2015), required of employers requesting temporary migrant workers in agriculture, but the SAWP employee-only bargaining unit comprised of just twenty-one members that season (a decline from thirty members on the successful certification of the unit in 2010). Then in 2017, according to a union staff representative, based on a review of listings of employer applications for LMIAs posted briefly online, Sidhu applied for approximately eighty LMIAs (staff representative, interview, July 19, 2017). Although this figure mirrored the size of its original agricultural workforce (i.e., seventy-one employees participated in the first unsuccessful 2008 certification vote for a wall-to-wall bargaining unit), during that season (and in 2018 as well) Sidhu still engaged only twenty-one workers migrating under the SAWP. Such gaps between the number of employer applications for LMIAs and the number of SAWP employees actually working raise concern about the potential presence of non-unionized temporary migrant workers on the farm. Specifically, they raise questions about whether Sidhu requested, and, if so, whether the grower gained approval for workers under a different and highly deregulated stream of Canada's TFWP—the agricultural stream that was created in 2011—that technically fall outside the circumscribed bargaining unit.[2]

It is worth noting that between 2013 and 2018, work permit holders under the Agricultural Stream grew from 9,800 to 16,520, a considerably faster growth rate than permit holders under SAWP in the same period (IRCC 2019).

In addition to this numeric attrition and mounting concern, ongoing at the time of writing, about further erosion of the bargaining unit, reports of employer surveillance of seasonal agricultural workers' living quarters at a very remote site impeded the union's access to bargaining unit members and thus their ability to share workplace concerns. According to the UFCW staff representative quoted in the epigraph to this chapter, "Sidhu & Sons claims that since the farm is out in Mission [BC], in a very rural area, for 'security reasons' the employer has also put up surveillance cameras outside of the [bunk] houses. . . . Those cameras are pointing right at the entrance door. We still do visits, but it's definitely very intimidating" (UFCW 1518 staff representative, interview, July 19, 2017).[3]

Despite evidence of a shrinking unit of SAWP employees and mounting employer surveillance at Sidhu, the dynamics of attrition are difficult to document given the grower's apparent adherence to CA provisions governing recall and the absence of formal grievances on the part of bargaining unit members. To demonstrate how attrition operates as a modality of deportability, this chapter therefore chronicles events following a 2015 application for decertification of a bargaining unit of SAWP employees at Floralia, also represented by Local 1518.[4] At Floralia, certain employees' application for decertification led to a protracted adjudicative process that revealed various manifestations of attrition. The analysis of this process, which puts into context attrition at Sidhu after the blacklisting affair, reveals that strategies directed to this end can entail both bold interference into a decertification vote and more subtle interventions. Here the grower used two such subtle tactics: namely, the manipulation of seniority-based recall processes codified in CAs—mediated and often constrained by the principles underpinning sending- and host-state officials' implementation of agreements surrounding the SAWP—and the resort to non-unionized employees of another entity, and hence outside the bargaining unit, a strategy that may or may not contravene CAs explicitly. The adjudication of an unfair labor practices complaint made by Local 1518 in 2016 after the LRB reinstated the union's certification at Floralia, and a related application the union made for a declaration that Floralia and S&G (a neighboring farm) are common employers, brought into view these potent yet often obscured tactics fostering attrition.[5] The goal of such subtle tactics, which included action deemed unlawful by the LRB, but that were difficult to substantiate, was to facilitate the dismissal of bargaining unit members with the prospect of return from future employment under the SAWP, thereby weakening the bargaining unit.

This chapter explores strategies aimed at increasing attrition. The first section analyzes possibilities for attrition under a TMWP founded on meeting host-state employers' labor supply needs and subject to a principle of hiring Canadians first. It begins by reviewing policies and procedures that employers seeking to retain SAWP employees are to follow, highlighting opportunities that this model TMWP offers employers for tailoring their requests for workers. Next, it explores how, and in what ways, CAs can affect employers' requests. This aspect of the inquiry shows that, in the absence of CAs, criteria governing employers' continuing engagement of SAWP employees protect access to jobs for Canadian citizens and/or permanent residents, but not for temporary migrant workers.[6] At the same time, these criteria grant employers experiencing ongoing labor shortages opportunities to hire temporary migrant workers, including their former employees, season to season. In an attempt to limit employers' arbitrary actions, CAs covering SAWP employees, and enforceable by labor law, seek to minimize discretionary aspects of employers' continuing requests for temporary migrant workers. They aim to regulate readmission criteria applicable to bargaining unit members who are SAWP participants through provisions for recall season to season based on seniority that inhibit employers' resort to strategies aimed at weakening and/or eliminating units of workers laboring transnationally.

Against this backdrop, section two charts the fraught history of the bargaining unit at Floralia, which is characterized by dynamics similar to those at Sidhu. It describes Local 1518's vexed pursuit of certification to represent an all-employee bargaining unit at Floralia, expanding on the synopsis offered in chapter 2, before chronicling certain employees' successive attempts at decertification. This aspect of the investigation exposes overt strategies directed at attrition and their origins, culminating in the LRB's decision that reinstated the union's certification on the basis that Floralia and certain employees improperly interfered with a 2015 decertification application (BC MOL 1996, s. 6(1)) by preventing bargaining unit members from meeting with a union representative (s. 33(6)b).

Moving to explore more subtle tactics revealing the *how* of attrition, the third section examines an unfair labor practices complaint and a concomitant application for a declaration that Floralia and S&G are common employers, launched by Local 1518 in 2016 after the LRB restored its certification. Examining dynamics surrounding this complaint, it documents Floralia's efforts to manipulate recall processes codified by the CA; this manipulation was facilitated by opportunities under the SAWP for employers to alter the size of their workforces with relative ease, while simultaneously using non-unionized workers, including SAWP employees, of another employer to perform bargaining unit work. On the basis of such evidence, the LRB delivered a two-pronged ruling in adjudicating the union's unfair labor practice complaint. On the one hand, it found that Floralia committed unfair labor practices (BC MOL 1996, s, 6(1), 6(3)(a)) by intentionally manipulating provisions of the CA (s. 49(1)) and mechanisms of the SAWP regarding recall and placement to free its workforce of any perceived union allegiance. On the other hand, it ruled that Floralia and S&G used "the direction and control exerted over two distinct entities to defeat bargaining rights" (BC LRB 2017, para. 110; see also BC MOL 1996, s. 38).

The severity of such breaches led the LRB to prescribe an extensive a set of remedies. The LRB recognized that simply upholding the certification was inadequate to the task of restoring bargaining unit stability, especially given the employer's continued contravention of the LRC after the LRB reinstated the union's certification; therefore adjudicators mandated every remedy sought by the union. Section four considers these remedies, assessing the extent to which a provincial LRB has the tools to respond meaningfully to forms of attrition targeting a unionized workforce of temporary migrant workers, particularly covert tactics and their effects. The analysis underscores the challenges of enforcing CAs on behalf of TMWP participants with the prospect of return in the presence of institutional mechanisms that operate at cross-purposes. Under the SAWP, such mechanisms include elements of its program design and operation, which are governed by an agreement between sending and host states that provides employers considerable flexibility in adjusting the size and composition of their temporary migrant workforces, that can conflict with how host-state labor relations tribunals typically approach the restoration of bargaining units and employee reinstatement.

Based on this somber assessment, the chapter concludes by emphasizing that attrition, as a modality of deportability, is integral to migration management. For temporary migrant workers with the prospect of return, unions' concerted efforts to sustain bargaining units may dampen threats and acts of workforce reduction, but they can never eliminate them fully. Evidence surfacing in the 2017 season—particularly that relating to the common employer's initial response to remedies that the LRB required Floralia/S&G to fulfill after engaging in unfair labor practices and to incremental changes in the composition of Sidhu's agricultural workforce—underscores this conclusion. It suggests that strategies directed at attrition, many of which are subtle but have far-reaching consequences, are even more numerous than those identified in the investigation of events surrounding the 2015 application for decertification of a bargaining unit at Floralia explored in this chapter. Indeed, in 2017, Sidhu seemingly sought to reduce the size of the already circumscribed bargaining unit by replacing SAWP employees with workers recruited under another more deregulated stream of Canada's TFWP.

Attrition under the SAWP: Employers' Ability to Alter the Size and Composition of Temporary Migrant Workforces

Attrition—or the process of reducing the strength or effectiveness of someone or something through sustained attack or pressure—is a term used typically to describe the incremental reduction of a workforce by various means other than de facto redundancy (i.e., layoffs; *Oxford Dictionary of English* 2010). In the context of the SAWP, it also functions as a modality of deportability implemented by unionized employers who may use strategies to weaken, shrink, and debilitate bargaining units encompassing temporary migrant workers, despite CA provisions regulating recall processes based on seniority season to season.

Achieving attrition among SAWP employees is possible, even in unionized contexts, primarily because of aspects of SAWP's program design and operation. The two preceding chapters described the (always qualified) means through which the SAWP accords participants with the prospect for return. In its focus on termination prompting repatriation during the term of an employment contract, chapter 2 highlighted how the evaluative process overseen by Mexican officials, and highly vulnerable to manipulation, operated as a threat.[7] Under this process, temporary migrant workers seeking to return, whose performance satisfies their former employers, are normally requested back by and reassigned to the same employer in the subsequent season, unless the employer has no work available, in which case they are usually placed elsewhere. In contrast, those terminated and promptly repatriated, or retained but evaluated negatively by their former employers, are rarely reassigned to a different employer in Canada. Chapter 3, in turn, focused on discretionary aspects of the readmission process and opportunities for blacklisting. Both chapters also showed that a central role of CAs is to regulate SAWP employees' terms and conditions of employment—in the first instance, to preempt unjust dismissal and, in the second instance, to limit blacklisting by constraining employers' ability to decline to invite back, or recommend for readmission to another farm, otherwise eligible bargaining unit members. There is nevertheless another angle on how the prospect for return is qualified. A fundamental premise of the SAWP, as an exemplar of migration management, is that employers may readily alter the size of their temporary migrant workforces. They are subject only to modest overarching parameters, such as the "Canadians first" hiring priority under the SAWP, and associated administrative procedures to which those seeking to engage SAWP employees must perpetually adhere.

To request workers under the SAWP and other TMWPs operating in Canada, an employer must submit an application for an LMIA. In this application, the employer is required to detail the efforts he or she has made to recruit workers domestically (i.e., those residing permanently in Canada). The most important criterion for a successful LMIA is to demonstrate that domestic workers are unavailable.[8] The employer must also specify the location of the work, because the temporary work permits granted are employer specific. Employers cannot transfer or loan workers without both the workers' consent and the express permission of agents of the Mexican government posted in Canada and of the Canadian federal government responsible for the TMWP (i.e., ESDC; ESDC 2018, vii.1, 2). The SAWP also stipulates that employers offer temporary migrant workers a minimum of four months' work and that SAWP employees leave Canada by December 15 each year.[9]

Through the LMIA employers can either request specific (normally former) SAWP employees by name or unnamed workers. Even named workers are assigned to specific employers by officials of Mexico's MOL if the LMIA is approved. If the named workers are unavailable, the employer may indicate whether or not he or she will accept substitutes and may indeed name acceptable substitutes.[10] This feature of the LMIA application enables employers to easily adjust the size of their temporary migrant SAWP workforces every year. In the absence of a CA, it also means that, from the perspective of Canadian federal officials (i.e., apart from any end-of-season evaluation process overseen by Mexico), provisions of SAWP agreements allow employers to decline to request some former SAWP employees eligible for readmission while requesting other employees. There is no requirement for employers to justify their requests for particular employees. Even though acts of anti-union animus contravene certain labor laws and policies, employers can make or withdraw requests for temporary migrant workers for unstated reasons, including, presumably, those related to former SAWP employees' perceived attitudes toward unions.

In response to such flexible parameters for readmission, and to preempt employers' resort to strategies aimed at weakening or eliminating bargaining units covering SAWP employees, those few groups of workers who have managed to unionize have negotiated CAs with provisions for recall based on seniority. In the case of Floralia, as with Sidhu, such provisions mean that the employer is required to abide fully by the LMIA process.[11] However, in instances in which the employer requests workers under the SAWP for subsequent seasons, in addition to fulfilling the requirements of LMIAs, there is a further step. Unlike most non-unionized SAWP employees, those that are unionized typically have CAs granting them unique rights to return for subsequent seasons. The CAs of unionized SAWP employees also often specify the means by which recall is to proceed, given the administrative processes governing the TMWP.

Under the first CA put in place between Floralia and its bargaining unit, recall procedures required all SAWP employees who wanted to be recalled for the following season to advise their employer by signing the recall list during the season (or within thirty days of a layoff notice). These employees were also entitled to submit their preference for either delayed recall (any time after the month of March for the subsequent season) or early recall (any time before the month of June for the subsequent season (Floralia Plant Growers Ltd. and UFCW Local 1518 2012, art. 20.05 (a), (c)). The CA required the employer, in turn, to submit, as per the terms of the SAWP, to officials of the Canadian government department responsible for the TMWP a "recall request list . . . 'in order of seniority' (subject to ability and availability) of SAWP employees requesting return employment" and to copy the union on all such requests (art. 20.05 (d)). There was, however, one condition: "where a substitution [was] made [by Mexico] beyond the control of the Employer, the Employer [was] not to be held in violation of the Agreement." When the employee requested was substituted in this manner, the employer was simply to "resubmit the missing named workers on subsequent recalls unless the Employer receive[d] confirmation or information of termination" as otherwise set out in the CA (art. 20.05 (d)). In essence, then, the CA required Floralia to request by name former SAWP employees with recall rights and to request by name such bargaining unit members in order of seniority.

In practice, each year between 2011 and 2015, Floralia requested between eighteen and twenty-eight employees via the SAWP (BC LRB 2017, para. 180). Typically, the employer submitted two sets of applications for LMIAs in a given season: the first, made in December or early January, included a list for early recall comprising members of its more senior SAWP workforce. The second, sent in by March, included a list for delayed recall comprised of less senior members. The CA thereby imposed restrictions on how this employer approached its annual requests of SAWP employees in its application for LMIAs. It did so, substantively, in terms of the workers it named and in what order, and, procedurally, by limiting the time frame in which to make such requests. These two critical restrictions, to which Floralia seemingly adhered for the first seven years of its CA with Local 1518, aimed to foster a principled and orderly recall process otherwise absent under the SAWP. However, the limits of this recall process became apparent in disputes arising in, and subsequent to, a 2015 application for decertification by certain employees at Floralia.

The Fraught History of Local 1518's Bargaining Unit at Floralia: Overt Strategies for Thwarting Certification and Fostering Decertification

The relationship between Floralia and Local 1518 was tumultuous from the start.[12] Just three years after the employer first hired temporary migrant workers under the SAWP, Local 1518 submitted an application in September 2008 for the certification of an all-employee bargaining unit; at that point, Floralia terminated fourteen SAWP employees who were subsequently repatriated (see chapter 2). In response, the union appealed to the LRB, arguing that the terminations constituted an unfair labor practice under the LRC because the single feature unifying the SAWP employees who were affected was their support of unionization during a certification drive. To diminish the union's claim, Floralia cited weather conditions as the reason for termination, which constitutes a "sufficient reason" for early cessation of employment under the Canada–Mexico Standard Employment Agreement (ESDC 2018). Ultimately, the LRB ruled in the employer's favor. Yet the future bargaining unit members' resolve was so strong that despite such attempts to undermine the certification drive, after the ballots were counted, the LRB certified a bargaining unit.[13] Furthermore, even after a subsequent attempt by Floralia to resort to the Jamaican/Caribbean SAWP program instead of its Mexican counterpart as a means of diluting union support, a first CA came into effect in 2009 (UFCW 1518 2016e, paras. 190–193).

The period following certification was also by no means quiet at Floralia. As chapter 3 described, in 2011 certain employees at Floralia, represented by the two most senior SAWP employees then placed at the farm, filed an application for decertification, which Local 1518 contested through a complaint of improper interference that it unsuccessfully sought to link to parallel allegations against Sidhu (Floralia 2015d, 2). Because of how events at Sidhu unfolded, in 2014 those representatives ultimately withdrew their decertification application.[14] However, just a year after the LRB decided not to cancel the certification at Sidhu, certain employees (of Floralia) that led the first decertification campaign, this time twelve in number, applied to revoke bargaining rights under s. 33(2) of the LRC. In their application, they appointed the second-most senior SAWP employee at Floralia, who co-represented certain employees in the 2011 attempt at decertification, as their sole representative. These employees claimed that more than 45 percent of the bargaining unit complement signed the application to cancel the certification, requiring the LRB to conduct and count a representation vote.

Not surprisingly, the union objected to the application and sought to prevent the LRB from counting the vote. From one angle, Local 1518 claimed that the twelve certain employees seeking to cancel the certification could not represent 45 percent of the employee contingent, because Floralia appeared to have either employed or intended to employ more employees than it disclosed. It argued that a larger number of employees recruited by Floralia domestically, whose names the employer did not disclose to the union, fell within its employ and thus within the scope of the wall-to-wall bargaining unit, thereby raising the threshold of de-certification (UFCW 1518 2015a, 1–2). Further disputing the validity of the 45 percent threshold, and prefiguring a subsequent claim of employer manipula-tion of the recall process, the union noted that, at the time of the decertification application (May 25), Floralia declined to have three recalled but unavailable em-ployees substituted by unnamed SAWP participants and thus potential bargain-ing unit members; this decision reduced Floralia's request for workers, thereby keeping the new SAWP employee contingent small enough to ensure that the decertification application remained valid (UFCW 1518 2015d, paras. 25–38). Flagging how overt strategies, such as improper interference, can be coupled with more subtle actions, Local 1518 suggested that the employer contravened CA pro-visions for seasonal contract renewal in an attempt to obtain sufficient support for decertification. Buttressing such contentions, the union also claimed that, on their entry into Canada on the eve of the decertification vote, the representative of certain employees prevented twelve bargaining unit members participating in the SAWP from discussing the vote with a representative of the union, thereby violating of s. 6(1) of the LRC on improper interference. Local 1518 also argued, for the first time, that Floralia and S&G, a neighboring non-unionized farm owned by members of the same family, were common employers (UFCW 1518 2016d, para. 90).[15] By the 2015 season, Local 1518 noted that S&G workers were per-forming work either on Floralia's premises or on its behalf (UFCW 1518 2015d, paras. 50–61) that should otherwise have been done by bargaining unit members. The LRB, however, did not accept any of these counterarguments, ruling that the vote be counted and canceling the certification on that basis.[16]

In response, the union immediately filed a successful application for leave and reconsideration of the LRB's original decision and pursued a partial stay of its Original Decision of 2015. The LRB granted Local 1518's request for this stay because it found that the involvement of a sovereign nation (i.e., Mexico) not sub-ject to the LRB's jurisdiction had complicated the case. Mexico's involvement, and presumably its ability to assist in the blacklisting of troublesome workers as documented in chapter 3, took matters of recall out of the control of the union and the employer. It meant that if a reconsideration of the Original Decision of 2015 were to lead the LRB to try to restore the parties to a pre-decertification state, the Board would need to be reliant on the "goodwill" of Mexican officials.[17]

After the LRB decided to reconsider its Original Decision of 2015 and grant the stay, the union offered additional evidence to support each of its major arguments through written submissions to which Floralia (and S&G) likewise objected (UFCW 1518 2016a, 2016b, 2016c; Floralia 2016a, 2016b; S&G 2016a). In the end, however, the LRB chose only to address Local 1518's claim of improper interference—and thus to register its strong disapproval of overt strategies of attrition—in its Reconsideration Decision. Choosing not to address how the employer used mechanisms available under the SAWP to manipulate the recall process in support of decertification, it found that "irrespective of the intent of what occurred," the fact that "twelve new employees from Mexico" were "den[ied] . . . the time and opportunity to properly ascertain the circumstances at issue and make inquiries and assess the views which were being presented to them . . . ultimately constitute[d] a breach of Section 6(1) of the Code" (BC LRB 2016b, paras 15–16). In rendering the Original Decision of 2015 null and void and restoring the union's certification, the LRB focused squarely on interference with the administration of a trade union.

The Unfair Labor Practices Complaint: Subtle Strategies Undermining Seniority-Based Recall

Even after the LRB restored Local 1518's certification at Floralia, the union remained concerned that the employer was manipulating the recall process and continued to question the grower's relationship to S&G, the neighboring farm of continued concern. Therefore it lodged an unfair labor practices complaint against Floralia, contending that the employer had violated Article 20.05 of the CA on recall. Local 1518 also applied, once again, to have Floralia and S&G be declared common employers for labor relations purposes on the basis of further evidence, drawn from the 2015 and 2016 seasons, of these employers' exertion of common direction and control to limit unionization (UFCW 1518 2016d; BC LRB 2017, paras. 1–7).

In adjudicating this complaint, the LRB admitted a large body of evidence, in the form of the parties' written submissions and documentation and oral testimony pertinent to Floralia's conduct before, during, and after certain employees' second attempt at decertification. Through this evidence, a picture emerged of manifestations, beyond de facto decertification, of attrition normally obscured from view. It shed light on how, without violating either the letter or the spirit of the SAWP, employers could both manipulate recall processes applicable to temporary migrant workers codified by CA and employ workers from other entities. It also demonstrated that host-state labor relations tribunals' capacity to secure the effective enforcement of CAs applicable to workers laboring transnationally is limited, even when unions mount successful challenges to manipulation. Together, these manifestations of attrition underscore the need for greater accountability among substantive economic beneficiaries—not only among direct beneficiaries, such as employers, but also sending and, especially, host states—of goods and services produced using temporary migrant workers' labor power.

Attrition via the Manipulation of Recall Processes Stipulated by the Collective Agreement

As noted in the first section, in submitting applications for LMIAs, under the SAWP employers are able to request either specific (i.e., normally former) employees by name or a specific number of unnamed workers under the SAWP.[18] Employers' ability to name specific workers on their applications for LMIAs allows them to adjust not only the size but also the composition of the SAWP workforces annually. Where they exist, however, provisions for recall based on seniority contained in CAs aim to constrain employers' flexibility in this regard. Accordingly, from its inception in 2009, the CA between Local 1518 and Floralia allowed SAWP employee bargaining unit members to indicate whether or not they wished to return in subsequent seasons and, if so, if they preferred early or delayed recall. The CA also required Floralia to copy the union when submitting this recall request list to Canadian government officials (Floralia Plant Growers Ltd. and UFCW Local 1518 2012, art. 20.05, (d)). Under this provision, Floralia was to request by name the previous season's SAWP employees with recall rights by order of seniority.

Local 1518's unfair labor practices complaint rested on its allegations that Floralia had defied these recall procedures prescribed by CA. The union claimed that, in the 2016 season, the employer "intentionally manipulated the mechanisms of the SAWP regarding the recall and placement of workers to ensure that its current compliment [sic] of employees is free of any perceived union allegiance," and that such manipulation interfered with the bargaining unit and the administration of a trade union (UFCW 1518 2016d, p. 1). According to the union, on learning that the LRB would reconsider its Original Decision of 2015, Floralia canceled LMIA applications for twenty-two of the twenty-four employees it requested previously, thereby requesting only two employees on its seniority list, both of whom were known not to support the union.[19] Local 1518 argued further that, once the union's certification was restored, Floralia delayed (and reduced) its requests for other bargaining unit members until known union supporters had been reassigned to other farms.

As evidence, the union drew on records of Floralia's applications for LMIAs from previous years and for the 2016 season, in which it claimed the most significant manipulation took place. Through such records, whose content went uncontested by the employer, the union demonstrated a dramatic departure from Floralia's usual pattern of recall, which was to request between eighteen and twenty-eight workers annually under the SAWP from 2011–2015. For the 2016 season, records showed that the SAWP workforce recalled by Floralia was only 37.5 percent the size of the previous season. They also revealed an unusual pattern of recall (see table 4.1), suggesting that the employer changed its plans after it learned that the union had applied for a reconsideration of the LRB's Original Decision, a partial stay of its decertification, and that the LRB uphold Article 20.05 addressing recall of the CA until it issued a Reconsideration Decision. Moreover, as the union also sought to show, the employer's approach to recall seemingly reflected its desire to recall as many senior employees as possible—specifically those senior employees known to have supported the 2015 application for decertification—while neglecting its responsibility to recall more junior employees who it presumed had not supported the decertification drive.

Specifically, on December 28, 2015, Floralia requested, for early recall, the worker who was first on the seniority list; the employer had secured this position for him on the list as a concession during the first CA negotiations, signaling his status as a loyal and trusted employee, despite gaps in his employment history at the farm (UFCW 1518 2016d, para. 47). Consistent with past practice, on January 12 and 14, 2016, Floralia then requested two groups of workers. The first group named was to arrive in two contingents in March and April and included eight senior SAWP bargaining unit members, starting with the second-most senior and the former representative of certain employees. There was, however, one hiccup: the fifth-most senior worker, and a known union supporter, was left off the list, and the tenth was included, a change in practice that the employer later characterized as an error (UFCW 1518 2016e, para. 82.1; BC LRB 2017, para. 31). Conversely, the union argued that this fifth-most senior employee's absence from this list of named workers had more to do with his being "instrumental in rallying the senior group of employees to the Union's cause" in the 2015 season and having had "a significant falling out" with the most-senior bargaining unit member (UFCW 1518 2016e, para. 82.1). The second group named was to arrive on June 7, 2016, and included fifteen workers. However, instead of requesting the remaining more junior group of employees on the seniority list, Floralia named two new workers and requested thirteen new unnamed workers (BC LRB 2017, para. 32).[20]

TABLE 4.1. Timeline of Floralia's LMIA Applications and their Outcomes, 2015–2016

DATE REQUESTED	NUMBER OF EMPLOYEES REQUESTED	RANKING ON SENIORITY LIST	REQUESTED DATE(S) OF ARRIVAL	OUTCOME
December 28, 2015	1	1	March 4, 2016	#1 on seniority list arrives
January 12, 2016	8	2–4, 6–10 (#5 omitted)	March 11, 2016, and April 8, 2016	**Canceled** January 15, 2016
January 14, 2016	15	No workers on seniority list named	June 7, 2016	**Canceled** January 15, 2016
January 21, 2016	1	2	April 4, 2016	#2 on seniority list arrives
April 1, 2016	7	3–9	June 8, 2016	7 substitutes arrive

At the same time, the employer indicated that it would not need more workers than the twenty-four requested in its application for the LMIAs.

On January 14, the same day that Floralia made its third request for workers under the SAWP, the union filed an application for reconsideration of the Original Decision of 2015 and a partial stay of the proceedings. That day, Local 1518 also sent by email a copy of its application to the employer, which the LRB followed up with a notice letter received by both parties on January 15. At this point, Floralia canceled the applications for LMIAs for SAWP employees it made on January 12 and 14 (UFCW 1518 2016e, paras. 93–99). To further substantiate its complaint, the union used cellphone records of the co-owner and, as she is referred to in submissions and rulings surrounding the complaint, the principal director at Floralia.[21] These records showed that the principal director of Floralia spoke with the most-senior bargaining unit member, and the only worker still scheduled to return to the farm later that season, for eleven minutes just hours after receiving notice of the union's application for reconsideration (para. 98; BC LRB 2017, para. 35). Notably, the principal director of Floralia also telephoned this most-senior bargaining unit member on the evening of March 1, 2016, the date that the LRB handed down the Reconsideration Decision and restored the union's certification, and again on March 30, 2016, immediately after Mexico reassigned all of Floralia's remaining former employees to new employers: these calls, the last call in particular, raised the possibility of coordination between representatives of the employer and the sending state (paras. 41–42, 49).

A week after the union filed its January application for reconsideration, Floralia's principal director had a nine-minute call with the second-most senior bargaining unit member and submitted a new LMIA requesting him for recall the following day, January 21, 2016 (BC LRB 2017, paras. 36–37). In this application, the employer requested this worker by name for arrival on April 4, 2016, indicating that substitutes would not be accepted if he were unavailable. Meanwhile (on January 22, 2016), after finding that "the Union demonstrated a serious case for reconsideration and would be irremediably prejudiced if the stay were not granted," the LRB granted the union its request for a partial stay of its Original Decision of 2015, protecting the recall provisions in Article 20.05 pending the outcome of its application for reconsideration (para. 38; see also BC LRB 2016a).

Having cancelled its previous applications for LMIAs and having held off requesting more than two SAWP participants holding first and second positions on the seniority list, the union pointed to Floralia's communications with Mexican authorities, without making any allegations against them.[22] It showed that the principal director had a seventeen-minute conversation with the Mexican consulate on March 3, 2015, two days after the LRB restored the union's certification. The union also placed into evidence those parts of SIMOL records of SAWP participants to which employers, workers, and consulate employees have access (e.g., information on workers' status). In testimony, a UFCW representative suggested that, in March 2016, each of Floralia's SAWP bargaining unit members' worker status would have been expected to be "*nominal, mismo empleador* (named, same employer), which indicates that the employer and the worker want the worker to return the following season." Instead, in contravention of SAWP workers' recall rights under Article 20.05, "with the exception of [the two most senior SAWP bargaining unit members], all of the SAWP Workers' SIMOL files showed a status of *reserva seleccion, no pedido por su empleador,* meaning that they had been reassigned to the reserve pool." This UFCW representative explained that "a worker would only have this status for one of two reasons: either the employer has refused to accept the worker back or has indicated that it is not accepting any more workers at all": the employer responded to this comment by noting that it had not communicated either of these decisions to the MOL, thereby demonstrating how inaction can cultivate attrition (BC LRB 2017, para. 47).

Once again, the union pointed to a connection between the employer and Mexican officials, which was pertinent to the LRB in establishing the facts of the case, while refraining from making a pleading against Mexico. After pursuing this link, Local 1518 demonstrated that, "starting at 5:52 a.m. local time on March 30, 2016 . . . with the exception of [the two most senior bargaining unit members], who Floralia had already requested by name . . . , the remaining eight senior SAWP Workers were assigned, within a 22-minute window, to new farms across Canada" (BC LRB 2017, para. 48). Despite the principal director's claim that the statuses of the workers on SIMOL were "changed without her knowledge or input" (para. 47), the union used cellphone records and testimony to illustrate that the principal director knew that the more junior bargaining members reassigned by Mexico had agreed to work on other farms after speaking with various senior bargaining unit members. Consequently, Floralia had this knowledge on April 1, 2016, when submitting applications for LMIAs for seven workers to arrive on June 8. In these applications, the employer named the same seven bargaining unit members it had named on January 12, except it included the fifthmost senior bargaining unit member, whose name was omitted from the list originally (i.e., it had named workers who had numbers three to nine on the seniority list). It also named more junior bargaining unit members as possible substitutes as per the requirements of the CA, but those "named workers and the substitutes had accepted positions with other farms and were no longer available to be assigned to Floralia" (para. 50).

Furthermore, the union entered into evidence documents suggesting that, in its application of April 1, Floralia requested that "if its named workers were unavailable, it wanted to be assigned employees that were new to the SAWP program," although the principal director denied making this request (para. 51).[23] In the final analysis, Mexico only assigned nine workers to Floralia under the SAWP for the 2016 season. Just two such workers were on the seniority list, the two most-senior bargaining unit members, one of whom had figured prominently in previous applications for decertification made by certain employees and both of whom had received calls from Floralia's principal director during the reassignment process. The remaining bargaining unit members with recall rights, many of whom were known to be union supporters based on evidence offered in the 2015 application for decertification, were reassigned elsewhere (para. 27). The primacy accorded to the labor supply needs of host-state employers under the SAWP, reflected in their considerable flexibility in adjusting the size and composition of their temporary migrant workforces, meant that mechanisms of the TMWP permitted—and arguably facilitated—this erosion of the bargaining unit.

In its overall response to Local 1518's claims, Floralia did not contest any of the union's evidence regarding its submission, withdrawal, and resubmission of applications for LMIAs for workers under the SAWP for the 2016 season. However, the employer sought to demonstrate that it "*did not conspire* with the Mexican Consulate or manipulate the recall process to avoid recalling the Union supporters*" (BC LRB 2017, para. 53, emphasis added). Consequently, its principal director, as the person chiefly responsible for organizing the employer's workforce, cited four reasons for altering and ultimately delaying recall in this unconventional way.[24] She cited, first, the desire to know the outcome of the decision before requesting employees.[25] Second, she cast attention to the availability of less work in spring 2016 than in previous years (para. 56). Third, she noted concerns relating to Floralia's financing.[26] Finally, she pointed to uncertainties surrounding the availability of housing for SAWP employees due to a dispute with the city of Abbotsford. The principal director argued that Floralia could not commit to recalling bargaining unit members until these four issues were resolved. Only in late March 2016 did it become clear that the employer would need a twelve-person crew for the rest of the season, at which point the two most-senior bargaining unit members were approved to arrive in April and three domestic workers had already been hired, leaving a need for just seven SAWP employees (Floralia 2016c, 4–5; BC LRB 2017, paras. 57–64).

The crux of the union's unfair labor practice complaint was that Floralia manipulated the recall process codified under the CA to rid itself of workers known, or perceived to be, pro-union in an attempt to weaken the bargaining unit. Local 1518 claimed that Floralia's actions were too calculated and well timed to be unintentional. In response, Floralia, largely through its principal director's testimony, sought to rationalize its actions in delaying the recall of bargaining unit members and reducing their numbers, based on otherwise understandable reasons, such as crop failure, inadequate housing, and the like.[27] But, once again, the employer did not question the union's account of its own actions (i.e., the facts) since, in prioritizing the labor supply needs of host-state employers, the SAWP permitted Floralia to pursue recall in this way. Against this backdrop, the second dimension of the union's complaint helped complete this circle: Floralia was only able to dramatically reduce the size of the bargaining unit by using workers from a non-unionized entity, namely S&G. Thus, the union argued that the LRB should declare the two growers common employers for a labor relations purpose. This joint contracting, in practice, not only undermined the credibility of Floralia's explanations for its approach to recall but also revealed yet another (related) strategy for achieving attrition among temporary migrant workers with the prospect of return who held a unique set of rights conferred by a CA.

Attrition via the Resort to Employees of a Non-Unionized Entity

A second dimension of the union's unfair labor practices complaint centered on its contention that Floralia was only in a position to delay submitting applications for LMIAs for the majority of SAWP workers until very late in the season, as well as to recall only half of its regular workforce, because it had contracted with another entity to perform work usually done by its bargaining unit members (BC LRB 2017, para. 65). The union thereby sought a declaration from the LRB that Floralia and S&G, a neighboring farm, are common employers for a labor relations purpose. It aimed to prove that these employers used their "direction or control" over two different entities to undercut bargaining rights (UFCW 1518 2016e, para. 287). To advance this claim, Local 1518 attempted to demonstrate, first, that, in practice, Floralia and S&G fell under common direction and control and, second, that non-unionized employees of S&G were performing work that would otherwise be undertaken by bargaining unit members at Floralia.

As evidence of the first contention, the union pursued two tracks—common ownership and shared direction—both of which these employers contested. Regarding common ownership, the union sought to show that both the land and capital of Floralia and S&G were owned jointly by members of a single extended family, with these relatives' specific roles and property ownership changing hands fluidly for pragmatic reasons. In a pivotal submission toward the end of the proceedings, the union summed up its position as follows: "[the] two entities are operated for the general benefit of . . . [the entire extended family] . . . all without much care as to who legally owns the title to those companies" (UFCW 1518 2016e, para. 304). In developing this claim, Local 1518 paid close attention to the activities and roles of one family member: the father of the principal director of Floralia who was also an uncle of the principal director of S&G (referred to henceforth as Floralia's head grower). Offering evidence that he was Floralia's representative dealing with farmers markets, federal food safety programs, and municipal zoning bodies, the union claimed that Floralia's head grower occupied a management role (BC LRB 2017, paras. 66–67; UFCW 1518 2016d, paras. 98–100; see also Floralia Plant Growers Ltd 2016c, 11–12; BC LRB 2017, para. 68, 70). At the same time, he was the largest shareholder (holding 36% of the shares), served as the board chair of S&G, directed S&G employees, and was one of two people with signing authority (UFCW 1518 2016d, paras. 92–94; UFCW 1518 2016e, para. 325). More narrowly, to demonstrate the two entities' common ownership of land, also mediated by the head grower, the union offered evidence that Floralia's line of credit was secured by property owned jointly by the principal director's parents (BC LRB 2017, para. 66). Furthermore, while Floralia's principal director and her mother owned an equal number of shares in the business, the employer's primary premises housed the residence of their nuclear family. It also housed a packing facility, cooler, and greenhouse used by both Floralia and S&G based on a facility-sharing agreement initiated by the head grower of Floralia, who also served as S&G's representative in negotiating the terms of this agreement with his own two children, who represented Floralia (see Tables 4.2–4.3; S&G 2016b, 1–2).

In response to arguments about common ownership that centered on the head grower of Floralia, the two entities emphasized his marginal role on both farms. Floralia claimed that he was effectively a consultant involved intermittently, taking years off due to illness, and only took on the role of head grower in late 2014

TABLE 4.2. Ownership Structure of Floralia (Located on Land Owned by the Parents of Floralia's Principal Director) following Incorporation, 1999–2017

DATE RANGE	OWNER(S) AND STAKE	
1999 (month unspecified)	Principal director of Floralia (100%)	
1999 (month unspecified) to February 2016	Principal director of Floralia (50%)	Principal director of Floralia's brother (50%)
February 2016 onward	Principal director of Floralia (50%)	Principal director of Floralia's mother (50%)

TABLE 4.3. Ownership of S&G (Located on Land Owned Originally by the Uncle of Floralia's Principal Director) following Incorporation, 2014–2017

DATE RANGE	OWNERS AND STAKE			
2014 (unspecified) to November 25, 2016	Head grower of Floralia and principal director of Floralia's father (36%)	Principal director of S&G's mother and principal director of Floralia's aunt (34%)	Principal director of S&G and principal director of Floralia's first cousin (15%)	Principal director of S&G's brother and principal director of Floralia's first cousin (15%)
November 25, 2016 onward	Principal director of S&G's mother and principal director of Floralia's aunt (34%)		Principal director of S&G and principal director of Floralia's first cousin (33%)	Principal director of S&G's brother and principal director of Floralia's first cousin (33%)

after his son left the business; in that role, moreover, the head grower did not "exercise control or direction" (Floralia 2016b, 19; see also Floralia 2016c, 10–11; Floralia 2015c, paras. 55–58). S&G, in turn, claimed that the head grower of Floralia was an "advisor and mentor" to young business owners and was "peripheral" to the employer's operations, serving as a minority stakeholder and consultant who never exercised control (S&G 2016b, 1–2; S&G 2016a, 2; BC LRB 2017, paras. 69–71).[28] Indeed, the principal director of S&G went so far as to testify that, in late November 2016, Floralia's head grower (i.e., his uncle) sold back his shares in S&G at his own initiative (at $1 per share). At this point, he also resigned as chair of S&G precisely to "avoid this type of dispute" over common ownership (BC LRB 2017, para. 71). This was S&G's response to the union's contention that the sale of these shares in S&G "betray[ed]" the "remarkably fluid . . . line between Floralia and S&G's operations" (UFCW 1518 2016e, para. 299).

To prove the shared operational aspects of the common employer declaration, the union presented evidence of the close ties between the two employers' principal directors, using cellphone records to show that they spoke regularly (UFCW 1518 2016e, paras. 313–316).[29] More concretely, Local 1518 offered evidence that Floralia's head grower, together with S&G's principal director and his mother, worked and held considerable responsibility over various farm stalls under Floralia's banner.[30] Moreover, they did so alongside employees of S&G for a labor relations purpose—to weaken the bargaining rights of Floralia's unionized employees—the union's second central contention (BC LRB 2017, para. 74). Among several examples offered by the union, a UFCW representative supporting the SAWP employees at Floralia who were pursuing unionization testified "observ[ing] and record[ing] two S&G SAWP employees working alongside [S&G's principal director's mother] selling Floralia's product at a Floralia stall at the Port Coquitlam farmers market" on July 21, 2016 (para. 75).[31] This representative also testified seeing and documenting S&G employees working alongside Floralia's head grower at a stall operated by Floralia in the River District on May 28, 2016.[32]

In terms of work in the fields, the UFCW representative testified that he observed and recorded a team of S&G workers picking in Floralia's fields on June 22, 2016. The principal directors of Floralia and S&G did not dispute this claim. Yet they insisted that Floralia had simply sold S&G the "afterpick," which they defined as "leftover crop once the premium product has been harvested," distinguishing it from the "premium product" picked initially by the Floralia crew: they characterized this sale as a "standard farming practice" performed by outside workers (BC LRB 2017, para. 77).

Also tied to the "afterpick" scenario, but occurring on September 22, 2015, to demonstrate the depth of the connection between the two entities, the UFCW representative observed and recorded S&G employees working on one of Floralia's fields directly next to the most-senior bargaining unit member at Floralia (BC LRB 2017, para. 78).[33] Several months earlier, on June 24, 2015, the UFCW representative reported seeing S&G employees alone on Floralia's premises, recognizing one as a SAWP participant previously assigned to Floralia and therefore a former member of the bargaining unit (UFCW 1518 2015d, 13–15). The representative also testified seeing Floralia's principal director working alongside these S&G workers and directing their work until the team detected the presence of the union. At that point, the representative saw S&G workers "fleeing" the premises. When he confronted Floralia's principal director, in a scene captured on video, she indicated that the worker in question, the former Floralia employee, was "just there to visit some of his friends from the Floralia crew and she had to tell him to stop interrupting their work" (para. 79; UFCW 1518 2016e, 32). Discussing the same encounter, S&G's principal director testified that his employees regularly performed packing work on behalf of S&G at Floralia's "Primary Premises"; indeed, his uncle, Floralia's head grower, arranged for S&G to have access to Floralia's cooler and packaging facility due to problems with access to their own (BC LRB 2017, para. 80).[34]

In such periods during which S&G employees, some of whom were SAWP participants, were working alongside Floralia employees and/or management, the union also used cellphone records to demonstrate that the principal directors' regular "phone calls increase[d] in both length and frequency when labour disputes ar[o]se"; for example, their telephone communications increased when Local 1518 filed its application for reconsideration and when the LRB published its decisions (BC LRB 2017, para. 74). Other evidence used by the union to suggest shared direction included evidence that S&G's principal director sometimes submitted his LMIAs from Floralia's fax machine, evidence countered by Floralia's principal director who noted that, from time to time, she mentored her cousin in preparing for his applications for the SAWP program. Floralia's principal director nevertheless left unaddressed the union's evidence, that, in preparing for the 2015 season, when LMIAs from both S&G and Floralia were faxed from Floralia's fax machine, "certain typographical errors occur[red] on both [LMIAs]"; for the union, her lack of response thereby implied that these entities were already coordinating their requests in advance of that season (para. 73). That there was shared direction was buoyed by the fact that, whereas at the time of Floralia's certification in 2008, there were thirty employees on the voter list, in 2016, Floralia had only eleven employees, and S&G—technically a different (and non-unionized) corporate entity also engaging temporary migrant workers under the SAWP—had fully eighteen (UFCW 1518 2016e, para. 360).

The LRB's Decision

In response to the union's unfair labor practice complaint, the LRB found Floralia to have committed unfair labor practices and concluded that Floralia and S&G were common employers for a labor relations purpose.

In its ruling that there was improper interference in contravention of s. 6(3)(a) of the LRC, the LRB cited previous decisions recognizing that "employers do not ordinarily advertise their unfair labour practices" (BC LRB 2017, 101). Thus, any employer in this situation must "positively establish *bona fide* reasons for its conduct"; if the employer establishes that it had *bona fide* reasons for its conduct, the onus is on the union to establish that "the employer's conduct was tainted by anti-union animus" (101). In this instance, Floralia was compelled to justify why it submitted applications for LMIAs for its typical complement of twenty-four workers by January 14, 2016, and promptly canceled them on January 15, 2016. Yet the employer's justifications were unsatisfactory to the LRB, specifically, its concerns over financing and its ability to provide sufficient housing to SAWP employees, and the state of its crops, facilities, and available land. It thereby noted that the employer was as "aware" of these issues on January 15 as it was in the preceding days (paras. 103–104). The LRB also agreed with the union that if Floralia was concerned with leaving the fifth-most senior bargaining unit member, a worker known to be sympathetic to the union (UFCW 1518 2016e, para. 82.1), off the list, "it would have recalled him before April 1, 2016" (BC LRB 2017, para. 103). Overall, then, the LRB concurred with the union that "the only thing that changed for Floralia between January 12, 2016 and January 15, 2016 was the filing of the Union's application for reconsideration of the 2015 Original decision," which "motivated Floralia" to cancel its requests (para. 105). Furthermore, the LRB found that when Floralia learned about the application for reconsideration, it immediately canceled its LMIAs and "delayed recalling its workers, other than [the two most senior bargaining unit members], while it waited to find out if the Union's certification was restored"; then, on learning that the bargaining unit was restored, the employer limited its recall to the nine most-senior employees, "the majority of whom Floralia knew would support its interests" (para. 107). For adjudicators, Floralia clearly violated s.6 (3)(a) of the LRC insofar as its motivation for proceeding with recall in this way—by manipulating mechanisms governing recall in the CA (without technically violating the rules of the SAWP, but arguably disregarding their spirit)—was to "avoid recalling the majority of the SAWP workers who continued to support the Union" and thereby tantamount to an unfair labor practice (paras. 106–108).

Whereas the LRB had effectively dismissed such subtle tactics in the 2015 Reconsideration Decision that restored the union's certification, which was informed by overt employer interference with the decertification vote, its 2017 decision responded to and further illuminated the effectiveness of subtle strategies of attrition, such as the manipulation of the processes governing recall codified by the CA. On the related question of whether or not Floralia and S&G were common employers for a labor relations purpose, a relationship between the two farms that, according to the union, enabled Floralia to rely on non-unionized SAWP employees, the LRB's focus was on s. 38 of the LRC. According to the LRB, s. 38 aims to prevent employers from using the control and direction they exert over two distinct entities to defeat bargaining rights and thereby gives adjudicators the discretion to declare two or more companies common employers. In this instance, while the LRB viewed Floralia and S&G to be distinct corporate entities, it found the union to have provided evidence that they were indeed under common control and direction, based on its assessment of Floralia's head grower's role as "mentor and advisor" to both principal directors, given that he lived and owned the property housing Floralia's primary premises and long served as the chair of S&G's Board of Directors (BC LRB 2017, paras. 110–112). Adjudicators also found the relationship between Floralia and S&G's principal directors to be exceptionally close and noted their tendency to communicate increasingly "when labour relations and staffing issues arise" and to share key office equipment (para. 113). Still, the LRB found it difficult to monitor the on-farm work performed by employees of Floralia and S&G, given the multiple fields farmed. For this reason, evidence of employee overlap was clearest at the farmers market, given both the local UFCW representative's testimony and video and photographic evidence showing "[t]hat work was performed by S&G employees in a season when Floralia failed to recall half of its usual complement of SAWP Workers" (para. 114). For the LRB, therefore, Floralia was using "a non-union company to perform bargaining unit work," necessitating a common employer declaration to prevent prejudicing bargaining unit rights (paras. 114–115).

Remedies Prescribed by the LRB and Their Limits

The severity of Floralia's breaches, coupled with the fact that the employer contravened the LRC in the foregoing ways, even after the 2015 Reconsideration Decision reinstated the union's certification, led the LRB to mandate an extensive set of remedies. Concurring with the union, the LRB's central concern in this case was to ensure that the remedies prescribed were in sync with the mechanics of the SAWP program, including its annual timelines for recall and placement. Whereas in cases involving domestic workers, the LRB would have ordered reinstatement in the 2017 season, given the union's rationale for CA provisions governing recall, the LRB recognized that it was unlikely that SAWP employee bargaining unit members denied recall could be reassigned before 2018 under the TMWP (UFCW 1518 2016e, paras. 407–409). Consequently, the LRB extended its remedies to the 2018 season and the term of the CA to the earlier of ten months from the date on which the last SAWP employee bargaining unit member returned to work at the common employer or the first began work in 2018; that is, until sometime in 2019 (BC LRB 2017, para. 117, no. 10).

In prefacing its substantive remedies, the LRB also declared deterrence to be vital "because Floralia managed to achieve through the manipulation of the recall process exactly what the Board's Stay Decision [which restored the union's certification in 2015] was intended to prevent; it decimated the bargaining unit" (BC LRB 2017, para. 117). Thus, in addition to requiring declarations of Floralia's breaches and a ten-month time bar on future applications for decertification (under s. 33 (6) of the LRC) going forward, for the purpose of the LRC, S&G and Floralia were to constitute one employer and be bound to the CA. Any employees of S&G in 2016 were also to be added to the seniority list. Additionally, the LRB issued a series of orders designed to ensure that the common employer used its seniority list of early March 2016 in recalling SAWP employee bargaining unit members and that it treat as "unbroken" the seniority of all workers on this list who returned before the end of the 2018 season (para. 117, nos. 6, 7, 8, 9, 11).

The LRB also directed the common employer to submit to ESDC/Service Canada clear lists of alternate workers, taking account of seniority, and to copy the union on all correspondence with this government agency, as well as to inform the union of flight confirmations (BC LRB 2017, para. 117, nos. 12–14). Additionally, the translation of the LRB's final decision into Spanish, and costs associated with sending copies to affected workers and the Mexican Consulate in Vancouver as well as to Service Canada, were to be covered by the common employer (para. 117, nos. 15–16).

Evidence presented in the union's complaint and taken as fact by the LRB in its final decision implied that the common employer had contravened immigration law and policy. At issue, in particular, was Part VII (1&2) of the Agreement for the Employment in Canada of Seasonal Agricultural Workers from Mexico in BC, 2016, which obliged employers not to move, transfer, or loan workers without the consent of the worker and approval in writing from ESDC/Service Canada and the Mexican government agent. Nevertheless, the LRB did not have the power itself to penalize Floralia and S&G for such breaches.[35] Nor was it able to confront Mexican officials responsible, administratively, for facilitating processes surrounding (re)assignment—by fulfilling employee requests for transfer, providing named and unnamed workers and substitutes, etc.—and for abrogating CA provisions on recall on the basis of seniority applicable to SAWP employees because such officials were not themselves bound by the CA. These Mexican officials, however, were able to access, and indeed were empowered to assess, employers' evaluations of former SAWP employees via the SIMOL. Pointing to the significance of deportability—in this instance, through the modality of attrition—as a condition of possibility under the SAWP, the LRB's remedial authority was constrained by the disjuncture between elements of the SAWP's design and operation and the application of labor laws and policies. In its decision, the LRB could merely highlight errors in the employers' ways, underscore these errors for the sending- and host-state officials responsible for administering a TMWP permitting employers to make requests for labor (and hence applications for LMIAs) year after year, and take the limited remedial actions available under the LRC.[36]

The LRB was also in no position to interfere with the SAWP's commitment to migration management—and, thus, to meeting host-state employers' ongoing labor supply needs with flexibility. As developments at Sidhu in the 2017 season would show, such constraints proved important going forward. They contributed to a climate of fear, heightening the threat of dismissal from future employment by way of the SAWP, by fostering strategies of attrition of a different order: the resort, by an employer with a history of recruiting and recalling SAWP participants, to another stream of Canada's TFWP as a means of maintaining a consistent supply of temporary migrant workers season to season while shrinking bargaining unit membership.

Conclusion: Developments at Floralia and Sidhu Going Forward

In December 2016, before the LRB ruled in the unfair labor practices case, S&G applied for sixteen LMIAs for SAWP workers and advertised accordingly for the upcoming 2017 season. However, it withdrew its applications after the LRB made its ruling. In the summer of 2017, S&G's operations lay dormant: its fields were neglected, and it appeared to be without employees. Similarly, in May 2017, Floralia initially applied for LMIAs for twelve SAWP employees to arrive in late July to pick its crops, but subsequently canceled six such requests. While the employer made its remaining six requests based on seniority, by that time presumably Mexico had already dispatched to other farms many bargaining unit members, including those located midway down the seniority list who were known to be pro-union (lawyer for UFCW 1518, interview, July 18, 2017). By late July 2017, Floralia had engaged only one SAWP employee on early recall—the second-most senior bargaining unit member on the 2016 recall list—and two domestic employees, principally to staff, along with its principal director, six farmers markets located throughout the province on a weekly basis (UFCW 1518 staff representative, interview, July 19, 2017). Technically, the common employer thus complied with the remedies mandated by the LRB, but navigated the LMIA process so as to permit further erosion in the bargaining unit.[37]

Meanwhile, Sidhu's recruitment practices, exposed by Local 1518 in 2017, revealed another novel strategy of attrition. In preparation for that season, after having reduced the size of its SAWP workforce beginning in 2010 after the certification of the SAWP employee-only bargaining unit, Sidhu made requests, in order of seniority, for the same number of SAWP employees (twenty-one) it had engaged during the previous season. Yet according to union staff representatives' review of employer applications for LMIAs, it applied for approximately eighty temporary migrant workers: a number closer to the size of the employer's agricultural workforce at its height in 2009 (seventy-four). To make up the difference (of approximately sixty) between the number of temporary migrant workers Sidhu requested and the number of SAWP employees arriving, the employer likely sought workers through another stream of Canada's TFWP (UFCW 1518 staff representative, interview, July 26, 2017).

Starting in 2014, Canada's TFWP program changed from categorizing labor streams by either low or high "skill" to low or high "wage," creating opportunities for employers to engage seasonal agricultural workers through a larger number of TMWPs. In the process, four options, described briefly in chapter 1, for requesting temporary migrant workers in agriculture became available to employers. Two were new: the stream for low-wage positions and the new stream for high-wage positions.[38] The others were the long-standing SAWP and the rapidly expanding agricultural stream introduced in 2011 (see appendix, table A.1) (which was structured to some degree around skill level and encompassing agricultural products such as fruits and vegetables). At the time of writing, the agricultural stream drew workers from the Philippines, Guatemala, and Thailand among other low-income countries, perpetuating long-standing institutionalized racialized inequalities in agriculture (Satzewich 1991).[39] Presumably, since Sidhu cultivates fruits, the employer made LMIA applications for the bulk of its migrant workforce under this highly deregulated stream, which provides for fixed-term contracts for a maximum of eight months that are renewable under certain conditions but are by no means circular by design.[40]

Broadly, this differentiated approach would explain Sidhu's ability to maintain its operation while reducing the size of the bargaining unit encompassing SAWP employees, as noted in the introduction to this chapter. The employer's decision to attempt to resort to temporary migrant workers participating in another stream of Canada's TFWP also helps reveal why, together with mounting employer surveillance at this worksite, the union did not immediately pursue an unfair labor practices complaint of the type that succeeded against Floralia. Presumably, Sidhu sought workers from a stream of the TFWP distinct from the SAWP on the assumption that the LRB's certification of a bargaining unit comprised exclusively of SAWP participants meant that the unit would not extend to other temporary migrant workers. Unlike the all-employee bargaining unit at Floralia, which, by definition, encompassed participants in any stream of the TFWP, as well as domestic employees for that matter, temporary migrant workers engaged by Sidhu outside the SAWP would most likely either have to gain certification and form a bargaining unit separately from the existing unit or pursue the extension of the existing bargaining unit to participants in other TMWPs: both were unlikely prospects given the considerable employer surveillance of the work-site, including of workers' living quarters. Their situation thus underscores the numerous shifting strategies available to employers, who benefit substantively from temporary migrant workers' labor power in pursuit of attrition. It reveals the significance of this modality of deportability for temporary migrant workers with the prospect of return, including unionized SAWP employees with other-wise unique seniority-based CA rights to recall, in the face of a labor relations tribunal with limited room to maneuver.

In the book's conclusion, I put forward some avenues for alternative means to curbing attrition among TMWP participants with the prospect of return. These interventions include the incorporation of provisions mandating adherence to host-state labor laws and policies in MOUs and operational guidelines as well as instituting stricter regulations applicable to host-state employers using the LMIA process and seeking to move to request migrant workers from more weakly regulated TWMPs.

Conclusion

The legal struggle of SAWP employees of Sidhu, together with that of Floralia, illustrates that deportability, as it applies to participants in a TMWP permitting circularity, is an essential condition of possibility for migration management. Despite the formal commitments to human, social, and civil rights to which this dominant global policy paradigm aspires, the possibility of removal is ever present, even under its associated "best practice" TMWPs. As demonstrated by the experiences of the SAWP employees pursuing unionization as a means of realizing and retaining their rights, threats of removal may be deployed and carried out by a variety of institutions and actors, with the effect of shoring up a TMWP that provides participants with relatively low wages and labor standards.

The temporary migrant workers of focus in these pages confronted and resisted three modalities of deportability, each characterized by a unique set of dynamics: termination without just cause during the term of a seasonal employment contract, followed typically by repatriation, or on the receipt of a negative employer evaluation limiting prospects for return; blacklisting despite being otherwise eligible for recall, often prompting expulsion from future employment in the host state; and attrition, either in workplaces ripe for unionization or in established bargaining units. These modalities are difficult to document and hence to investigate. They often operate through subtle processes and practices, the analysis of which is enhanced by building on the insights of the prominent bodies of scholarly literature reviewed in chapter 1: sociological studies of temporary migrant workers' experience, critical legal and policy analyses of TMWPs, and scholarship on the political economy of labor migration. Departing from the

central preoccupations of these bodies of literature and their respective procedures for inquiry, however, this book has examined how the design and administration of the SAWP, as a model of migration management, produces threats and
acts of removal. By sketching the contours of the three modalities of deportability
confronting participants in this TWMP, it has aimed to fill the lacuna regarding
legal and administrative processes and practices and the underlying dynamics affecting their shape. Placing the *how* of deportability at the center of the investigation has entailed re-creating a narrative about the construction of this social
condition—which operates as a means of control—among temporary migrant
workers who have the prospect of return and have decided to exercise their rights
to organize and bargain collectively. The reconstruction of this narrative has
aimed, in turn, to connect such realities to knowledge production in practice—
making space for revealing truths that may be evident to deportability's subjects,
but are otherwise concealed by administrative processes and governing strategies.

In tracing what deportability does, and therefore what it is, chapters 2–4 ana-
lyzed the attempts of UFCW Local 1518, working against the odds on behalf of
SAWP employees of Sidhu, as well as of Floralia, to use legal channels in the host
state to help realize and retain the labor rights of workers migrating to participate in a TMWP permitting circularity. Indeed, Local 1518 made such efforts despite the limitations of a Wagnerian-style LRC and the primacy of the SAWP as
an intergovernmental agreement governing working across borders. Through the
analysis of such efforts, each chapter revealed key dissonances between immigration and labor laws, policies, and administrative practices that shape modalities
of deportability. Dissonances surfaced amid laws and policies on the books, such
as between provisions of the Canada–Mexico standard employment agreement
under the SAWP that, in permitting termination without just cause, are at odds
with various labor laws and polices operating in the host state, as well as with collective bargaining practice. They also featured prominently in aspects of TMWP
design and administration that give employers the ability to request the number
of SAWP participants they require seasonally, as well as to name the participants
they seek to rehire—yet leave the oversight of readmission processes to Mexican
officials under no obligation to adhere to host-state labor laws, including those
prohibiting anti-union interventions such as blacklisting.

By way of conclusion, this last chapter reflects on dissonances identified with
each modality under study as a means to envision incremental changes directed
ultimately at transformation. Obstacles to limiting deportability writ large will
persist so long as migration management dominates paradigmatically—driven
by the exploitive dynamics of global capitalism and thus prioritizing the interests
of socioeconomic beneficiaries of temporary migrant workers' labor power, including host states and host-state employers and, to a lesser extent, sending states

dependent on remittances.[1] Nevertheless, in combination with the forward-looking organizing efforts already being undertaken by unions and worker centers, in areas where unionization is difficult to achieve partly because of the still-dominant Wagnerian-styled model of unionization, certain modest interventions in policy and practice hold promise in forging change and curbing deportability among temporary migrant workers. Because the foregoing case study focused on the SAWP, the alternatives outlined in this chapter primarily address this TMWP.[2] Given, however, that the SAWP is often touted as a model of migration management, they seek to provide meaningful avenues toward incremental change in other TMWPs in Canada and elsewhere. There are mounting calls for broad-based policy responses to increase the accountability of substantive socioeconomic beneficiaries of temporary migrant workers' labor power, such as policies mandating that "the state that provides the institutional setting for addressing wrongs . . . to its territorial insiders . . . open its dispute resolution processes to all those who assert substantive claims on its labor market" (Mundlak 2009, 214). These responses dispense with methodological nationalism (Wimmer and Schiller 2002) and gesture toward global labor market membership or the freeing of labor rights and protections from the exclusive domain of nation-states (Vosko 2011, 380). In line with this book's overarching concern to address growing incongruities between the persistently national framing of labor laws and policies and the challenges confronting workers laboring transnationally in the face of migration management, the proposed suite of alternatives gives particular consideration to how to scale up innovative features of CAs and other promising practices linked to collective representation to the level of intergovernmental agreements, policies, and guidelines with a focus on those governing the SAWP.[3]

Scaling up Promising Practices Tied to Collective Representation

At the core of each modality of deportability confronting SAWP employees at Sidhu lie conflicts and tensions between intergovernmental agreements, policies, and operational guidelines governing the TMWP and labor laws and policies in the host state; these dissonances exist in a context in which the intergovernmental agreements and accompanying policies and guidelines supersede provisions of CAs encompassing temporary migrant workers, with the effect of upholding sending and host states' sovereign power over emigration and immigration, respectively. Such dissonances are real: their effects are concrete, rather than abstract. Some rest in inconsistencies between the terms of arrangements forged in intergovernmental agreements and the MOUs to which they give rise, such as the

Canada–Mexico standard employment agreement that animates the SAWP's purpose—to support the "hiring of temporary support" on a seasonal basis "when Canadians or permanent residents are not available"—and employment standards legislation in the host state (Sidhu & Sons Nursery Ltd. and UFCW Local 1518 2010, paras. A–D, art. 4.03). Others are a product of conflicting practices adopted in governing migration, such as those surrounding the (re)admission of temporary migrant workers and labor relations acts that provide not only for the certification and recognition of unions but also the enforcement of terms and conditions codified in CAs. Still others lie in tensions at the interface of provisions of labor relations acts, such as BC's LRC, and the leading assumptions of intergovernmental agreements, MOUs, and the like relating to the SAWP that are shaped by the dynamics of global capitalism. Whereas the former bar certain employment practices for labor relations purposes, the latter give primacy to employers' interests: they do so by giving FARMS/FERME a seat at the institutional table without according organized labor a parallel status and, more broadly, by upholding employers' demands for temporary migrant workers without applying clear criteria for evaluating applications for LMIAs based on past employer conduct and the effects of such conduct on temporary migrant workers eligible for recall.

Mitigating Termination with Principled Parameters around Dismissal and Open Work Permits with Pathways to Permanency

With regard to termination prompting premature repatriation during the term of the seasonal employment contract, chapter 2's analysis of the bid by SAWP employees of Sidhu to organize and bargain collectively revealed that, under this TMWP, temporary migrant workers residing in the host state can be terminated at will and summarily repatriated. An examination of this modality of deportability in operation shows how, true to migration management, the SAWP accords considerable authority to nonstate actors to manage the flows of TWMP participants, extending new modes of control to private actors, rather than providing meaningfully for greater openness. The Canada–Mexico standard employment agreement provides that an employer may cease seasonal employment contracts for any reason at any time, without allowing for the possibility of appeal, so long as there has been consultation with a Mexican government agent: while a SAWP employee is placed with a specific employer (and bound to that employer via a closed work permit), the employer in question is also entitled to terminate "employment for non-compliance, refusal to work, or *any other sufficient reason*" (ESDC 2016a, X.1, emphasis added). Reasons for termination offered by employers bound to the Canada–Mexico SAWP, and its BC variant, include diminishing demands for products contributing to reduced labor needs and, especially, poor weather conditions leading to declining crop yields. While such customary "official reasons" may be acceptable at a programmatic level, they are questionable on their own terms; given the fixed nature of all seasonal employment contracts under the SAWP, employers accrue minimal labor cost savings by terminating employees early.

In addition to documenting employers' common resort to such official reasons, chapter 2 offered clear evidence of employers' exercise of their ability to terminate without just cause as a means of eliminating SAWP employees perceived to be pro-union. This objective departs sharply from employment standards legislation in Quebec and Nova Scotia, which protects, in some measure, employees against unjust dismissal, as well as the Canada Labour Code, which extends such protection to non-unionized employees in the federal jurisdiction. It also runs counter to the tenor of laws and policies governing collective bargaining, which promote procedural fairness and acknowledge and seek to mitigate power imbalances inherent in the employment relationship by facilitating the negotiation of CAs, in operation in such jurisdictions and elsewhere. In supporting the rights of employees to be members of trade unions and to participate in union activity (and employers to likewise be members of and to participate in employer associations' lawful activities), and in promoting procedural fairness in the provision of these individual and collective rights, labor relations laws across Canada enable CAs to provide and supplement protection against unjust dismissal through provisions governing hiring, promotion, and termination procedures, as well as recall in instances of layoffs (see, e.g., BC MOL 1996, s. 4(1) and (2)). As a means of curbing arbitrary behavior, CAs are vitally important in regulating practices surrounding termination in industries such as agriculture where hiring and hence layoffs are often seasonal.

Not surprisingly, the permissibility of termination without just cause under intergovernmental agreements whose terms effectively govern SAWP employees was a central factor motivating the effort to unionize and negotiate a CA at Sidhu. Nevertheless, as subsequent developments showed, extending such protection by a CA has limits. Not only are novel CA provisions superseded by the SAWP and subject to a Wagner Act–inspired LRC that tends to prioritize industrial stability and citizen-workers or "territorial insiders" (Mundlak 2009), a CA enforceable only in the host state is insufficient to the task of eliminating the possibility of removal under intergovernmental agreements, even if such repatriation flows from workers' perceived support of unions and unionization. At best, such CA protections discourage termination prompting repatriation on such explicit bases, yet they cannot foreclose the resort to other modalities of deportability.

The practice of termination without just cause was nevertheless central to enabling certification of the union in its quest for dignity and respect for SAWP employees of Sidhu. Indeed, this quest for dignity and respect among workers laboring transnationally served as a defining feature of SAWP employees' common community of interest, notably, given the Wagnerian orientation of BC's LRC that has impeded unionization among workers in secondary industries and small firms, who are recent immigrants or hold tenuous residency status, have limited power, and may only be permitted to engage in seasonal employment. Similarly, mitigating this modality was a central focus of the CA, pointing to an obvious avenue for limiting SAWP employees' insecurity; namely, by formally prohibiting dismissal without just cause in the Canada–Mexico standard employment agreement, a move defensible on the principled basis that temporary migrant agricultural workers engaged under programs such as the SAWP constitute a highly vulnerable group.

Alongside banning dismissal without just cause, another avenue for improvement involves introducing a proactive complaint mechanism, building on the most developed arbitral processes outlined in CAs, into the Canada–Mexico standard employment agreement and its provincial variants, and providing guidelines for its implementation in MOUs and operational guidelines. Administered ideally by a tribunal overseen by the federal government of Canada, this complaint mechanism would be triggered every time a SAWP employee is fired before the conclusion of a fixed-term (i.e., seasonal) employment contract. Under its auspices, a workers' advocate would then be assigned to take on individual cases, thereby eliminating the need for (otherwise risky) worker-initiated complaints. A substantive feature of the complaint mechanism would involve introducing a reverse burden of proof, which would require the employer to verify that any termination (of either a union and non-union SAWP employee) is warranted and is in no way linked to the employee's beliefs about or involvement in unions.

These proposed measures, built on the recognition of the racialized and gendered geopolitical inequalities surrounding temporary migration for employment, effectively challenge the notion that TMWPs necessarily produce net positives for all the involved parties: temporary migrant workers, low-income sending states, high-income host states, and host-state employers seeking to minimize labor costs. By calling for socioeconomic beneficiaries of temporary migrant workers' labor power, such as host state employers, to bear more of the burden of labor protection (Mundlak 2009), they also address the inevitably precarious situation of SAWP employees in terms of both their employment and immigration statuses. Moreover, because seasonal contracts are limited in duration, implementing this set of measures would not result in excessive employer obligations. Optimally, it would also cultivate the creation and oversight of a broader range of fair grievance procedures and adherence to them and prevent repatriation without a hearing. To be effective, such measures would need to be binding on all parties: not only employers and unions but also sending and host states.

Eliminating the requirement for a closed work permit under the SAWP and other TMWPs, providing for open work permits, and enabling more expansive and more effective pathways to permanent residency would complement setting such principled parameters around termination prompting premature repatriation.[4] One promising way to counteract the new modes of control characteristic of migration management is to have unions, rather than employers, apply for such permits and, akin to a hiring hall model, play a central role in dispatching and reassigning workers to eligible employers. The advantages of this approach, promoted by representatives of Local 1518, are that it would encourage a freer flow of temporary migrant workers, limit their deportability, and reduce the erosion of their conditions of work and employment by putting institutions promoting workers' rights and protections at the center of placement and readmission processes (UFCW 1518 staff representative, interview, July 12, 2018).[5] As a way to strengthen the terms and conditions of standard employment agreements, representatives of Local 1518, together with community organizations and workers' centers concerned with increasing migrant workers' rights, should advocate the complementary introduction of broader-based bargaining, specifically, provisions for sectoral bargaining.[6]

Limiting Blacklisting by Institutionalizing Seniority-Based Recall and Fair, Enforceable Procedures for Readmission

By making it possible for SAWP participants to change employers, the provision of open work permits would also go some distance to mitigating threats and acts of employer reprisal against employees supportive or perceived to be supportive of unions. But while open work permits could enable these participants to remain in the host state until the end of their fixed-term contract, they would do little to limit blacklisting—a modality whose operation highlights how the design and administration of TMWPs permitting circularity allow sending and host states, together with employers, to inhibit meaningful collective representation among temporary migrant workers with the prospect of return, even where unionization is permissible in agriculture. As chapter 3 illustrated, the central dissonance is between, on the one hand, oversight of the readmission processes for SAWP participants by Mexican officials, who are not bound by host-state labor laws and policies because of the systemic principle of sovereignty, and, on the other hand, provisions of the BC LRC prohibiting blacklisting. An oblique, disciplinary evaluation, completed by employers and overseen by Mexican officials aware of the economic significance of remittances (described in chapter 2), is one scarcely scrutinized mechanism, among others, identified in chapter 3 that can block the readmission of participants identified as troublemakers, but who are otherwise eligible for recall. Yet, under BC's LRC (1996), actions by "an employer *or person acting on behalf of an employer*" to interfere with the formation, selection, or administration of a union are deemed unfair labor practices (s. 6(1), emphasis added). So too are the discharge, discipline, or dismissal of a person because of his or her decision to become a member a trade union, as well as the attempt—by intimidation, dismissal, threat of dismissal, or any other kind of threat or by the imposition of a penalty or a promise—to compel or to induce an employee to refrain from becoming or continuing to be a member of a trade union (s. 6(3)). The LRC likewise prohibits coercion and intimidation by "a person" "that could reasonably have the effect of compelling or inducing a person to become or to refrain from becoming or to continue . . . to be a member of a trade union" (s. 9).

In light of such dissonances between the LRC and the design and administration of the SAWP, Local 1518's bid to unionize employees at Sidhu (as well as Floralia) was designed to counter mechanisms institutionalized in the administration of the SAWP aimed ostensibly at fostering "ordered legal migration," but instead effectively impeding access to and the exercise of labor rights. In a novel attempt to create fair and standardized contract renewal and recall procedures—while considering the seasonal period in which migrant workers return to the sending state as a feature of the employment relationship—the union negotiated a CA specifying that "seniority of SAWP employees in prior seasons shall be maintained": it required the employer to keep a seniority list and to maintain the priority of foreign workers in prior seasons.[7] Season-to-season seniority was thus the CA's means of providing workers greater assurances of future employment. Prevailing to date, this first CA also contained corresponding provisions on layoffs, dictating that they be conducted "in reverse order of seniority," unless there are volunteers, with the caveat that SAWP employees may be laid off before Canadian citizens and/or permanent residents in accordance with MOUs, operational guidelines, and the standard employment agreement (Sidhu & Sons Nursery Ltd. and UFCW Local 1518 2010, arts. 16.03, 16.04). With respect to recall, in requesting employees through the SAWP (i.e., by way of LMIAs), Sidhu and likewise Floralia under its similar CA were also to list those who have completed the probationary period "in order of seniority" and to send a copy to the union (arts. 16.07, 16.08).

Together, these features of the CA covering SAWP employees of Sidhu created a procedure for regulating recall based on season-to-season seniority in the face of the persistent threat of blacklisting. Yet, chapter 3 showed how sending-state officials still managed to support the excise and/or discipline of SAWP participants perceived to be pro-union. Thus CA provisions promoting season-to-season seniority and recall on such bases proved inadequate in significantly weakening this modality of deportability. It is therefore necessary to provide the right to recall in the Canada–Mexico standard employment agreement and its provincial variants and to make readmission processes under SAWP more transparent. With regard to the former recommendation, which addresses the host-state side of the equation, safeguards protecting the number of temporary migrant workers engaged through the program each year should be put into place annually: these are warranted particularly if the long-standing labor shortages that characterize Canada's agricultural industry are to persist and if more highly deregulated TMWPs in agriculture are to remain. Such safeguards would aim not only to preserve openings for eligible SAWP employees to return but also to limit employers' resort to other (more highly) deregulated TMWPs in an effort to preempt the exercise or enforcement of labor rights and weaken the model program's worker-centered aspects. To accompany such measures, with respect to the situation of the sending-state, modified MOUs would do well to mandate both increased transparency in admission as well as readmission processes and adopt a seniority- or job tenure-based approach to readmission (characterizing job tenure as unbroken season to season). Optimally, the MOUs would also include guidelines for fostering circularity that would be applicable to both sending states and host-states and host state employers, as well as monitoring measures to ensure that they are applied fairly. For example, intergovernmental agreements could mandate that the federal government of Canada publish all applications for LMIAs (with individuals' identities concealed to protect those workers who are named) and require that the Mexican government likewise make available data obtained from the employer evaluation. To achieve the greatest effect, such guidelines, which could also contribute to limiting attrition, would further mandate that employees' union status, activity or perceived views about unions are not to interfere with standardized tenure-based readmission procedures. Moreover, in instances in which parties sought to deviate from tenure-based procedures (e.g., employers, sending- and host-state officials, etc.), they would be required to demonstrate that the proposed departure is in no way influenced by the union status, activity, or perceived views about unions of the temporary migrant workers affected. Otherwise, the workers affected would receive automatic readmission.

Preempting Attrition by Bolstering the Capacity to Organize and Bargain Collectively

Incorporating the most innovative features of CAs aimed at preventing blacklisting into intergovernmental agreements would help curtail this modality in places where employers rely on the labor of the SAWP participants. However, these scaled-up provisions would not solve problems linked to the equally thorny problem of attrition: actions aimed at gradually reducing the strength of bargaining units covering temporary migrant workers, some of which may be certified to cover participants in a particular TMWP exclusively. As chapter 4 demonstrated in the case of the SAWP, achieving attrition is possible, including to some degree in unionized contexts, primarily because of further aspects of program design and operation pertinent to recall and readmission season to season. A starting assumption of this exemplar of migration management is that employers may readily alter the size of their temporary migrant workforces. Because employers must adhere to the "Canadians first" hiring priority and associated administrative procedures, those requiring seasonal agricultural workers can readily replace SAWP employees with domestic employees and with workers drawn from other TMWPs. Herein marks the central dissonance underpinning the modality of attrition: in the absence of a CA and, in some cases, even in its presence (i.e., if an employer decides to either reduce or eliminate its SAWP workforce and/or to resort to another TMWP), employers may decline to hire SAWP participants who are otherwise eligible for readmission. At the same time, BC's LRC, like labor relations laws operating in other jurisdictions in Canada and elsewhere, prohibits interference with the formation, selection, or administration of a union (unfair labor practices), as well as intimidation and coercion. It also bans the exercise of direction and control over two (or more) entities directed at defeating bargaining rights (BC MOL 1996, s. 38).

In the case of Floralia, this friction came to the fore with the grower's resort to non-unionized temporary migrant workers, some of whom migrated under the SAWP, from a neighboring farm and related entity. Although the LRB was careful to emphasize that subcontracting, in and of itself, is not illegal, engaging in this practice to undermine collective bargaining is prohibited. Floralia was called to account for contravening the LRC and for manipulating the recall process under the CA. Still, attrition may take more subtle forms. As developments at Sidhu in the late 2010s suggest, it may involve the gradual reduction of a workforce of SAWP employees, as well as incremental attempts to resort to temporary migrant workers through other TMWPs. The apparent adoption of this strategy by Sidhu (i.e., limited to SAWP participants) was especially troubling, given the highly circumscribed bargaining unit, confined to SAWP employees exclusively, certified in this workplace.

Eliminating this last dissonance with the aim of reducing attrition as a modality of deportability entails a suite of changes at the level not only of intergovernmental agreements but also of policies and guidelines governing the TMWP (e.g., MOUs and operational guidelines). First, it calls for revising intergovernmental agreements to increase TMWP participants' capacity to organize and bargain collectively in contexts where unionization is permissible and, accordingly, to affirm that practices aimed at preempting unionization, weakening bargaining units, or defeating bargaining rights contravene agreements between sending and host states. To make such provisions meaningful, with respect to the admission, oversight, and readmission of temporary migrant workers under the SAWP, relevant MOUs, operational guidelines, and standard employment agreements would incorporate elements mandating adherence to host-state labor relations laws and policies by all the involved parties (i.e., host- and sending-state officials, employers, union representatives, etc.) and establishing penalties for nonadherence. Implementing such mutually agreed measures would amount to a partially deterritorialized solution to vexed labor law and policy problems in the face of deterritorialized capitalism (Mundlak 2009). It would eliminate sending and host states' concerns about undermining their respective sovereign authority over emigration and immigration. At the same time, for such measures to have the desired effects, at the level of the host state, rules addressing recruitment set out in policies governing TMWPs—specifically those governing the Canadian federal government's LMIA process that, in providing employer-centered "flexibility," creates openings for manipulation—would set limits on employers' ability to request temporary migrant workers from different (and differentially (de)regulated) TMWPs; in the context of agriculture and the SAWP in particular, strict limitations on switching TMWPs would apply to growers where unionization is permissible, and these rules would be monitored closely where TMWP participants are seeking to realize or retain their rights to organize and bargain collectively.

Scaling up innovative features of CAs and other promising practices linked to collective representation to the level of intergovernmental agreements, policies, and guidelines, and then adjusting administrative practices accordingly, would contribute to limiting the strength of these modalities of deportability. Of necessity, such measures, given their tenor and substance, seek to destabilize deportability as a condition of possibility for TMWPs characterized as exemplars of migration management. They would also contribute to reducing the degree of authority extended to private actors in managing the flows of temporary migrant workers under this paradigm. As demonstrated by the legal cases of SAWP employees at Sidhu and Floralia, deportability's effects cannot be ignored, including by proponents of a paradigm committed formally to upholding human, social, and civil rights. Given the paradoxes engendered by these commitments when paired with the goal of generalizing a global orderly migration model through arrangements fostering new modes of control, the measures described here offer but modest starting points for disrupting deportability's most severe consequences for temporary migrant workers with the prospect of return.

Notes

INTRODUCTION

1. The number of temporary migrant workers in Australia and Canada doubled in the period between 2005 and 2013, despite the recession. But, while remaining higher than 2005 levels, flows declined and/or fluctuated somewhat in both countries shortly thereafter because of domestic political developments (OECD 2008, 2010, 2012 [35, table 1.2], 2014 [25, table 1.2], 2015 [23, table 1.2; 24, table 1.3; 26, table 1.4], 2017, 2018).

Although temporary migrant workers' documented presence (e.g., via the provision of work permits) continued to decline in the EU after the 2008–2009 recession because of the elimination of internal mobility restrictions, in practice the phenomenon of *temporary* migration for employment remained alive and well (OECD 2014, 25; OECD 2016, 23; see also Hunt 2014).

2. Henceforth Sidhu & Sons Nursery Ltd. is referred to as "Sidhu," and Local 1518 of the UFCW is referred to as "Local 1518."

3. The legal term "certain employees" denotes a group of people involved in a formal process of the LRB (e.g., an application for decertification, a complaint of unfair labor practices, etc.).

4. After it was granted immunity, this sending state appealed, on similar grounds, first to the BC Supreme Court (BC SC) and later to the BC Court of Appeal (BC CA), to have all evidence related to its actions suppressed. However, it lost its case in both venues (*United Mexican States v. BC LRB* [2014]; *United Mexican States v. BC LRB* [2015]).

5. Henceforth Floralia Plant Growers Ltd. is referred to as "Floralia."

6. I first used the notion of modalities of deportability, developed further in this book, in an article examining threats and acts of blacklisting of SAWP employees at Sidhu (Vosko 2015).

7. In many host-state contexts, even if migrant workers are protected by national or subnational labor laws, they can be denied suitable remedies when their labor rights are violated. One U.S. example that pertains to undocumented workers is found in federal labor law, which provides most workers in the private sector the right to create and join unions without interference from their employers. Normally, under the National Labor Relations Act, if a worker is fired unlawfully for engaging in union activities, he or she is to be reinstated with back pay. However, as Wishnie (2007, 1453, emphasis added) explains, "Reinstatement of an illegally discharged immigrant worker is mandatory *only* upon the employee's proof of work authorization"; furthermore, because it is assumed by the courts that an employee without proof of work authorization should not have been employed in the first place, in some circumstances, undocumented workers who have been illegally discharged for engaging in union activity are ineligible for back pay (e.g., where they provide false employment documents and their unauthorized immigration status is unknown to the employer; see also Bosniak 2006; Gleeson 2016). Indeed, in a 5–4 decision in *Hoffman Plastic Compounds* (2002), the U.S. Supreme Court found that this otherwise normal remedy for unlawfully firing an employee for engaging in union activities (i.e., reinstatement with back pay) would "encourage [undocumented workers'] successful evasion of apprehension by immigration authorities, condone prior violations of the immigration laws,

and encourage future violations" (Opinion of the Court, *Hoffman Plastic Compounds, Inc., Petitioner v. National Labor Relations Board* [March 27, 2002]; for reflections on this decision, see especially Fisk and Wishnie 2005 and Bosniak 2006; for a discussion that sets the dissonance between immigration and labor law in the United States revealed in *Hoffman Plastic Compounds* in the context of institutions and regulations governing low-skilled migrant labor internationally, see also Kuptsch and Martin 2011).

8. This book uses the terms "sending" and "host" states of migrants for practical reasons, rather than to suggest that migration is a uni- or bidirectional process; in other words, the use of these terms is meant to reflect the self- and mutual characterization of, in this case, the Mexican and Canadian states and how their roles in the migration process are understood and depicted by the actors whose actions are chronicled in these pages. A central point of departure for the ensuing analysis is the rejection of methodological nationalism—or the assumption that "the nation/state/society is the natural social and political form of the modern world" (Wimmer and Schiller 2002, 302)—and the related view of migration, which "sees immobility and the life-long inhabitancy of one nation as the 'normal' human condition," and to acknowledge, instead, the existence of transnational "concurrent unequal life chances" (Lutz 2018, 582). Accordingly, the following chapters aim to contribute to the deterritorialization of the scholarly imaginary and thereby to reject approaches that tend to reduce analytical focus to the boundaries of nation-states.

1. DEPORTABILITY AMONG TEMPORARY MIGRANT WORKERS

1. Arguably, they date to the late nineteenth-century attempts by sovereign nations to "br[ea]k away from the principle of free circulation ... [and] forbid the entrance of foreigners and decide who can be admitted" (Chetail as cited by Piché 2012, 113) and, subsequently, the coordinated efforts by, for example, the League of Nations to "regulate international exchange of labour" in the Depression era (Trachtman 2009, xvii).

2. In his analysis of the situation of guest workers drawn into different low-wage sectors in the U.S. context, Ness (2011) analogously terms the dual process of creating conditions cultivating both the emigration of migrant workers and their exploitation in destination states as "corporate despotism."

3. The four intergovernmental organizations most centrally involved in migration management—the International Organization for Migration (IOM), the International Centre for Migration and Policy Development, the United Nations High Commission on Refugees, and Frontex—are very different from one another. Whereas one is a UN agency and the International Centre for Migration and Policy Development was established by the European Council, the other two lie outside established interstate systems.

4. That is, an alternative often posed to the model of migration originating in the seventeenth century, when nation-states came to be "imagined" as ethnically and culturally homogeneous political entities or "communities" (Anderson 1983), and operating throughout the Cold War, under which national governments held the "monopoly of the legitimate means of movements" (Torpey 2000, 2).

5. Notably, in an era of migration management, in practice, migration under permanent and temporary statuses does not alone determine whether or not labor migrants remain in host states or return to sending states. For example, in Canada, as elsewhere, under the Provincial Nominee Program, the temporary-to-permanent track is a prevalent model of migration that accounts for a considerable share of permanent migrants.

6. Although evident, the movement away from permanent immigration is less marked in newer countries of immigration in Latin America, Africa, the Middle East, and especially Asia that nevertheless resort increasingly to temporary migration for employment (e.g., South Korea, Malaysia, and Taiwan; see, e.g., Castles 2014; OECD 2014).

7. In 2012, women made up only 3.8 percent of Mexican SAWP workers in Canada (Becerril 2016, 156).

8. The multiplication of the categories through which various countries permit entry creates difficulties in comparing data across OECD countries, thwarting fine-grained analyses of trends (see Lemaitre et al. 2007).

9. The OECD's three other groupings are (1) intercompany transferees migrating to work temporarily in another branch or organization of a transnational corporation and often exempt from labor market tests and part of regional mobility arrangements (i.e., NAFTA, TPP etc.; OECD 2014, 173, 192); (2) trainees migrating to work temporarily under types of work-experience measures meant to help integration into the labor market (OECD 2014, 39); and (3) working-holiday makers, a group comprised of youth and young adults migrating to work temporarily, possibly for tourism or work experience, under bilateral youth mobility agreements concluded between countries, often on condition of reciprocity. Note: this last category exists in Australia, Canada, New Zealand, and the United States, among other countries (OECD 2014, 154), and, at the time of writing, its Canadian iteration was known as "International Experience Canada."

10. The OECD makes no official claim that this measure is comparable to circular temporary migration for employment. Because of the short duration of seasonal employment, however, it stands to reason that circularity occurs when it is not blocked by caps or other restrictions, and thereby represents a sizable subset of seasonal temporary migration for employment in the OECD.

11. According to the OECD (2014, 25), "seasonal workers, who numbered half a million in 2007, fell by 64% between 2007 and 2012. The main reason behind this substantial drop is the fact that seasonal workers from new EU countries no longer require a permit to work in EU countries (in particular, Germany). Further, two of those countries that, previously, received large numbers of seasonal labor migrants from outside of the EU— Italy and Spain—now each receive fewer than 10 000 annually. In other OECD countries, seasonal worker flows were stable." This pattern continued well into 2016 (OECD 2018, 27).

12. While Canada admits tens of thousands of immigrants as permanent residents under family and humanitarian classes annually, the majority of permanent residents coming each year enter under the heading of "economic immigrants" (IRCC 2016a). These newcomers are granted permanent residency on the basis of their occupation, skills, or investments. Still, permanent residents admitted as economic immigrants are increasingly being outnumbered by the annual admission of those on temporary work permits.

13. This test was known as a Labour Market Opinion (LMO) before June 2014; thereafter it was redesigned and relabeled as a Labour Market Impact Assessment (LMIA). The number of positions approved, formerly by Human Resources and Skills Development Canada (HRSDC)—a department created in 2003 and renamed Employment and Social Development Canada (ESDC) in 2015 having been reconstructed several times in the interim—to be filled by a migrant worker is contingent on various conditions, including no displacement of work for Canadian nationals.

14. Issued by the federal ESDC, LMIAs involve the evaluation of whether there is a genuine need for workers, often determined on the basis of the presence or absence of a labor shortage, defined in relation to the availability of workers domestically. The number of positive LMIAs issued annually is typically larger than the number of entries.

Indicative of the significance of the SAWP vis-à-vis other agricultural streams, there were only 880 positive labour market opinions granted in the latter in BC in 2012.

15. Even in the context of widespread public concern about Canada's TFWP as a whole, the SAWP is so well entrenched that an extensive 2016 Report of the Standing

Committee on Human Resources, Skills and Social Development and the Status of Persons with Disabilities that was highly critical of the TFWP did not recommend radical reforms to the SAWP.

This is not to suggest that this Standing Committee did not hear criticisms of the SAWP, but rather that it judged feedback on this TFWP to be, on balance, more positive than that received on other programs. On the one hand, the Standing Committee reported receiving positive feedback from representatives of sending states, such as Jamaica, who asserted that "the SAWP provides many cultural and financial benefits and does not need to be reformed" (HUMA 2016, 19). It also heard from Canadian agricultural organizations, including the Canadian Agriculture Human Resource Council, which conveyed that "programs like the SAWP contribute to filling a labour gap that exists in the agricultural industry despite significant recruitment and retention efforts" (19) and recommended building on SAWP's success by "establishing a dedicated Canadian Agriculture and Agri-Food Workforce Program" (19). On the other hand, although they did not recommend elimination of the SAWP, migrant workers, as well as advocacy groups and labor organizations, drew attention to "specific features of the program [that] place temporary foreign workers in a vulnerable position" (19); for example, representatives of the Migrant Worker Solidarity Network of Manitoba criticized employers' "discretionary power to repatriate workers when they do not comply with some aspect of the work or 'for any other sufficient reason,'" as did representatives organizations such as the Caregivers' Action Network (19).

16. Contrary to this assumption, as Hanley and Wen (2017) illustrate, the rise of TMWPs in Canada more generally has been accompanied by a tightening of immigration controls, a development that can, in turn, contribute to a rise in the number of undocumented migrant workers.

17. As Satzewich (2007) shows, at this time there was particular concern about Mexican Mennonites holding Canadian citizenship; many of these workers were illiterate and otherwise highly disadvantaged, working under exploitive conditions on Ontario farms.

18. Bilateral agreements exist between Canada and Mexico, BC and Mexico, and Canada and the Commonwealth Caribbean, including Jamaica, Trinidad and Tobago, and members of the Organization of Eastern Caribbean States. However, the agreements between Canada and Mexico and BC and Mexico are the focus here.

19. Strictly speaking, under the Canadian Constitution, provincial legislatures possess the ability to make immigration laws and policies alongside the federal government "as long and as far only" as they "are not repugnant to any Act of the Parliament of Canada" (Government of Canada 1867). In practice, however, the provinces hold "greater powers in the area of immigrant *integration* and settlement, because these tend to fall under the exclusively provincial jurisdictions of property and civil rights" (Black and Hagan 1993, cited in Boushey and Luedtke 2006, 214). The result is that, under the SAWP, the federal government has agreements with participating sending states that are often then transposed, modified, or supplemented by provinces that participate in the TMWP, such as BC.

20. Although they are often assisted by representatives of FERME and FARMS, individual employers must make initial and subsequent applications for LMIAs in which they are required to demonstrate, through various forms of documentation (e.g., job ads), that they have attempted unsuccessfully to find domestic workers to fill positions available, to provide copies of employment contracts prepared in a manner consistent with standard employment agreements, and to have their applications signed by a liaison officer for the sending-state government.

21. Only about 10 percent of Canada's labor force falls in industries regulated federally under the Canada Labour Code, which sets out minimum employment standards akin to those established under provincial employment standards acts.

22. Workers engaged and transported by farm labor contractors have still fewer entitlements to minimum rates where sufficient work is not available to send them into the fields. In such instances, they are only eligible for two hours of pay as opposed to the standard four-hour minimum. Employers are also exempt from liability for employees' unpaid wages when farm labor contractors are in default.

23. After being employed for twelve consecutive months, farm workers paid an hourly rate or a salary are entitled to two weeks' vacation and, after five years of consecutive employment, are entitled to three weeks. However, most farmworkers are employed seasonally.

24. Significantly, immigrants holding citizenship or permanent residency status, many of whom are of South Asian heritage, comprised most of BC's agricultural workforce, including nursery workers, from the early twentieth century through to the early 2000s.

25. On the politics behind agricultural workers' inclusion in BC, see Jensen 2013, chap. 2.

26. On the significance of statutory recognition, see Doherty 2013, 369.

27. In addressing dispute resolution, broadly the LRC imposes a duty to bargain in good faith, prohibits strikes and lockouts while a CA is in force and until negotiations have reached an impasse, and supports the resolution of disputes over the interpretation and application of CAs through binding arbitration.

28. In engaging in large-scale organizing efforts in the 1980s (Jensen 2013), the primary challenges confronting the CFU were (1) the farm labor contractor system, where a contractor is understood, in the language of S.1 of the ESA, to be "an employer whose employees work for or under the direct control of another person" but functions as an intermediary, which impeded the identification of employers and bargaining unit members; and (2) intimidation, which thwarted organizing, given that many immigrants in agriculture faced language barriers and many young women endured sexual abuse by farm labor contractors (Berggold 2011, 11; Former leader of CFU, interview, July 30, 2013).

29. The first decision is the 2001 *Dunmore* case, where the SCC heard a challenge to Ontario-based agricultural workers' exclusion from protection of their right to join unions and collectively represent themselves to employers. This case resulted in what Fudge (2012a, 4) aptly characterizes as an "incremental" expansion of the scope of protection. According to Fudge (7), the SCC held in *Dunmore* that "freedom of association imposes a positive obligation on the government to protect the rights of vulnerable workers . . . to join and participate in unions"; because agricultural workers represent one such group, the decision opened political space for the UFCW to organize in other provinces. The decision was circumscribed, however, by the SCC's determination that Canada's Charter of Rights and Freedom's freedom of association guarantee did not protect collective bargaining. Ontario thus created the Agricultural Employees Protection Act (AEPA), legislation that, as Fudge (7) shows, offers only "the narrowest interpretation of the constitutional requirements set out in that [i.e., the Dunmore] decision"; the SCC nevertheless affirmed its constitutionality subsequently (i.e., in the Fraser case).

The second notable decision involves the BC Health Services case of 2007 in which the SCC concluded that a right to collective bargaining is, under the Charter of Rights and Freedoms, a "limited right"—a verdict suggesting that though the charter protects the right of union members seeking to engage in "collective bargaining on workplace issues," it does not provide a right to any specific model of collective bargaining (e.g., Wagner Act model), or to a particular method of bargaining, an interpretation upheld by the SCC in the Fraser Decision of 2011, which confirmed the constitutionality of the AEPA.

On these rulings, see other contributions to Faraday, et al. 2012. On the relationship between them and Wagnerism in Canada, see especially Tucker 2014. On such rulings' significance in BC, see Russo 2012.

30. After workers voted to unionize, Greenway Farms applied to have the certification canceled, arguing that, because SAWP is administered federally, the LRC did not pertain to these TMWP participants. As Russo (2012, 129–32) demonstrates, the employer's argument focused on immigration being under federal jurisdiction, the role of foreign government agents in representing SAWP employees, and conditions of work being set in their entirety in advance by host and sending states (see also Russo 2011). In response, Local 1518 countered that the SAWP only mandates minimum terms, focusing on temporary migrant workers' entry, stay, and exit, rather than the range of terms that might otherwise be included in agreements pertaining to workers holding permanent residency or citizenship, that CAs may supplement; therefore, it argued that the LRC does not conflict with the SAWP. Furthermore, in the view of the union, the SAWP was not "law" in the form of a treaty, but rather an administrative arrangement (BC LRB 2009b, 28). In the end, the LRB agreed to apply the LRC, concluding that, in providing a minimum of rights, the SAWP employment contract in no way forecloses the negotiation of additional rights through collective bargaining.

31. For example, in Canada, the number of formal detentions reported by the Canadian Border Services Agency grew from just under 11,000 in 2004/2005 to 14,362 in 2008/2009 (CBSA 2010); meanwhile, the number of deportations in the United Kingdom increased twofold, from approximately 30,000 in 1997 to 68,000 in 2008, and tripled in the United States where deportations rose from 114,432 in 1997 to 319,382 in 2007 (Anderson et al. 2011, 550). Considering the United States, Anderson and colleagues also found growing numbers under the Obama administration, and the use of detentions is expected to rise further as promised by the Trump administration.

32. As developed and used here, the term "deportability" builds on De Genova's (2002) theorization. However, as Plascencia (2009) shows, Sayad also provides a helpful expanded analyses of deportation, first published in French, which encompasses not only acts but also threats of removal, or what Sayad calls "liability to deportation" (Sayad, in an English translation of the original 1996 article in which he adopts the corresponding term "expellable," as cited by Plascencia 2009, 382–383).

33. For example, in exploring developments in 1930s that took parallel expression in the 1950s, De Genova (2007, 427) found that "inasmuch as the mass expulsion of Mexicans during the 1930s proceeded with no regard to 'legal' residence or US citizenship or even birth in the US—and migrant and citizen alike were deported simply for being 'Mexicans'—the more plainly racist character of the illegalization and deportability of Mexican labor became starkly manifest."

34. Here, De Genova's claim reflects Sassen-Koob's (1981) formative insight, which predates, yet foresees, the multiplication of TMWPs: namely, that migrant labor is a distinct component of the labor supply defined by the institutional differentiation of its processes of reproduction and maintenance, a feature that mobilizes insecurity as a means of spurring self-disciplining behavior.

35. For a notable exception, see a new and provocative book by Nyers (2018) on "irregular citizenship," which enlarges this focus in a different direction than my own by focusing on the "unmaking of citizenship" through deportation.

36. There are, however, a few exceptions found in contributions of sociologists using ethnographic approaches to the study of deportability among undocumented migrants and identifying legal and institutional practices giving rise to this social condition; see, e.g., contributions to a special issue of the *Journal of Ethic and Migration Studies* addressing new ethnographic perspectives edited by Drotbohm and Hasselberg 2014.

37. This body of scholarship is vast and varied. It includes interventions into the history of Canada's TMWPs (see, e.g., Sharma 2006), the evolution of particular variants (see, e.g., Satzewich 1988, 1989a, 1989b, 1991; Arat-Koç 1989, 1999, 2006; Valiani 2012;

contributions to Choudry and Smith 2016), the relationship between the push toward North American integration and the growth of TMWPs in Canada (see, e.g., Gabriel and Macdonald 2004a, 2004b, 2004c, 2012; Gabriel 2011), how TMWPs contribute to labor market deregulation (see, e.g., Bauder 2006), and forms of resistance among TMWP participants (see, e.g., Gabriel and Macdonald 2014; contributions to Vosko et al. 2014 and to Choudry and Smith 2016).

38. In studying deportability among SAWP employees who are exercising their rights to organize and bargain collectively, I use the language "structure . . . the field of action" loosely, rather than in the sense used by Bourdieu or, for that matter, Foucault. Nevertheless, for Bourdieu, the notion of the "field" speaks to similar phenomena related to the symbolic and social constraints on the range of avenues available to workers in reacting to or resisting institutionalized possibilities of removal.

39. While I adopt a methodological approach rooted in feminist objectivity and acknowledge the gendered male character of the SAWP, gender relations in and of themselves are not the central focus of the analysis in these pages. For an analysis of the degree to which this program targets men and the consequences of its gendered (male) policies and practices on the few women who migrate under its auspices, see, for example, Becerril 2016.

40. In elaborating on the notion of reflexivity, as it is invoked, by those espousing feminist objectivity, Jackson (2011) suggests further that the practice has an extensive history in the social sciences—and indeed often serves as a foundation for arguments for the natural and social sciences given the capacity of researchers to reflect on their own situations: "the argument is that because human beings, unlike rocks or plants, have cultures and identities and volition, human beings cannot be studied in the way that rocks or plants are studied. When studying human beings, *researchers are necessarily internal to their objects of analysis in a way that they are not when they study non-human objects*" (157, emphasis added). This sentiment, too, is foundational to feminist objectivity as it is engaged here.

41. In adopting this approach, Haraway (1988) seeks to account for the enduring "objective" qualities of social structures of domination, without attributing to them some immutable character.

42. The research involving human subjects conducted as part of this book was approved by York University's, Human Participants Review Sub-Committee (certificate #: e2013–139) and subscribes to Canada's Tri-Council Policy on Ethical Conduct for Research Involving Human Subjects.

43. Questions posed in in-depth interviews of such key informants aimed to discern actions and events that the parties identified with deportability as it is lived by temporary migrant workers with the prospect of return. They queried informants' knowledge of how such workers' labor rights and their exercise are perceived and received, as well as of the mechanics of central modalities of deportability.

44. Because the identities of individual actors themselves do not advance the central aim of this analysis—that is, apprehending the *how* of deportability—the following chapters do not use the names of individual employees, consular employees, union personnel, and employers. Gender pronouns are, however, used in some circumstances. For example, in chapter 4, such pronouns are used to help clarify complex familial relations between employers at Floralia and a neighboring farm S&G. They are also used in the identification of SAWP participants to acknowledge the gendered (male) character of the entirely male SAWP workforce at the farms under study.

45. In a different context, that of airline carriers and shipping enterprises, Torpey (2000, 9–10) aptly characterizes such actors as "sheriff's deputies" engaged in "quasi-governmental activities," emphasizing the same point: namely, that their proliferation

does not amount to a loss of state sovereignty over migration, but rather to the introduction of more indirect (and often perverse) forms of its enforcement.

46. On the issue of early cessation of employment, the agreement simply stipulates that when an employee has to return to Mexico due to medical reasons, "The EMPLOYER must pay the cost of reasonable transportation and subsistence expenses except in instances where the WORKER's return home is necessary due to a physical or medical condition which was present prior to the WORKER'S arrival in Canada in which case the Government of Mexico will pay the full cost of the WORKER'S return" (ESDC 2016, IX).

47. In their *Dictionary of Human Resource Management,* Heery and Noon (2018) associate blacklisting with the practice of employers, employment agencies and business organizations taking note of the names of persons known to be trade union activists to, for example, allow for vetting of job applications and exclusion of union militants from employment more broadly (see also Segal 2009; Van den Broek 2003). Scholarly literature on the use of blacklisting as a means of expressing anti-labor or anti-union sentiments suggests that it can involve monitoring processes, such as so-called labor espionage, whereby paid agents are introduced into a given workplace "to inform [employers] on union and other dissident worker activity" (Segal 2009, 37), as well as recruitment strategies that seek to identify and filter out candidates with unionist tendencies or backgrounds or formerly employed in unionized firms or in highly unionized industries (Van den Broek 2003). Common to most literature documenting the contours of blacklisting in workplaces is the observation that its power and effects grow when associated acts are pursued collectively by employers (Segal 2009, 39), although blacklisting is increasingly recognized to involve a complex web of actors that may be tied to business, social or civil society organizations, and other groups (Spaulding 2009).

48. Between 2002 and 2011, Canada introduced two new TMWPs encompassing the agricultural sector with the official aim of making temporary migrant work genuinely temporary: (1) the Low Skill Pilot Project (2002), renamed the Pilot Project for Occupations Requiring Lower Levels of Formal Training, National Occupational Classification C & D in 2007, and (2) the Agricultural Stream of the Pilot Project for Occupations Requiring Lower Levels of Formal Training, National Occupational Classification C & D (2011). Focusing on "low-wage positions," these programs, some of which remain in place, not only put the SAWP under pressure but also impeded unionization or reduced the force of provisions on seniority and recall contained in existing collective agreements in three ways. First, they were open to workers migrating from an unlimited number of countries, prompting competition between sending states and, hence, incentives among such states to provide migrant workers who are compliant and thereby reluctant to organize. Second, although they entailed "forced rotation" (Wong 1984, 85), they limited the tenure of migrant workers' employment in Canada by requiring them to leave for a minimum period, limiting continuity in employment and thereby affecting unions' ability to organize and maintain bargaining unit strength (Government of Canada 2014, 12). Third, they permitted private labor brokers to recruit and place workers, cultivating debt bondage and triangular employment relationships thwarting unionization (Hennebry 2008).

2. GETTING ORGANIZED

1. Initially, Local 1518 lost a bid to represent a bargaining unit comprised of Sidhu's entire agricultural workforce due to disputes (similar to those that occurred in other certification drives at BC farms, such as Greenway, BC, but to different ends) over whether employees of farm labor contractors and administrative personnel should fall within its ambit. Yet, as key informant interviews and scholarly literature suggest, the social origins of BC agriculture provide further context for the union's inability to organize the entire

workforce at Sidhu, specifically for why some domestic employees, with ties to farm labor contractors, were ostensibly reluctant to support unionization.

Since the beginning of the 1970s, immigrants, have comprised a sizable segment of BC's agricultural labor force; these workers have migrated mainly from Punjab, India, and many are women. Even though these workers are permanent residents or citizens of Canada, many labor under the highly exploitive farm labor contracting system permissible in the province, a system that shares many features with the SAWP. Amplifying their labor market insecurity, historically, immigrant agricultural workers hired by farm labor contractors, as well as those engaged directly by growers, have also faced, and continue to confront, obstacles to unionization due to the "strong regional kinship ties which continue from Punjab" that constrain their access to employment in Canada and to the growers' and contractors' use of religious values to control workers (Bush 1995). As a leader of the CFU at the time of early unionization drives reflected in retrospect, such dynamics affected the union's lack of success in organizing Sidhu's entire workforce (Former leader of CFU, interview, July 30, 2015).

2. In this case, in response, the union representing the SAWP employees seeking certification, UFCW Local 1518, appealed to the LRB, arguing that the terminations constituted an unfair labor practice, as defined by the LRC. The reason: the single feature uniting the affected group of SAWP employees was their vociferous support of unionization in the context of a certification drive. However, the LRB ruled in favor of the employer since, under the Canada–Mexico standard employment agreement, weather conditions constitute a "sufficient reason" for early cessation of employment (ESDC 2016a).

3. In this case, the employer took the SAWP employees to the airport (and had their baggage checked), but was prevented from repatriating them to Mexico upon the arrival of a (Mexican) consular official, who had been notified by a call from the union and who claimed not to have been consulted (UFCW 1518 2009c).

4. For evidence of the effects of the evaluation process gathered by scholars before 2010, see, e.g., Basok 2002, 120, 141–143; Binford 2009, 511.

5. The primary goal of this chapter is to illustrate how termination without just cause functions as a modality of deportability under the SAWP. However, the LRB's prioritization of industrial stability, alongside facilitating access to collective bargaining, is central to understanding the challenges temporary migrant workers face in their organizing efforts. For a fuller analysis of how the LRB sought to reconcile these sometimes competing goals in this case, and the contradictory implications of its ultimate stance for SAWP employees of Sidhu, see Vosko 2014, an article upon which this chapter builds.

6. However, in some subsequent instances, when unions attempted to tie the traditionally difficult-to-organize designation to single employers, adjudicators affirmed that the doctrine rests on evidence of "the nature of the sector"; for example, in a Reconsideration Decision in *Wal-Mart Canada Corp.* (BC LRB 2006, para. 38), where the notion of "traditionally difficult to organize" is discussed at length, the LRB ultimately canceled a certification partly on the basis that the designation originally made by LRB was "only applicable to a single employer, not the (retail) sector."

7. In so doing, the union noted that this code shares the same "essential ambition"— that is, ensuring the freedom to organize—as the SCC expressed in the *Dunmore* case and other provincial labor relations legislation (UFCW 1518 2008c, paras. 1.2, 1.3, 1.5).

8. The union considered the second *IML* factor of physical and administrative structure of the employer to be redundant and the fourth factor of geography to be, at a minimum, neutral to the question at hand. In response, however, the employer countered that the very fact that it has one administrative structure for all agricultural workers discredited the union's application.

9. To justify the argument that the LRB incorporate the traditionally difficult-to-organize doctrine as part of the *IML* test for determining bargaining unit appropriateness, the union also emphasized its consistency with labor relations policies throughout North America (UFCW 1518 2008c, para. 2.6).

10. This concern was consistent with the LRB's reluctance to certify cross-classification units in previous cases in which unions sought to have the LRB apply the traditionally difficult-to-organize doctrine. See for example, a Reconsideration Decision in *Wal-Mart Canada Corp.* (BC LRB 2006, para. 30).

11. Further discussion about whether or not a unit of SAWP employees is appropriate should be set aside, the union argued, because *IML* states that "'the same community-of-interest factors that we have outlined as applying in initial applications for certification are to be applied in determining an application for certification in traditionally difficult to organize situations. *However, they are to be applied in a more 'relaxed' fashion*'" (UFCW 1518 2009a, para. 3.18, emphasis added).

12. Repudiating Local 1518's contentions that provisions of the SAWP impede workers' organizing, the employer claimed, for example, that SAWP employees have job mobility, safe drinking water, and decent living accommodations (Sidhu 2009a, submission B, para. 35).

13. They contended that fewer than half of all SAWP employees in BC lived on-farm; thus, they were no more difficult for unions to reach than other workers (BCAC and WALI 2009).

14. To demonstrate that SAWP employees are difficult to reach, the union offered evidence that no more than 10 percent live off-farm. It also used evidence from an AWA organizer to show that unions did not have easy access to on-farm accommodations and that only one local grower regularly brought SAWP workers to its Surrey-based workers' center.

15. Before the BC LRB ruled in the Sidhu case, the union withdrew this complaint against Village Farms in exchange for an agreement from the employer to do the following: distance itself from a person allegedly acting on its behalf and both communicating anti-union sentiments to workers and connecting particular workers' visits to the AWA with their threatened repatriation; support the transfer of a worker threatened with repatriation to another farm; and, compensate the foregoing worker for a week's lost wages (UFCW 1518 2009e).

16. Workers' centers, such as those affiliated with the AWA, combine strategies from union and community organizing to support and make interventions on behalf of workers, typically those engaged in precarious employment or holding insecure residency status (on the nature and roles of workers' centers in the U.S. context, see, e.g., Fine 2006; in Canadian context, see, e.g., Cranford et al. 2006; Choudry and Heneway 2012). By offering worker members a combination of services (e.g., legal representation) and advocacy, and engaging in organizing related not only to workplace issues, narrowly defined, but also larger social issues, such as challenges unique to migrant workers laboring transnationally, these institutions of labor market regulation aim to develop "an organizational form that allows for a worker-centred philosophy of organizing" (Cranford et al. 2006, 366). However, as shown by the example of Village Farms terminating employees for visiting the AWA office, such organizations, even though they are often membership based, are limited in their capacity to protect workers from the retaliation of employers empowered by the SAWP to terminate without just cause.

17. Divisions over work jurisdiction were minor with one exception: Local 1518 sought a provision addressing the distribution of overtime among SAWP employees to ensure that bargaining unit members were treated fairly. However, Sidhu countered successfully that the allocation of overtime exceeded the scope of collective bargaining (UFCW

1518 staff representative, interview, July 25, 2013; UFCW/AWA representative, interview, July 12, 2013).

18. In the case of wages, for instance, the CA contained provisions providing that all employees are to receive the applicable "prevailing" rates for SAWP employees in BC (i.e., under governmental agreements), as determined annually by ESDC, plus additional payments to be introduced incrementally for each of the three-year terms of the CAs.

19. Furthermore, in instances where a substitution (of a worker) was made beyond the control of the employer (i.e., by Mexican officials), the employer was not to be held in violation of the CA (Sidhu & Sons Nursery Ltd. and UFCW Local 1518 2010, art.16.08).

20. The experience of a group of SAWP employees at Floralia described earlier gives credence to this contention. Recall that Floralia repatriated these TMWP participants just as this employer was being made aware of a unionization drive. In this instance, because a CA was not yet in place, there was no provision for expedited grievance and arbitration processes in instances of alleged unjust termination through collective bargaining. Furthermore, even though the timing of the group termination, together with grower's prompt action to repatriate the SAWP participants, suggested that anti-unionism could have triggered such action, SAWP agreements do not require sending states to reinstate in future seasons participants repatriated for reasons such as weather conditions in the host state, either to place them, in conjunction with their Canadian counterparts, at a given grower's farm or elsewhere in Canada.

3. MAINTAINING A BARGAINING UNIT OF SEASONAL AGRICULTURAL WORKER PROGRAM (SAWP) EMPLOYEES

1. This section builds on and is derived, in part, from an article published in the *Journal of Ethnic and Migration Studies* on November 20, 2015, available online (https://www .tandfonline.com/doi/abs/10.1080/1369183X.2015.1111134). Specifically, it develops the narrative traced originally therein in which I first examined some of the unique empirics pertaining to the blacklisting case in order to reveal threats and acts central to this modality deportability.

2. The union contended as well that each of Mexico's actions amounted to interference with the commercial activity of the workers and the union, as well as damaging the union's property.

3. It argued that this charter characterizes states as sovereign and equal on the basis that they "have the right to operate in their territory with no restrictions other than those existing under international law" and comity, or the general principle of non-infringement of national sovereignty (United Mexican States and its Consular Representative in Vancouver 2011, 5–6).

4. Here, the union pointed specifically to Mexico's ratification of the International Covenant on Economic, Social and Cultural Rights (1966), the International Covenant on Civil and Political Rights (1966), and the ILO Convention on Freedom of Association and the Protection of the Right to Organize (1948), each of which recognizes workers' rights to organize and to benefit from collective organization, and to "Mexico's gross violation of these treaties" (UFCW 1518 2011c, para. 3.53). It also argued that Mexico's resort to the comity of nations was misplaced given the lack of competing jurisdictional claims over the governance of labor relations in BC.

5. From the LRB's perspective, "[t]he nature of Mexico's involvement in that program consists of making available a pool of 300 Mexican workers who are ready to work for agricultural employers in Canada . . . [whereas] the commercial exception was meant to capture situations where the state itself is participating in commercial activity" (BC LRB 2012, paras. 36–37).

6. Even after gaining immunity from the LRB, Mexican officials were sufficiently concerned with having their actions revealed that they appealed, on the basis of state immunity, first to the BC SC and then to the BC CA, to have all evidence related to its actions suppressed, but these appeals were unsuccessful. In a decision upheld by the BC CA, the BC SC rejected this sending state government's arguments with regard to the scope of immunity (*United Mexican States v. BC LRB* [2014]; *United Mexican States v. BC LRB* [2015]).

7. This section aims to reveal practices constituting blacklisting motivating Local 1518's complaints to the LRB, rather than to call attention to the actions of individuals. Consequently, as explained in chapter 1, the analysis avoids naming names in describing and analyzing documentary and oral evidence (e.g., testimony) offered by former Mexican consular officials in hearings in the union's case against the employer and certain employees.

Similarly, the section avoids naming the SAWP participants involved in the case because of this chapter's focus on the *how* of blacklisting. However, according to the legal proceedings, and consistent with the gendered character of the workforce, he/him pronouns apply to all the SAWP employees in this case. Hence, in the analysis to follow, for ease of reading, where pronouns are necessary, he and him are used to refer to the workers concerned.

8. Initially, two of these former employees were engaged by the Mexican consulate in Vancouver, technically a Canadian employer, under Canada's TFWP; reflecting their own deportability, one reported fearing that failing to comply with supervisory demands would risk forfeiting prospects for permanent residency (Former (Mexican) consular employee, interview, July 26, 2014).

9. Notably, however, Local 1518 indicated that, after participating in a May 2011 press conference at the Mexican Senate denouncing the blacklisting of union activists from the SAWP, this former employee received a call from Mexico's MOL offering him work in Quebec (UFCW 1518, 2011b, paras. 10–13). As a result, the blacklisted bargaining unit member did eventually travel to Canada under the SAWP that summer to work on another farm.

4. SUSTAINING BARGAINING UNIT STRENGTH

1. In 2008, seventy-one employees participated in a first certification vote for a wall-to-wall bargaining unit, and the number of employees at Sidhu increased to fully seventy-four in 2009. However, the SAWP employee-only unit (in 2010) comprised just thirty members on formal certification, twenty-five when the initial application for decertification was made by certain employees (in 2011), and twenty-three with its dismissal in the context of blacklisting (in 2014), after which point the numbers continued to wane (UFCW 1518 staff representative, interview, July 26, 2017).

2. At the time of this book's completion, it was impossible to access definitive information on the situation at Sidhu in 2017, even after consulting lists of employer applications for LMIAs and positive (i.e., approved) LMIAs published typically by ESDC online. It is nevertheless reasonable to conclude both that Sidhu continued to rely heavily on temporary migrant workers and that there is merit to union representatives' suspicions that this employer made requests for LMIAs for workers participating in TMWPs outside the SAWP, and thereby the ambit of the bargaining unit certified by the LRB.

3. In addition to making this observation, the following year, the same UFCW staff representative observed that, after a brief hiatus, in summer 2018 Sidhu recalled the chief instigator of the initial application for decertification as a bunkhouse lead (or a leader of a crew sharing accommodation) (UFCW 1518 staff representative, interview, July 12, 2018). Given that this individual testified to being acutely aware of whether or not bargaining unit members were union supporters in the LRB proceedings that found improper interference in a decertification application (as documented in chapter 3), this union

staff representative characterized his presence as heightening the already intense monitoring of bargaining unit members at this site.

4. Recall that the union had initially tried to draw this employer into its complaint of unfair labor practices and coercion and intimidation (i.e., blacklisting) against Sidhu, investigated in chapter 3.

5. Common employer is a legal term used by labor relation boards, among others, to denote, broadly, shared ownership of an entity or entities as well as typically shared direction and control of its/their workforce(s).

6. Since the LRB characterizes this group as "domestic workers," the chapter adopts this term for the sake of consistency.

7. It described how this process initially took the form of an end-of-season paper evaluation that employers completed and SAWP employees were required to present to MOL officials on their return to the sending state. Chapter 2 then demonstrated that, beginning in 2012, employers were required to enter their evaluations into workers' SIMOL records, which were readily accessible to Mexican officials charged with recruitment and placement (i.e., based at the Mexican consulate in the receiving state and the MOL in Mexico).

8. The employer must also note the type of work to be performed to ensure that it falls within the definition of agricultural work under the SAWP, which excludes certain activities (e.g., driving and other nonagricultural work) and work with certain commodities (e.g., corn).

9. Effectively, therefore, all SAWP employees must arrive before August 15.

10. In such cases, the employer may indicate, in addition, whether or not he or she will accept unnamed substitutes if those who are named are unavailable.

11. The CA between Sidhu and Local 1518 has long mirrored that in place between Floralia and Local 1518, with two main exceptions: first, there is no provision for members of Sidhu's SAWP employee-only bargaining unit to request early or delayed recall, and second, the CA operating at Sidhu requires that, if a requested employee is substituted beyond the control of the employer (i.e., at the behest of the sending state), the employer will resubmit the missing name(s) on subsequent recall lists submitted within the following ninety days.

12. As in chapter 3, the ensuing discussion does not name individual SAWP employees of Floralia; rather, it describes them on the basis of their placement on the seniority list, the relevant variable in studying this aspect of the legal case. Also mirroring the earlier approach to refer to officials of the Mexican consulate in Vancouver and Mexico's MOL in the interior, whose names are irrelevant to the larger goal of documenting the how of deportability, the narrative refers to persons tied to the ownership structure of Floralia and S&G by their position or title and familial relations. However, in this instance, I use gender pronouns consistent with those used in legal proceedings to navigate the complexity of familial ownership structure.

13. Though the employer made efforts to hold counting the certification vote in abeyance by questioning the appropriateness of the bargaining unit, the LRB rejected this request, counted the votes, and certified the bargaining unit (Floralia 2008).

14. After the LRB decided not to cancel the certification of a bargaining unit of SAWP employees at Sidhu, it brokered a settlement agreement between Local 1518 and Floralia. This settlement involved the withdrawal of certain employees' application for decertification on the understanding that, without the LRB's rejection of the application, which would impose a time bar on a future application, certain employees could reapply to decertify at the unit in the near future (Lawyer for UFCW 1518, interview, July 18, 2017).

15. S&G was founded just a year before the 2015 decertification application, and it became operational after an informal facility-sharing agreement with Floralia was negotiated

by family members in spring 2014, including one family member who held positions in both companies (S&G 2015, 3). See also table 4.2 in this chapter.

16. With regard to the union's attempt to demonstrate that the employer had reported to the federal government that it was both advertising for and engaging domestic employees, the LRB found that while the union offered evidence of the employers' lack of credibility, it did not provide "*actual evidence* of hidden domestic workers" (BC LRB 2015c, paras. 26). For this reason, adjudicators could not determine if the number of workers participating in the representation vote was inaccurate (under s. 33(6)(b) of the BC LRC); furthermore, for the LRB, the absence of evidence of "'build-up' of the employee complement subsequent to the representation vote" meant that the union's claim that certain employees did not meet the requisite threshold was "without merit" (BC LRB 2015c, para. 28).

The LRB also found that Floralia and S&G were not common employers because they did not satisfy the test for common direction and control; according to adjudicators, the union provided insufficient evidence that employees of the latter were performing bargaining unit work (BC LRB 2015c, para. 50). The LRB further concluded that calculated manipulation, on Floralia's part, was unlikely since Mexico reassigned the three bargaining members whom the employer declined to invite back (para. 38).

Additionally, the LRB was unconvinced that the second most-senior bargaining unit member and representative of certain employees and his employer deliberately kept employees away from the farm before the vote with the intention of preventing them from talking to a representative of the union. For the LRB, the errands that the member undertook together with the SAWP employees on their arrival were typical: "it was not unreasonable for the recently arrived foreign workers to spend their first day engaging in banking, purchasing supplies and eating a meal" (BC LRB 2015c, para. 64).

17. In coming to this conclusion, the LRB concurred with the union's application for a partial stay, in which it noted, "[t]he decision to place SAWP employees with the Employer is not ultimately the Employer's but instead rests with the sovereign state of Mexico over which the Board has no jurisdiction. . . . The Union will, as a result have no access to a remedy. The Board will not, we respectfully submit, have jurisdiction to restore the previous state of affairs" (UFCW 1518 2016a, paras. 190–191).

18. Recall that in the case of the former, in applying for an LMIA, employers may also indicate whether they will accept substitutes if named workers are unavailable and may indeed name substitutes. Where substitutes are acceptable to employers, they may in addition indicate whether they will accept unnamed substitutes if those they named are unavailable.

19. These employees were known to be anti-union because they had initiated the previous application for decertification; they were also absent from the list, submitted into evidence in the 2015 legal proceedings, of those affirming the union as their chosen representative. Additionally, as the LRB's unfair labor practices decision suggests, in the course of the earlier decertification hearings, the union introduced membership cards signed by all but five of Floralia's SAWP employees, indicating that they wished to remain certified (BC LRB 2017, para. 27). As a result of this evidence, which was not central to the LRB's ruling, the employer became aware of which SAWP employees did not support the union, all of whom were among its nine most-senior workers.

20. LRB proceedings reveal that these two workers were suggested by an employee who was number ten on the seniority list and was only recalled because of the erroneous omission of the fifth-most senior bargaining unit employee (BC LRB 2017, para. 32).

21. The term "principal director" is that used by the LRB, and hence adopted herein. However, elsewhere, including in this individual's own testimony, she is described as "managing director" and "owner and shareholder."

22. In its final arguments, Local 1518 emphasized that the LRB "need not find there to have been collusion [between 'Floralia and the Mexican authorities'] in order to find a breach of Section 6" of the LRC (UFCW 1518 2016e, para. 11).

23. Nevertheless, all seven workers ultimately assigned to Floralia were new to the SAWP; through the principal's testimony it also became clear that five such new SAWP participants were blood relations, even though close relatives are not permitted to work on the same farm under the rules of the TMWP (BC LRB 2017, paras. 50–51; lawyer for UFCW 1518, interview, July 18, 2017).

24. Before doing so, she explained that she inadvertently left one senior bargaining unit member, who was essential to running a piece of equipment formerly operated by her departing brother, off the recall list on January 12, 2016.

25. In the words of the LRB, Floralia was "concerned about running afoul of whatever order the Board might make"; accordingly, the principal director "testified that she felt she would be safer if she waited to see what the Board decided before making any commitments" (BC LRB 2017, para. 55).

26. According to its principal director, Floralia had been secured based on her brother and former co-owner's personal guarantee and his farming expertise, but when he left the farm, she had to qualify for financing on her own. Moreover, the financing arrangement was delayed partly because of her brother's antagonistic behavior in the negotiations about her takeover, including his sale of land that Floralia planned to lease for the raspberry crop. Adding to the problems related to the raspberry crop and the crew required to cultivate, pick, and maintain it, Floralia's principal director claimed that she discovered that the strawberry crop failed in March 2016 and that, among other crop problems, its greenhouse had suffered significant damage during a windstorm that month as well (BC LRB 2017, paras. 57–61).

27. In the process, this employer also aimed to dispel concerns about the purpose of its principal director's communications (via cellphone) with senior bargaining unit members and officials of the Mexican consulate.

28. Indeed, S&G's principal director testified that he was so young (19) when he and his brother (20) sought to incorporate that the bank was "unlikely to lend him the money necessary to get S&G up and running without an experienced farmer on the board [of directors]," leading him to seek assistance from his uncle, although the uncle only ever acted as a consultant in practice (BC LRB 2017, para. 70; see also S&G Fresh Produce Ltd. 2015, 3; S&G Fresh Produce Ltd. 2016a, 2). This was the primary reason that he and his brother brought their mother and uncle on board as shareholders. He also testified that his uncle's farming knowledge was not up to date (BC LRB 2017, para. 70).

29. This illustration, on the part of the union, however, was met with resistance from the first cousins, who suggested that their telephone conversations were of a personal nature (UFCW 1518 2016e, paras. 313–316; BC LRB 2017, para. 74).

30. According to the LRB, the principal testified that, because farmers markets operate in cash without any security or surveillance, she needed help from her parents because "it is important to have someone she trusts in charge of the cashbox" (BC LRB 2017, para. 68).

31. In her defense, Floralia's principal director testified that she was simply "referenc[ing] in" S&G, explaining that "'referencing in' is when you allow another farmer to operate your stall at a market to test whether they would be interested in taking it over" (BC LRB 2017, para. 75).

32. Here, Floralia's principal director responded that her father was working alone one day and fell ill; when her aunt, a shareholder of S&G, came and brought him medication, an S&G worker accompanied her; she merely left that worker to assist at Floralia's stall while she went and closed her own stall (Floralia 2016c, 10; BC LRB 2017, para. 76).

33. In response, the principal of Floralia claimed that this most-senior bargaining unit member was there to perform the inventory count in order to complete this "commercial" sale of suboptimal produce (BC LRB 2017, para. 78).

34. S&G's principal director also attested that the worker in question was working for S&G on Floralia's premises that day; indeed, he made this claim and noted that four of his workers were performing S&G work at Floralia's operation that day, and explained that he was on its premises to bring them pizza for lunch (BC LRB 2017, para. 81). He also took this opportunity to explain that the S&G workers, whom the UFCW representative assumed were attempting to leave the premises on his arrival, were actually picking up their pizza lunch (BC LRB 2017, para. 81).

35. Nor was it able to penalize these employers' representatives for providing false information, an offense under the Immigration and Refugee Protection Act (2001) (Government of Canada 2001, s. 126 & 127).

36. That said, having received a translated version of the LRB's final decision as part of the remedies it prescribed, Mexican officials, according to one union representative, were unlikely to "kick these workers out" or risk transgressing the recall process as they know "these workers will contact us, and we will make an issue of it" (UFCW 1518 staff representative, interview, July 12, 2018).

37. A year later, in summer 2018, most of the fields operated by Floralia/S&G lay dormant, and this common employer made no requests for workers under the SAWP. Meanwhile all former SAWP employees of Floralia/S&G (i.e., bargaining unit members) were sent to farms across Canada, leaving only two potential scenarios—the entity ceased operation altogether or ceased operating for the period during which the LRB declared it would not entertain any applications for decertification (i.e., until the end of 2018)—only to be revealed in the future (UFCW 1518 staff representative, interview, July 12, 2018).

38. Complicating assignment to the streams for low-wage and high-wage positions after the 2014 changes, every agricultural commodity, in every province, was to be assigned a fluctuating wage rate updated several times a year, which would determine the category under which a given worker is placed.

39. The agricultural stream did not undergo any major changes in the transition of 2014. At its inception, this stream was initially part of the TFWP and involved an LMIA; it therefore remained part of a reduced TFWP encompassing exclusively LMIA-tested positions.

The following agricultural products are covered by this stream: apiary products; fruits and vegetables (including canning/processing of these products if grown on the farm); mushrooms; flowers; nursery-grown trees, including Christmas trees, greenhouses/ nurseries; pedigreed canola seed; sod; tobacco; bovine; dairy; suck; horse; mink; poultry; sheep; and, swine.

40. The design of the agricultural stream makes unionization challenging. That said, in the province of Quebec, the UFCW has negotiated CAs for wall-to-wall bargaining units encompassing workers migrating from Guatemala under this TMWP. These CAs provide for inclusive grievance and arbitration procedures, as well as rights to recall and seniority in some measure. For instance, the CA applicable to agricultural workers who are members of UFCW Local 501 in Portneuf, Quebec, has a provision stating that "the most senior employees will be the last laid off and the first recalled to work, *in all cases*" (Savoura and UFCW Local 501 2012, art. 5.09, appendix B, emphasis added). This provision attempts to guarantee, subject to the limits of the TMWPs in question, such as the SAWP's Canadians first hiring priority, that for every employee—regardless of citizenship status, whether or not they are migrant workers, and which TMWP they migrate under—recall is based on seniority (thereby providing theoretically for future employment for workers

migrating under TMWPs that are not circular by design, such as the agricultural stream); it also provides for wage increases on such bases.

CONCLUSION

1. As the union representative for Local 1518 put it, "For all of the TWMPs, instead of moving the factories elsewhere to have cheap labor, it is way better to have cheap labor here [i.e., domestically]. If you're working within that program [i.e., mindset or model], that's what you do" (UFCW 1518 staff representative, interview, July 12, 2018).

2. As they are imagined herein, such incremental changes by no means seek to replace, but rather aim to support, long-term campaigns to make TMWPs obsolete and thereby provide for secure residency status and full labor rights to workers laboring transnationally by "liberating temporariness" (Vosko et al. 2014) and forging strong transborder labor solidarities founded on revitalized (and arguably rebuilt) institutions of organized labor (Ness 2011).

3. I first offered preliminary iterations of several proposals developed in this chapter in my 2018 article on the limits of collective bargaining among participants in Canada's SAWP (Vosko 2018).

4. In instances in which SAWP employees are themselves in search of alternative employment or employers have justifiable reasons for termination, open work permits would minimize costs to both the temporary migrant worker and the original sponsoring employer. Additionally, as Migrant Workers Alliance for Change (2018), a coalition of advocacy and community groups, worker centers, and unions, has noted in defense of its calls for open work permits, "comprehensive policy needs to be developed to ensure that migrant workers are able to access healthcare, social assistance and other provincial benefits when in-between jobs."

Nevertheless, pathways to permanency are ultimately more desirable. In a joint policy submission to Immigration, Refugees and Citizenship Canada Caregiver Pilot Program Consultations in 2018, the Migrant Workers Alliance for Change and a coalition of migrant caregiver worker and worker centers, thus called for permanent status on landing for all low-waged migrant workers to ensure family unity, workers' access to labor and human rights, and also protect temporary migrant workers, such as migrant caregivers, who were promised permanency but have become undocumented due to a backlog in permanent residency applications (Caregivers Action Centres et al. 2018).

5. In promoting what she calls "transnational labor citizenship," a notion premised on the idea that "given the choice, a significant number [of temporary migrant workers] would opt to be 'circular' migrants, traveling north to work for part of each year and returning home regularly to tend to their businesses and families," Gordon (2008, 57) advocates a version of this model to address the situation of Mexican migrant workers in the United States. Taking, as an example, the case of Brazilian welders who migrated to Alberta in the early 2000s under Canada's TFWP through the International Labor Management Alliance's Global Union Hiring Hall, which enabled Canadian welders to train their unionized Brazilian counterparts to meet Canadian standards on the agreement that the Brazilians would receive full benefits and the same wages and working conditions as nationals and that the latter would preserve their pay and workplace protections, she contends that hiring halls of this sort would "facilitate the enforcement of baseline labor rights and allow migrants to carry benefits and services with them as they move" (Gordon 2007, 504; see also Gordon 2008, 63).

Elsewhere, I (Vosko 2011) critique Gordon's (2008, 60) model on several grounds: in particular, I raise concerns about the protectionist character of her proposal that migrant workers be required to take a "workplace standards [or solidarity] oath" promising not to accept lower wages and levels of protection than their national counterparts. I also question this model's closed shop approach, which, by replacing national citizenship with compulsory membership in a union of paid workers, "risks perpetuating another set of exclusions tying rights recognition to one's status as worker ... [with] obvious gendered implications for migrants whose work in caring roles is not recognized within the scope of the formal economy" (Vosko 2011, 383; on the gendered character of this boundary, see, especially, McNevin 2009, 163). As an interim measure in limiting deportability among SAWP participants, aspects of Gordon's hiring hall model nevertheless hold promise.

So too do the complementary initiatives of other trade unions attempting to work across borders to protect migrant workers. One example is the Union Network International Passport. Developed by this global union federation, which organizes craft and service workers (engaged in postal, tourism, electricity, telecom, social security, commerce, finance, media, cleaning, and security industries), this passport allows unionized migrants to be "hosted" by a Union Network International-affiliated union in the destination country and makes them eligible for a range of benefits, which range from the provision of information on working conditions, the banking system, and tax regulations to opportunities to participate in local union training courses and receive advice on labor issues and legal support.

Another innovative initiative is the European Migrant Workers' Union: founded by German trade union IG BAU in 2004 in response to the underpayment of migrant workers from Poland laboring in Berlin, the European Migrant Workers' Union organizes temporary migrant workers, principally in agricultural and construction, of all nationalities who work for a limited period of time in one or several EU member states (other than their own; Schmidt 2006, 197–198).

6. The proposal for broader-based bargaining, specifically sectoral bargaining, is by no means new in the BC context where, in 1992, a report commissioned by the provincial government, prepared by John Baigent, Vincent Ready, and Tom Roper, called for amending the BC LRC to allow for a form of sectoral certification. As MacDonald (1997, 268–269), in a study probing the utility of sectoral bargaining in BC observed at that time, had it been implemented, this measure would have allowed, "unions at small enterprises which have been historically under represented by trade unions ... to amalgamate their bargaining units for the purpose of bargaining jointly with their employers." If the union could show sufficient support from additional locations within the sector in question, the form of sectoral certification proposed would also have allowed for the extension of sectoral agreements to new workplaces midway through a CA (Vosko 2000, 268). Although a measure of this sort has yet to be adopted in BC, and the stipulation that each workplace in a given sector could not employ more than fifty employees (or their equivalent) is a limitation of the proposal as I argue elsewhere (269), the significance of the Baigent, Ready, and Roper recommendation, and of sectoral bargaining more generally, is its movement beyond the Wagner Act model of industrial unionism by, in particular, enabling a "breakthrough contract," such as the CA between Sidhu & Sons and Local 1518, to serve as a lead (or master) CA for workplaces and employers in the same industry or sector (British Columbia 1992). As MacDonald (1997, 271) contends, this form of collective bargaining "would therefore enable those [workers in workplaces] too small to afford the costs of negotiating and enforcing separate collective agreements [or, in the case of SAWP employees, too afraid to do so,] to negotiate jointly ... [as it] ... recognizes that it is more difficult to intimidate a whole sector of working people than it is a small group of employees working in close proximity to management." In this way, sectoral bargaining would facilitate standardizing decent wages and working conditions within an industry.

Up to the time of this book's completion, the proposal by Baigent, Ready, and Roper continued to be cited in appeals by many unions for labor law reform in the province. For instance, in March 2018, in a submission to a government-commissioned review of

BC's LRC, the province's Hospital Employees' Union explicitly asked special advisors to consider amendments providing for broader-based bargaining through multiemployer sectoral certifications (British Columbia 1992). Notably, in its submission, this union also called attention to the fact that a broad provision of this order had been in place (with modest modifications) for approximately twenty years between 1973 and 1992 and that provision for sectoral certification continues to provide for "stable labour relations and collective bargaining" for employees in the health care sector under the province's Health Authorities Act (1996) (Hospital Employees' Union 2018). In an independent submission to this review also referencing the Baigent-Ready-Roper model (British Columbia 1992) and the Health Authorities Act, as well as the Community Social Services Labour Relations Act (2003), and illustrating how strategies of workers' centers and entities subscribing to similar organizing models partly because of limited access to Wagner Act–style unionization can complement efforts to forge—and indeed scale up—other important policy changes, such as the provision of open work permits, the Vancouver-based Migrant Workers' Centre (2018) likewise appealed for measures allowing for broader-based bargaining among care workers, many of whom are migrants. This worker's center's submission also demonstrated that creating a list of migrant care workers in private homes to enable broader-based bargaining would be straightforward given the existence of a mandatory registry under BC's ESA and the LMIA process through which employers of caregivers have historically (i.e., until as recently as February 2019, when changes were announced to provide a pathway to permanent residency for a modest number of care workers alongside eliminating the latest iteration of the TMWP long known as the Live-in Caregiver Program) had to provide information about the workers sought initially, as well as those who arrive later, a process that remains applicable to workers migrating under the SAWP and the Agricultural Stream.

7. Recall that, under the relevant provisions of the CA, seniority was only considered broken if the SAWP employee was duly discharged and not reinstated through the grievance procedure or arbitration, voluntarily quit or resigned, was absent from work without prior written approval from the employer, or failed to return to work on the completion of an authorized leave without a satisfactory reason (Sidhu & Sons Nursery Ltd. and UFCW Local 1518 2010, arts. 7.01, 7.02).

Appendix: Tables

TABLE A.1. Total Annual Temporary Labor Migration Flows (in thousands), Selected OECD Countries, 2005–2016

	AUSTRALIA	CANADA	NEW ZEALAND	UNITED STATES	TOTAL (4 COUNTRIES)
2005	183	107.1	78	635.2	1,003.3
2006	219.1	146.4	86.6	678.1	1,130.2
2007	257.6	164.9	99.2	483.6	1,005.3
2008	300.1	192.6	99.1	443.1	1,034.9
2009	325.8	169.2	87.4	453.1	1,035.5
2010	276.6	173	84.8	468.2	1,002.6
2011	303.8	179.8	81	460.8	1,025.4
2012	371.1	201.4	89.1	457.3	1,118.9
2013	411.8	206.1	102.5	505.7	1,226.1
2014	370.6	162.6	109.1	550.1	1,192.4
2015	409.1	134	114.6	595.2	1,252.9
2016	387.8	149.4	123.4	658.2	1,318.8
Factor of Change (2016/ 2005)	2.1	1.4	1.6	1.0	1.3

Sources: OECD 2008; OECD 2010; OECD 2012, 35, table 1.2; OECD 2014, 25, table 1.2; OECD 2015, 23–6, tables 1.2, 1.3, 1.4; OECD 2017; OECD 2018. Compiled from figures for working holiday makers, seasonal workers, intra-company transferees, and other temporary workers provided in "Country Notes" for Australia, Canada, New Zealand, and the United States.

TABLE A.2. Seasonal Temporary Labor Migration (in thousands), Selected OECD Countries, 2007–2016

	2007	2008	2009	2010	2011	2012	2013	2014	2015	2016
Australia	—	0.1	0.1	—	0.4	1.1	1.5	2.0	3.2	4.5
Canada	22	24.2	23.4	24.1	25.3	25.8	27.8	29.9	30.8	34.2
New Zealand	7	10.4	7.8	7.7	7.8	8.2	8.4	9.4	9.8	11.1
United States*	51	64.4	60.1	55.9	55.4	65.3	74.2	89.3	108.1	134.4
Non-EU OECD Total **	238	218	168	165	170	174	187	216	240	-
OECD Total***	720	574.9	523.7	583	372.5	208.5	212	362.6	527.2	685.4

Sources: OECD 2017, table 1.2; OECD 2018, table 1.2.
* Numbers for all years include only H-2A visa holders migrating under the Temporary Seasonal Agricultural Worker Program.
** Numbers include the United States, Canada, Mexico, New Zealand, Australia, and Norway. Numbers for the US component of this measure include both agricultural and nonagricultural H-2A and H-2B visa holders.
*** Numbers for the US component of this measure seemingly include H-2A visa holders exclusively.

TABLE A.3. Entries of Temporary Work Permit Holders and Permanent Residents to Canada, Selected Substatuses, and Their Comparative Ratio, by Selected Year

	2000	2005	2009	2012	2015	2017
Entries of Temporary Work Permit Holders	11,6540	12,2365	17,6745	213,573	249,765	302,821
Seasonal Agricultural Worker Program	16,710	2,0281	2,3393	2,5414	3,0740	3,5175
Mexican	9,235	11,871	15,739	17,765	21,430	24,765
Caribbean	7,475	8,410	7,654	7,649	9,310	10,500
Entries of Permanent Residents— Economic Class	136,287	15,6313	153,491	160,819	170,367	159,262
Ratio Temporary vs. Permanent	0.86	0.78	1.15	1.32	1.47	1.90

Sources: CIC 2010, 6, 66; CIC 2012, 6, 66; IRCC 2015b, tables 3.1, 3.2; IRCC 2015a, 4; IRCC 2016c tables 3.1 and 3.2; IRCC 2016b, 5; IRCC 2018a,13, 29; IRCC 2019.

TABLE A.4. Temporary Work Permit Holders in Canada by Selected Temporary Migrant Work Program and Year, 2004–2017

	AGRICULTURAL WORKERS*	LIVE-IN CAREGIVERS	OTHER HIGHER-SKILLED/ HIGH-WAGE	OTHER LOWER-SKILLED/ LOW-WAGE	TEMPORARY FOREIGN WORKER PROGRAM (LMO/ LMIA REQUIRED)	INTERNATIONAL MOBILITY PROGRAM (LMO/ LMIA EXEMPT)	TOTAL TEMPORARY WORK PERMIT HOLDERS
2004	19,880	16,670	31,124	2,753	70,471	66,757	**137,228**
2005	21,867	18,889	33,211	3,086	77,131	72,689	**149,820**
2006	24,328	22,526	36,573	4,572	88,281	81,312	**169,593**
2007	27,996	29,577	44,009	12,656	116,587	97,407	**213,994**
2008	31,468	23,281	48,788	25,002	131,414	118,608	**250,022**
2009	30,929	20,057	41,559	18,280	114,387	121,744	**236,131**
2010	31,761	17,114	40,540	16,349	109,506	138,432	**247,938**
2011	33,862	16,721	42,347	19,957	116,452	159,568	**276,020**
2012	35,035	12,707	47,117	22,715	117,522	173,676	**291,198**
2013	37,794	11,043	44,863	25,416	118,446	193,381	**311,827**
2014	39,452	11,822	26,423	16,721	94,621	194,160	**288,781**
2015	40,096	7,389	19,469	5,995	73,040	176,168	**249,208**
2016	45,185	7,787	19,727	5,878	78,535	208,582	**287,117**
2017	48,095	3,320	**	**	78,788	224,033	**302,821**
Factor of Change (2017/ 2004)	2.42	0.20	0.63*	2.14*	1.12	3.36	**2.21**

Sources: CIC 2014, tables 3.1, 3.2; IRCC 2016c, tables 3.1, 3.2; IRCC 2018a, 29; IRCC 2018b.

*This category includes SAWP participants as well as participants in the Streams for Other High-skilled/High-wage and Other Low-skilled/Low-wage positions in agriculture.

**2017 data unavailable for Other Higher-Skilled and Other Lower-Skilled subcategories of TFWP.

Bibliography

PRIMARY SOURCES

Legal Proceedings, Rulings/Decisions, and Written Testimony

British Columbia. 1992. *Recommendations for Labour Law Reform: A Report to the Honourable Moe Sihota, Minister of Labour.* Victoria, BC: The Sub-Committee of Special Advisors.

British Columbia Labour Relations Board (BC LRB). 1974. *Insurance Corporation of British Columbia & CUPE, Local 1695 & Office and Technical Employees' Union, Local 378 & BC Government Employees Union & Miscellaneous Workers', Wholesale and Retail Delivery Drivers' and Helpers' Union, Teamsters Local 351.* BC LRB 63.

——. 1993. *Island Medical Laboratories Ltd & Dueck Chevrolet Oldsmobile Cadillac Limited & Teamsters Local Union No.213 & Health Sciences Association of British Columbia.* BC LRB 308.

——. 1999. *Sears Canada Inc & Local 213 of the International Brotherhood of Electrical Workers.* BC LRB 47, February 12.

——. 2006. *Wal-Mart Canada Corp. & UFCW, Local 1518* BC LRB 153, June 30.

——. 2008. *Sidhu & Sons Nursery Ltd & UFCW, Local 1518.* BC LRB B159, October 14.

——. 2009a. *Sidhu & Sons Nursery Ltd & UFCW, Local 1518.* BC LRB B63, March 14.

——. 2009b. *Greenway Farms Ltd. -and- United Food and Commercial Workers International Union, Local 1518 -and- Attorney General of Canada -and- Attorney General of British Columbia.* BC LRB B135/2009, July 16.

——. 2010. *Sidhu & Sons Nursery Ltd. -and- UFCW, Local 1518 -and- Western Agriculture Labour Initiative (WALI) and British Columbia Agriculture Council (BCAC).* BC LRB B26/2010, February 9.

——. 2012a. *Sidhu & Sons Nursery Ltd. [Certain Employees of] -and- Floralia Plant Growers Limited [Certain Employees of] -and- Sidhu & Sons Nursery Ltd. -and- Floralia Plant Growers Limited -and- UFCW, Local 1518 -and- United Mexican States and Consulado General de Mexico en Vancouver.* BC LRB B28/2012, February 1.

——. 2012b. Testimony. *Sidhu & Sons Nursery Ltd. and United Food and Commercial Workers International Union, Local 1518* BC LRB 61942 & 61973, February 23, 24, 27, 28.

——. 2014. *Sidhu & Sons Nursery Ltd. Certain Employees of and United Food and Commercial Workers International Union, Local 1518.* BC LRB 61942 & 61973, March 20.

——. 2015a. Order. *Certain Employees of Floralia Plant Growers Limited and UFCW, Local 1518 and Floralia Plant Growers.* BC LRB 68534/15L, June 30.

——. 2015b. *Certain Employees of Floralia Plant Growers Limited and UFCW, Local 1518 and Floralia Plant Growers.* BC LRB 68534/15L & 68603/15, July 21.

——. 2015c. *Certain Employees of Floralia Plant Growers Limited and UFCW, Local 1518 and Floralia Plant Growers and S&G Fresh Produce.* BC LRB B248/2015, December 30.

——. 2016a. *Certain Employees of Floralia Plant Growers Limited and UFCW, Local 1518 and Floralia Plant Growers and S&G Fresh Produce.* BC LRB B17/ 2016, January 22.

——. 2016b. *Certain Employees of Floralia Plant Growers Limited and UFCW, Local 1518 and Floralia Plant Growers and S&G Fresh Produce.* BC LRB B34/ 2016, March 1.

——. 2017. *Certain Employees of Floralia Plant Growers Limited and UFCW, Local 1518 and Floralia Plant Growers and S&G Fresh Produce.* BC LRB B17/2017, January 20.

Floralia Plant Growers Ltd. v. United Food and Commercial Workers International Union, Local 1518 (Vacation Pay Grievance) [2015] B.C.C.A.A.A. No. 135 No. X-021/15. http://www.labourlawoffice.com/wp-content/uploads/2016/05/Floralia_Plant _Growers_Ltd-_v- United_Food_a.pdf.

Opinion of the Court. *Hoffman Plastic Compounds, Inc., Petitioner v. National Labor Relations Board* [March 27, 2002] No. 00.1595. Supreme Court of the United States.

United Mexican States v. British Columbia Labour Relations Board (BC LRB) [2014]. BC LRB. BCSC 54. https://www.courts.gov.bc.ca/jdb-txt/SC/14/00/2014BCSC0054.htm.

United Mexican States v. BC LRB [2015]. BC LRB. BCCA 32. https://www.courts.gov.bc .ca/jdb-txt/CA/15/00/2015BCCA0032.htm.

International Agreements

Canada and United Mexican States. 2001. *Seasonal Agricultural Worker Program: Memorandum of Understanding.*

International Labour Organization (ILO). 1948. *Freedom of Association and Protection of the Right to Organize Convention.* No. 87. https://www.ilo.org/dyn/normlex/en /f?p=NORMLEXPUB:12100:0::NO::P12100_INSTRUMENT_ID:312232.

United Nations (UN). 1945. *Charter of the United Nations.* 1 UNTS XVI, October 24. http://www.un.org/en/charter-united-nations.

UN General Assembly. 1966. *International Covenant on Civil and Political Rights*, United Nations Treaty Series, 999: 171, December 16. https://treaties.un.org/doc/Treaties /1976/03/19760323%2006-17%20AM/Ch_IV_04.pdf.

——. 1966. *International Covenant on Economic, Social and Cultural Rights.* United Nations, Treaty Series, 993: 3, December 16. https://treaties.un.org/doc/Treaties/1976/01 /19760103%2009-57%20PM/Ch_IV_03.pdf.

UN General Assembly Vienna Convention on Consular Relations (VCCR). 1963. United Nations. Treaty Series 596: 261–290. http://legal.un.org/ilc/texts/instruments /english/conventions/9_2_1963.pdf.

Submissions

British Columbia Agricultural Council (BCAC) and Western Agricultural Labour Initiative (WALI). 2009. *Sidhu & Sons Nursery Ltd & UFCW, Local 1518* BC LRB 58243, June 22.

Caregivers Action Centre, Caregiver Connections Education and Support Organization CCESO, Eto Tayong Caregivers (ETC), GABRIELA Ontario, Migrant Workers Alliance for Change, Migrante Ontario and Vancouver Committee for Domestic Workers and Caregivers Rights, et al. 2018. *Permanent Status on Landing: Real Reform for Caregivers.* Joint submissions, April 6. http://www.migrantworkersalliance .org/wp-content/uploads/2018/06/Caregiver-Reform-Submissions_April-2018 .pdf.

Certain Employees. 2015a. Submission to BC LRB. *Floralia Plant Growers Limited and United Food and Commercial Workers International Union Local 1518 and Certain Employees.* BC LRB 68534, June 16.

——. 2015b. Submission to BC LRB. *Floralia Plant Growers Limited and United Food and Commercial Workers International Union Local 1518 and Certain Employees.* BC LRB 68534, August 14.

———. 2015c. Submission to BC LRB. *Floralia Plant Growers Limited and United Food and Commercial Workers International Union Local 1518 and Certain Employees.* BC LRB 68534, September 29.

Floralia Plant Growers Ltd. 2008. Submission to BC LRB. *Floralia Plant Growers Limited and United Food and Commercial Workers International Union Local 1518.* BC LRB 58370, October 8.

———. 2015a. Response to BC LRB. *Floralia Plant Growers Limited and United Food and Commercial Workers International Union Local 1518.* BC LRB 68534 & 68603, June 17.

———. 2015b. Submission to BC LRB. *Floralia Plant Growers Limited and United Food and Commercial Workers International Union Local 1518.* BC LRB 68534 & 68603, July 20.

———. 2015c. Submission to BC LRB. *Floralia Plant Growers Limited and United Food and Commercial Workers International Union Local 1518 and Certain Employees and S&G Fresh Produce Limited.* BC LRB 68534, 68603, & 68783, August 14.

———. 2015d. Submission to BC LRB. *Floralia Plant Growers Limited and United Food and Commercial Workers International Union Local 1518 and Certain Employees and S&G Fresh Produce Limited.* BC LRB 68783, September 29.

———. 2016a. Submission to BC LRB. *Floralia Plant Growers Limited and United Food and Commercial Workers International Union Local 1518 and S&G Fresh Produce Limited.* BC LRB 69263, January 20.

———. 2016b. Submission to BC LRB. *Floralia Plant Growers Limited and United Food and Commercial Workers International Union Local 1518 and S&G Fresh Produce Limited* BC LRB 69263, January 27.

———. 2016c. Submission to BC LRB. *Floralia Plant Growers Limited and United Food and Commercial Workers International Union Local 1518 and S&G Fresh Produce Limited.* BC LRB 69263, August 15.

Hospital Employee's Union. 2018. Submission to the Special Advisers to the Minister of Labour. *Labour Relations Code Review.* https://engage.gov.bc.ca/app/uploads/sites/332/2018/03/Hospital-Employees%E2%80%99-Union.pdf.

Migrant Workers Alliance for Change. 2018. *Expanding Worker Rights—Open Work Permit Program for Migrant Workers Facing Risk.* http://www.migrantworkersalliance.org/wp-content/uploads/2017/12/Open-Work-Permit-Program-for-Migrant-Workers-Facing-Risk.pdf.

Migrant Workers' Centre. 2018. Submission to the Special Advisors to the Minister of Labour. *Labour Relations Code Review.* https://engage.gov.bc.ca/app/uploads/sites/332/2018/03/Migrant-Workers-Centre-1.pdf.

S&G Fresh Produce Ltd. 2015. Submission to BC LRB. *Floralia Plant Growers Limited and United Food and Commercial Workers International Union Local 1518 and Certain Employees and S&G Fresh Produce Limited.* BC LRB 68534 & 68603, August 12.

———. 2016a. Submission to BCLRB. *Floralia Plant Growers Limited and United Food and Commercial Workers International Union Local 1518 and S&G Fresh Produce Limited.* BC LRB 69263, January 26.

———. 2016b. Submission to BCLRB. *Floralia Plant Growers Limited and United Food and Commercial Workers International Union Local 1518 and S&G Fresh Produce Limited.* BC LRB 69861, August 12.

Sidhu. 2008a. Submission to BC LRB. *Sidhu & Sons Nursery Ltd & UFCW, Local 1518* BC. LRB 58243, August 8.

———. 2008b. Submission to BC LRB. *Sidhu & Sons Nursery Ltd & UFCW, Local 1518.* BC LRB 58243, August 15.

——. 2009a. Submission to BC LRB. *Sidhu & Sons Nursery Ltd & UFCW, Local 1518*. BC LRB 58243, May 27.

——. 2009b. Submission to BC LRB. *Sidhu & Sons Nursery Ltd & UFCW, Local 1518*. BC LRB 58243, June 3.

——. 2009c. Submission to BC LRB. *Sidhu & Sons Nursery Ltd & UFCW, Local 1518*. BC LRB 58243, June 5.

——. 2010. Submission to BC LRB. *Sidhu & Sons Nursery Ltd & UFCW, Local 1518*. BC LRB 61167, September 15.

UFCW 1518. 2008a. Submission to BCLRB. *Greenway Farms Ltd. and United Food and Commercial Workers Union Local 1518*. BC LRB B135, October 3.

——. 2008b. Submission to BCLRB. *Floralia Plant Growers Limited and United Food and Commercial Workers International Union Local 1518*. BC LRB 58370, October 14.

——. 2008c. Submission to BC LRB. *Sidhu & Sons Nursery Ltd & UFCW Local 1518*. BC LRB 58243, August 15.

——. 2008d. Submission to BC LRB. *Sidhu & Sons Nursery Ltd & UFCW, Local 1518*. BC LRB 58243, August 20.

——. 2008e. Submission to BC LRB. *Sidhu & Sons Nursery Ltd & United Food and Commercial Workers International Union, Local 1518*. BC LRB 58243, November 3.

——. 2009a. Submission to BC LRB. *Sidhu & Sons Nursery Ltd & UFCW, Local 1518*. BC LRB 58243, May 27.

——. 2009b. Submission to BC LRB. *Sidhu & Sons Nursery Ltd & UFCW, Local 1518*. BC LRB 58243, June 5.

——. 2009c. Submission to BC LRB. *Sidhu & Sons Nursery Ltd & UFCW, Local 1518*. BC LRB 58243, June 12.

——. 2009d. Submission to BC LRB. *Sidhu & Sons Nursery Ltd & UFCW, Local 1518*. BC LRB 58243, July 2.

——. 2009e. Submission to BC LRB. *Sidhu & Sons Nursery Ltd & UFCW, Local 1518*. BC LRB 58243, August 6.

——. 2009f. Submission to BC LRB. *Sidhu & Sons Nursery Ltd & UFCW, Local 1518*. BC LRB 58243, August 13.

——. 2010. Submission to BC LRB. *Sidhu & Sons Nursery Ltd & UFCW, Local 1518*. BC LRB 61167, August 31.

——. 2011a. Submission to the BC LRB. *United Mexican States and Canéulado General de Mexico en Vancouver and Sidhu & Sons Nursery Ltd. and Certain Employees and United Food and Commercial Workers International Union, Local 1518*. BC LRB No. 61966/11, 61995/11, April 19.

——. 2011b. Submission to BC LRB. *United Mexican States and Canéulado General de Mexico en Vancouver and Sidhu & Sons Nursery Ltd. and Certain Employees and United Food and Commercial Workers International Union, Local 1518*. BC LRB No. 61966/11, 61995/11, April 28.

——. 2011c. Submission to BC LRB. *United Mexican States and Canéulado General de Mexico en Vancouver and Sidhu & Sons Nursery Ltd. and Certain Employees and United Food and Commercial Workers International Union, Local 1518*. BC LRB No. 61966/11, 61995/11, September 6.

——. 2015a. Submission to BC LRB. *Floralia Plant Growers Limited and United Food and Commercial Workers' International Union*. BC LRB 68534/15L, June 10.

——. 2015b. Submission to BC LRB. *Floralia Plant Growers Limited and United Food and Commercial Workers' International Union*. BC LRB 68534/15L, June 11.

——. 2015c. Submission to BC LRB. *Floralia Plant Growers Limited and United Food and Commercial Workers' International Union*. BC LRB 68534/15L & 68603/15, June 19.

———. 2015d. Submission to BC LRB. *Floralia Plant Growers Limited and United Food and Commercial Workers' International Union and Certain Employees and S&G Fresh Produce Limited.* BC LRB 68534/15L & 68603/15, July 28.

———. 2015e. Submission to BC LRB. *Floralia Plant Growers Limited and United Food and Commercial Workers' International Union.* BC LRB 68534/15L, August 5.

———. 2015f. Submission to BC LRB. *Floralia Plant Growers Limited and United Food and Commercial Workers' International Union and Certain Employees and S&G Fresh Produce Limited.* BC LRB 68763/15, August 25.

———. 2015g. Submission to BC LRB. *Floralia Plant Growers Limited and United Food and Commercial Workers' International Union and Certain Employees and S&G Fresh Produce Limited.* BC LRB 68534/15L, 68603/15, 68763/15, October 1.

———. 2015h. Submission to BC LRB. *Floralia Plant Growers Limited and United Food and Commercial Workers' International Union and Certain Employees and S&G Fresh Produce Limited.* BC LRB 68534/15L, 68603/15, 68763/15, October 16.

———. 2016a. Application to BC LRB for Stay and Reconsideration. *Floralia Plant Growers Limited and United Food and Commercial Workers' International Union and Certain Employees and S&G Fresh Produce Limited.* BC LRB 68534/15L, 68603/15, 68763/15, January 13.

———. 2016b. Submission to BC LRB. *Floralia Plant Growers Limited and United Food and Commercial Workers' International Union and Certain Employees and S&G Fresh Produce Limited.* BC LRB 69263/16L, January 21.

———. 2016c. Submission to BC LRB. *Floralia Plant Growers Limited and United Food and Commercial Workers' International Union and Certain Employees and S&G Fresh Produce Limited.* BC LRB 69263/16L, February 2.

———. 2016d. Submission to BC LRB. *Floralia Plant Growers Limited and United Food and Commercial Workers' International Union and S&G Fresh Produce Limited.* BC LRB 69861/16T, July 25.

———. 2016e. Written Argument in the Matter of an Application and Complaint to the Labour Relations Board. *United Food and Commercial Workers, Local 1518 and Floralia Plant Growers and S&G Fresh Produce Limited.* BC LRB 69861/16T, December.

United Mexican States and Consulado General de Mexico en Vancouver (2011). Submission to the BC LRB. *United Mexican States and Consulado General de Mexico en Vancouver and Floralia Plant Grower Limited and UFCW Local 1518.* BC LRB 61966/11 & 61995/11, August 19.

Collective Agreements

Floralia Plant Growers Ltd. and UFCW Local 1518. 2012. *Collective Agreement. Duration of September 23, 2012-September 22, 2016.*

Savoura and UFCW Local 501. 2012. *Collective Agreement. Duration of March 1, 2012-May 1, 2017.*

Sidhu & Sons Nursery Ltd. and UFCW Local 1518. 2010. *Collective Agreement. Duration of November 2, 2010–November 2, 2013.*

Government Documents

British Columbia Ministry of Labour (BC MOL). 1996. *Labour Relations Code.* RSBC 1996. Victoria: BC Ministry of Labour.

BC MOL. 2002. *Guide to the British Columbia Labour Relations Code.* Victoria: Ministry of Labour and Citizen's Services. http://www.lrb.bc.ca/codeguide/guide.pdf.

Employment and Social Development Canada (ESDC). 2016a. *Agreement for the Employment in Canada of Seasonal Agricultural Workers from Mexico in British Columbia for the Year 2016.* Ottawa: Employment and Social Development Canada.

Government of British Columbia. 1996. *Health Authorities Act.* RSBC 1996, c. 180. Victoria: Queen's Printer. http://www.bclaws.ca/civix/document/id/complete/statreg/96180_01.

———. 2003. Community Services Labour Relations Act. SBC 2003, c. 27. Victoria: Queen's Printer. http://www.bclaws.ca/Recon/document/ID/freeside/00_03027_01.

Government of Canada. 1867. *The Constitution Act* 30 & 31 Victoria, c 3. http://canlii.ca/t/ldsw.

———. 1985. *State Immunity Act* R.S.C., 1985, c. S-18. Ottawa. https://laws-lois.justice.gc.ca/eng/acts/S-18/.

———. 2001. *Immigration and Refugee Protection Act* S.C. 2001, c. 27. Ottawa. https://laws-lois.justice.gc.ca/eng/acts/I-2.5/.

———. 2014. *Overhauling the Temporary Foreign Worker Program: Putting Canadians First.* Ottawa: Employment and Social Development Canada.

Human Resources and Skills Development Canada (HRSDC). 2013. *Agreement for the Employment in Canada of Seasonal Agricultural Workers from Mexico in British Columbia.* Ottawa: Human Resources and Skills Development Canada. http://www.hrsdc.gc.ca/eng/jobs/foreign_workers/agriculture/seasonal/sawpmc2013_bc.shtml. Permanently archived at: http://web.archive.org/web/20130607213953/http://www.hrsdc.gc.ca/eng/jobs/foreign_workers/agriculture/seasonal/sawpmc2013_bc.shtml

Secretaría del Trabajo y Previsión Social (STPS). 2011. *Online Evaluation User's Manual.* Dirección General de Inspección Federal del Trabajo. Accessed July 20, 2017. http://simol.stps.gob.mx:204/html/info_empleador.html/.

———. (n.d.). *Notice to the Employer (Employee Evaluation Form)—Seasonal Agricultural Workers' Program.* Departamento de Migratories a Canada. Accessed July 20, 2017.

Standing Committee on Human Resources, Skills and Social Development and the Status of Persons with Disabilities (HUMA). 2016. *Temporary Foreign Worker Program: Report of the Standing Committee on Human Resources, Skills and Social Development and the Status of Persons with Disabilities.* Ottawa.

STATISTICAL SOURCES

Citizenship and Immigration Canada (CIC). 2010. *Facts and Figures: Immigration Overview Permanent and Temporary Residents.* Ottawa: Citizenship and Immigration Canada.

———. 2012. *Facts and Figures 2012: Immigration Overview Permanent and Temporary Residents.* Ottawa: Citizenship and Immigration Canada.

———. 2014. *Facts and Figures 2013: Immigration Overview: Temporary Residents.* Ottawa: Citizenship and Immigration Canada.

Employment and Social Development Canada (ESDC). 2014a. "Number of Temporary Foreign Worker Positions on Positive Labour Market Opinions under the Agricultural Occupations, by Location of Employment." Accessed January 28, 2014. http://www.esdc.gc.ca/eng/jobs/foreign_workers/lmo_statistics/annual-agriculture.shtml. Permanently archived at: https://web.archive.org/web/20150401174636/http://www.esdc.gc.ca/eng/jobs/foreign_workers/lmo_statistics/annual-agriculture.shtml

———. 2014b. "Number of Temporary Foreign Worker Positions on Positive Labour Market Impact Assessments (LMIAs) under the Agricultural Occupations, by Location of Employment." Accessed November 17, 2014. http://www.esdc.gc.ca:80

/eng/jobs/foreign_workers/lmo_statistics/annual-agriculture.shtml. Permanently archived at: https://web.archive.org/web/20160114021550/http://www.esdc.gc .ca:80/eng/jobs/foreign_workers/lmo_statistics/annual-agriculture.shtml.

———.2016a. *Agreement for the Employment in Canada of Seasonal Agricultural Workers from Mexico in British Columbia for the Year 2016.* Ottawa: Employment and Social Development Canada.

———. 2016b. "Annual Labour Market Impact Assessment Statistics 2008–2015, Primary Agriculture Stream." Accessed August 2, 2016. https://www.canada.ca/en/employ ment-social-development/services/foreign-workers/reports/2014/lmia-annual -statistics/agricultural.html. Permanently archived at: https://web.archive.org/ web/20170907184226/https://www.canada.ca/en/employment-social -development/services/foreign-workers/reports/2014/lmia-annual-statistics /agricultural.html.

———. 2017. "Number of Temporary Foreign Worker (TFW) Positions on Positive Labour Market Impact Assessments (LMIAs) under the Primary Agriculture Stream by Province/Territory." Accessed October 2, 2017 at: http://www.edsc.gc.ca/ouvert -open/bca-seb/ae-ei/TFWP2016_Q4_Table_09_e.csv.

———. 2018. "Number of Temporary Foreign Worker (TFW) Positions on Positive Labour Market Impact Assessments (LMIAs) under the Primary Agriculture Stream by Province/Territory" Dataset. Accessed December 4, 2018 at: https://open.canada .ca/data/en/dataset/e8745429-21e7-4a73-b3f5-90a779b78d1e.

Immigration, Refugees and Citizenship Canada (IRCC). 2015a. *Facts and Figures 2015: Immigration Overview—Permanent Residents.* Dataset. Accessed January 28, 2019. https://open.canada.ca/data/en/dataset/2fbb56bd-eae7-4582-af7d-a197d185 fc93.

———. 2015b. *Facts and Figures 2015: Immigration Overview–Temporary Residents.* Dataset. Accessed January 28, 2019. https://open.canada.ca/data/en/dataset/052642bb-3fd9 -4828-b608-c81dff7e539c.

———. 2016a. *Canada: Admissions of Permanent Residents by Immigration Category, 1980– Q2 2016, June 30.* http://open.canada.ca/data/en/dataset/ad975a26-df23-456a-8ada -756191a23695.

———. 2016b. *Facts and Figures 2016: Immigration Overview—Permanent Residents.* Ottawa: Immigration, Refugees and Citizenship Canada.

———. 2016c. *Facts and Figures 2016: Immigration Overview–Temporary Residents.* Ottawa: Immigration, Refugees and Citizenship Canada.

———. 2018a. *2018 Annual Report to Parliament on Immigration.* Custom Dataset, January 21. Request tracking number: CR-18-0594. Ottawa: Immigration, Refugees and Citizenship Canada.

———. 2018b. "Canada: Temporary Foreign Worker Program (TFWP) Work Permit Holders by Program, Country of Citizenship and Year in Which Permit(s) Became Effective, January 2015–August 2018." Dataset. Accessed December 4, 2018. https://open.canada.ca/data/en/dataset/360024f2-17e9-4558-bfc1-3616485d65b9.

———. 2019. "Canada: Temporary Foreign Workers Program (TFWP) Work Permit Holders under Agricultural Worker Program by Program, Country of Citizenship, and Year in which Permit(s) Became Effective, 2013–November 2018." Custom Dataset, January 21. Request tracking number: CR-18-0594. Ottawa: Immigration, Refugees and Citizenship Canada.

Organization for Economic Co-operation and Development (OECD). 2008. *International Migration Outlook 2008.* Paris: OECD Publishing.

———. 2010. *International Migration Outlook: SOPEMI 2010.* Paris: OECD Publishing.

———. 2012. *International Migration Outlook 2012.* Paris: OECD Publishing.

———. 2014. *International Migration Outlook 2014*. Paris: OECD Publishing.
———. 2015. *International Migration Outlook 2015*. Paris: OECD Publishing
———. 2016. *International Migration Outlook 2016*. Paris: OECD Publishing.
———. 2017. *International Migration Outlook 2017*. Paris: OECD Publishing.
———. 2018. *International Migration Outlook 2018*. Paris: OECD Publishing.

Interviews

Former leader of CFU (Canadian Farm Workers Union). 2015, July 30. Burnaby, BC.
Former (Mexican) Consular Employee. 2014, July 26. Vancouver, BC.
Lawyer for UFCW Local 1518. 2013, July 25. Vancouver, BC.
Lawyer for UFCW Local 1518. 2014, July 25 Vancouver, BC.
Lawyer for UFCW Local 1518. 2015, July 20. Vancouver, BC.
Lawyer for UFCW Local 1518. 2016, July 25. Vancouver, BC.
Lawyer for UFCW Local 1518, 2017, July 18. Vancouver, BC.
President, UFCW Canada. 2014, March 11. Toronto.
President, UFCW Local 1518. 2013, July 12. New Westminster, BC.
UFCW Local 1518, staff representative. 2013, July 25. Vancouver, BC.
UFCW Local 1518, staff representative. 2016, July 26. Vancouver, BC.
UFCW Local 1518, staff representative. 2017, July 19. Vancouver, BC.
UFCW Local 1518, staff representative. 2018, July 12. Vancouver, BC.
UFCW/AWA, staff representative. 2013, July 12. New Westminster, BC.

SECONDARY SOURCES

Alboim, Naomi, and Karen Cohl. 2012. *Shaping the Future: Canada's Rapidly Changing Immigration Policies*. October. Toronto: Maytree Foundation. http://maytree.com/wpcontent/uploads/2012/10/shaping-the-future.pdf.
Anderson, Benedict. 1983. *Imagined Communities: Reflections on the Origin and Spread of Nationalism*. New York: Verso.
Anderson, Bridget, Mathew J. Gibney, and Emanuela Paolettic. 2011. "Citizenship, Deportation and the Boundaries of Belonging." *Citizenship Studies* 15, no. 5: 547–563.
Andrijasevic, Rutvica, and William Walters. 2010. "The International Organization for Migration and the International Government of Borders." *Environment and Planning D: Society and Space* 28, no. 6: 977–999.
Aradau, Claudia, and Jef Huysmans. 2013. "Critical Methods in International Relations: The Politics of Techniques, Devices and Acts." *European Journal of International Relations* 20, no. 3: 596–619.
Arat-Koc, Sedef. 1989. "In the Privacy of Our Home: Foreign Domestic Workers as a Solution to the Crisis of the Domestic Sphere in Canada." *Studies in Political Economy* 28: 33–58.
———. 1999. "'Good Enough to Work but Not Good Enough to Stay': Foreign Domestic Workers and the Law." In *Locating Law: Race/Class/Gender Connections*, edited by Elizabeth Comack, 125–151. Halifax: Fernwood Publishing.
———. 2006. "Whose Social Reproduction? Transnational Motherhood and Challenges to Feminist Political Economy." In *Social Reproduction: Feminist Political Economy Challenges Neo-Liberalism*, edited by Kate Bezanson and Meg Luxton, 75–92. Montreal: McGill-Queen's University Press.
Basok, Tanya. 1999. "Free to Be Unfree: Mexican Guest Workers in Canada." *Labour, Capital and Society* 32, no. 2: 192–222.
———. 2002. *Tortillas and Tomatoes: Transmigrant Mexican Harvesters in Canada*. Montreal: McGill-Queen's University Press.

——. 2007. *Canada's Temporary Migration Program: A Model despite Flaws*. Washington, DC: Migration Policy Institute.

Basok, Tanya, Danièle Bélanger, and Eloy Rivas. 2014. "Reproducing Deportability: Migrant Agricultural Workers in South-Western Ontario." *Journal of Ethnic and Migration Studies* 40, no. 9: 1394–1413.

Bauder, Herald. 2006. *Labour Movement: How Migration Regulates Labour Markets*. Oxford: Oxford University Press.

Becerril, Ofelia. 2016. "Gendered Policies, Single Mothers and Transnational Motherhood: Mexican Female Migrant Farmworkers in Canada." In *Women Migrant Workers: Ethical, Political and Legal Problems*, edited by Zahra Meghani, 154–176. New York: Routledge.

Berggold, Craig. 2011. "The Colour of Food: A History Photo Essay." *Briarpatch Magazine*, September 1. https://briarpatchmagazine.com/articles/view/the-colour-of -food.

Binford, Leigh. 2009. "From Fields of Power to Fields of Sweat: The Dual Process of Constructing Temporary Migrant Labour in Mexico and Canada." *Third World Quarterly* 33, no. 3: 503–517.

——. 2013. *Tomorrow We're All Going to the Harvest: Temporary Foreign Worker Programs and the Neoliberal Political Economy*. Austin: University of Texas Press.

Bosniak, Linda. 2006. *The Citizen and the Alien: Dilemmas of Contemporary Membership*. Princeton, NJ: Princeton University Press.

Boucher, Gerard. 2008. "A Critique of Global Policy Discourses on Managing International Migration." *Third World Quarterly* 29, no. 7: 1461–1471.

Bourdieu, Pierre. 1990. "A Lecture on the Lecture." In *In Other Words: Essays towards a Reflexive Sociology*, 177–198. Stanford: Stanford University Press.

Bourdieu, Pierre, and Loïc J. D. Wacquant. 1992. *An Invitation to Reflexive Sociology*. Cambridge: Polity Press.

Bourdieu, Pierre, and Shaun Whiteside. 1996. *Photography: A Middle-Brow Art*. Translated by Shaun Whiteside. Stanford: Stanford University Press.

Boushey, Graeme, and Adam Luedtke. 2006. "Fiscal Federalism and the Politics of Immigration: Centralized and Decentralized Immigration Policies in Canada and the United States." *Journal of Comparative Policy Analysis* 8, no. 3: 207–224.

Brown, Wendy. 2010. *Walled States, Waning Sovereignty*. Cambridge, MA: MIT Press.

Budworth, Marie-Hélène, Andrew Rose, and Sara Mann. 2017, March. *Report on the Seasonal Agricultural Worker Program*. Ottawa: Inter-American Institute for Cooperation on Agriculture Delegation in Canada. http://www.iica.int/sites/default/files /publications/files/2017/bve17038753i.pdf.

Burawoy, Michael. 1976. "The Functions and Reproduction of Migrant Labour: Comparative Material from Southern Africa and the United States." *American Journal of Sociology* 81, no. 5: 1050–1087.

Bush, Murray. 1995. *A History of the Canadian Farmworkers' Union*. http://www.vcn.bc .ca/cfu/about.htm.

Canadian Borders Services Agency (CBSA). 2010. *CBSA Detentions and Removals Programs: Evaluation Study*. http://www.cbsa-asfc.gc.ca/agency-agence/reports-rapports/ae -ve/2010/dr-rd-eng.html#s02.

Castles, Stephen. 2006. "Guestworkers in Europe: A Resurrection?" *International Migration Review* 40, no. 4: 741–766.

——. 2014. "International Migration at a Crossroads." *Citizenship Studies* 18, no. 2: 190–207.

Castles, Stephen, and Mark J. Miller. 2003. *The Age of Migration: International Population Movements in the Modern World*, 3rd ed. New York: Palgrave Macmillan.

Castles, Stephen, and Derya Ozkul. (2014). "Circular Migration: Triple Win, or a New Label for Temporary Migration?" In *Global and Asian Perspectives on International Migration: Global Migration Issues*, edited by Graziano Battistella, 27–49. New York: Springer.

Choudry, Aziz, and Mostafa Henaway. 2012. "Agents of Misfortune: Contextualizing Migrant and Immigrant Workers' Struggles Against Temporary Labour Recruitment Agencies." *Labour, Capital and Society* 45, no. 1: 36–65.

Choudry, Aziz, and Adrian Smith, eds. 2016. *Unfree Labour? Struggles of Migrant and Immigrant Workers in Canada*. Oakland, CA: PM Press. Collyer, Michael. 2012. "Deportation and the Micropolitics of Exclusion: The Rise of Removals from the UK to Sri Lanka." *Geopolitics* 17, no. 2: 276–292.

Cornelisse, Galina. 2010. "Immigration Detention and the Territoriality of Universal Rights." In *The Deportation Regime: Sovereignty, Space, and the Freedom of Movement*, edited by Nicholas De Genova and Nathalie Peutz, 101–122. Durham, NC: Duke University Press.

Coutin, Susan B. 2015. "Deportation Studies: Origins, Themes and Directions." *Journal of Ethnic and Migration Studies* 41, no. 4: 671–681.

Cranford, Cynthia J., Tania Das Gupta, Deena Ladd, and Leah F. Vosko. 2005. "Thinking through Community Unionism." In *Precarious Employment: Understanding Labour Market Insecurity in Canada*, edited by Leah F. Vosko, 353–378. Montreal: McGill-Queens University Press.

De Genova, Nicholas. 2002. "Migrant "Illegality" and Deportability in Everyday Life." *Annual Review of Anthropology* 31, no. 1: 419–447.

——. 2005. *Working the Boundaries: Race, Space, and "Illegality" in Mexican Chicago*. Durham, NC: Duke University Press.

——. 2007. "The Production of Culprits: From Deportability to Detainability in the Aftermath of 'Homeland Security.'" *Citizenship Studies* 11, no. 5: 421–448.

——. 2010. "The Deportation Regime: Sovereignty, Space, and the Freedom of Movement." In *The Deportation Regime: Sovereignty, Space, and the Freedom of Movement*, edited by Nicholas De Genova and Nathalie Peutz, 33–68. Durham, NC: Duke University Press.

De Genova, Nicholas, and Nathalie Peutz, eds. 2010. *The Deportation Regime: Sovereignty, Space, and the Freedom of Movement*. Durham, NC: Duke University Press.

Doherty, Michael. 2013. "When You Ain't Got Nothin', You Got Nothin' to Lose.... Union Recognition Laws, Voluntarism and the Anglo Model." *Industrial Law Journal* 42, no. 4: 369–397.

Drotbohm, Heike, and Iness Hasselberg. 2014. "Deportation, Anxiety, Justice: New Ethnographic Perspectives." *Journal of Ethnic and Migration Studies* 41, no. 4: 551–562.

European Migration Network. 2011. *Temporary and Circular Migration: Empirical Evidence, Current Policy Practice and Future Options in EU Member States*. European Migration Network, September. http://ec.europa.eu/dgs/home-affairs/what-we -do/networks/european_migration_network/reports/docs/emn-studies/circular -migration/0a_emn_synthesis_report_temporary__circular_migration_final_sept _2011_en.pdf.

Faraday, Fay. 2012. *Made in Canada: How the Law Constructs Migrant Workers' Insecurity*. September. Toronto: Metcalf Foundation. http://metcalffoundation.com/wp -content/uploads/2012/09/Made-in-Canada-Full-Report.pdf.

Faraday, Fay, Judy Fudge, and Eric Tucker, eds. 2012. *Constitutional Labour Rights in Canada: Farm Workers and the Fraser Case*. Toronto: Irwin Law.

Fine, Janice. 2006. *Worker Centers: Organizing Communities at the Edge of the Dream.* Ithaca, NY: ILR Press/Cornell University Press.

Fisk, Catherine, and Michael J. Wishnie. 2005. "The Story of 'Hoffman Plastic Compounds v. NLRB': Labor Rights without Remedies for Undocumented Immigrants." *Labor Law Stories.* https://scholarship.law.duke.edu/faculty_scholarship/1243/.

Fleras, Augie. 2014. *Immigration Canada: Evolving Realities and Emerging Challenges in a Postnational World.* Vancouver: University of British Columbia Press.

Foucault, Michel. 1977. *Discipline and Punish: The Birth of the Prison.* New York: Pantheon Books.

Fraser, Nancy. 2018. CBSA. *Economic Geography* 94, no. 1: 1–17.

Fudge, Judy. 2012a. "Introduction: Farmworkers, Collective Bargaining Rights, and the Meaning of Constitutional Protection." In *Constitutional Labour Rights in Canada: Farm Workers and the Fraser Case,* edited by Fay Faraday, Judy Fudge, and Eric Tucker, 1–29. Toronto: Irwin Law.

——. 2012b. "Precarious Migrant Status and Precarious Employment: The Paradox of International Rights for Migrant Workers." *Comparative Labor Law & Policy Journal* 34: 95–132.

Fudge, Judy, and Fiona McPhail. 2009. "The Temporary Foreign Worker Program in Canada: Low-Skilled Workers as an Extreme Form of Flexible Labour." *Comparative Labor Law & Policy Journal* 31: 5–46.

Gabriel, Christina. 2008. "A 'Healthy' Trade? NAFTA, Labour Mobility and Canadian Nurses." In *Governing International Labour Migration: Current Issues, Challenges and Dilemmas,* edited by Christina Gabriel and Hélène Pellerin, 112–127. London: Routledge.

——. 2011. "Migration and Globalized Care Work: The Case of Internationally Educated Nurses in Canada." In *Feminist Ethics and Social Policy: Towards A New Global Political Economy of Care,* edited by Rianne Mahon and Fiona Robinson, 39–59. Vancouver: University of British Columbia Press.

Gabriel, Christina, and Laura Macdonald. 2004a. "Chrétien and North America: Between Integration and Autonomy." *Review of Constitutional Studies* 9, nos. 1–2: 71–91.

——. 2004b. "Of Borders and Business: Canadian Corporate Proposals for North American 'Deep Integration.'" *Studies in Political Economy* 74: 79–100.

——. 2004c. "The Hypermobile, The Mobile and the Rest: Patterns of Inclusion and Exclusion in an Emerging North American Migration Regime." *Canadian Journal of Latin American and Caribbean Studies* 29, nos. 57–58: 67–91.

——. 2012. "Debates on Temporary Agricultural Worker Migration in the North American Context." In *Legislated Inequality: Canada's Temporary Migrant Worker Program,* edited by Patti Tamara Lenard and Christine Straehle, 95–116. Montreal: McGill-Queen's University Press.

——. 2014. "Domestic Transnationalism: Legal Advocacy for Mexican Migrant Workers' Rights in Canada." *Citizenship Studies* 18, no. 3: 243–258.

Geddes, Andrew. 2015. "Temporary and Circular Migration in the Construction of European Migration Governance." *Cambridge Review of International Affairs* 28, no. 4: 571–588.

Geiger, Martin, and Antoine Pécoud. 2010. "The Politics of International Migration Management." In *The Politics of International Migration Management,* edited by Martin Geiger and Antoine Pécoud, 1–20. Basingstoke: Palgrave Macmillan.

——, eds. 2013. *Disciplining the Transnational Mobility of People.* London: Palgrave Macmillan.

Ghosh, Bimal. 2000. "New International Regime for Orderly Movements of People: What Will It Look Like?" In *Managing Migration: Time for a New International Regime*, edited by Bimal Ghosh, 220–248. Oxford: Oxford University Press.

——. 2012. "A Snapshot of Reflections on Migration Management: Is Migration Management a Dirty Word?" In *The New Politics of International Mobility: Migration Management and its Discontents*, edited by Martin Geiger and Antoine Pécoud, 25–30. Osnabrück, Germany: Institute for Migration Research and Intercultural Studies, University of Osnabrück.

Gibney, Matthew. 2008. "Asylum and the Expansion of Deportation in the United Kingdom." *Government and Opposition* 43, no. 2: 146–167.

Gleeson, Shannon. 2016. *Precarious Claims: The Promise and Failure of Workplace Protections in the United States.* Berkeley: University of California.

Goldring, Luin, and Patricia Landolt. 2013a. "The Conditionality of Legal Status and Rights: Conceptualizing Precarious Non-Citizenship in Canada." In *Producing and Negotiating Non-Citizenship: Precarious Legal Status in Canada*, edited by Luin Goldring and Patricia Landolt, 3–30. Toronto: University of Toronto Press.

——. eds. 2013b. *Producing and Negotiating Non-Citizenship: Precarious Legal Status in Canada.* Toronto: University of Toronto Press.

Gomberg-Muñoz, Ruth, and Laura Nussbaum-Barberena. 2011. "Is Immigration Policy Labor Policy? Immigration Enforcement, Undocumented Labor, and the State." *Human Organization* 70, no. 4: 366–375.

Gordon, Jennifer. 2007. "Transnational Global Citizenship." *Southern California Law Review* 80, no. 3: 503–588.

——. 2008. "Towards a Freer Flow of Labor (with Rights)." *Americas Quarterly* Summer: 58–63.

Greer, Ian, Ciupijus Zinojius, and Nathan Lillie. 2013. "The European Migrant Workers Union and the Barriers to Transnational Industrial Citizenship." *European Journal of Industrial Relations* 19, no. 1: 5–20.

Guild, Elspeth. 2009. *Security and Migration in the 21st Century.* Cambridge: Polity Press.

Hanley, Jill, and Ya Wen. 2017. "Social Policy Frameworks of Exclusion: The Challenge of Protecting the Social Rights of 'Undocumented Migrants' in Quebec and Shanghai." *Journal of Asian Public Policy* 10, no. 3: 249–267.

Haraway, Donna. 1988. "Situated Knowledges: The Science Question in Feminism and the Privilege of Partial Perspective." *Feminist Studies* 14, no. 3: 575–599.

Harvey, David. 2003. *The New Imperialism.* Oxford: Oxford University Press.

Heery, Edmund, and Mike Noon. 2018. *A Dictionary of Human Resource Management.* New York: Oxford University Press.

Hennebry, Jenna. 2008. "Bienvenidos A Canadá? Globalization and the Migration Industry Surrounding Temporary Agricultural Migration in Canada." *Canadian Studies in Population* 35, no. 2: 339–356.

——. 2010. "Who Has Their Eye on the Ball? Jurisdictional 'Futbol' and Canada's Temporary Foreign Worker Program." *Policy Options* July/August: 62–67.

——. 2012. *Permanently Temporary? Agricultural Migrant Workers and Their Integration in Canada.* IRPP Study No. 26. Montreal: Institute for Research on Public Policy.

Hennebry, Jenna, and Janet McLaughlin. 2012. "The Exception that Proves the Rule: Structural Vulnerability, Health Risks and Consequences for Temporary Migrant Farmworkers in Canada." In *Legislated Inequality: Canada's Temporary Migrant Worker Program*, edited by Patti Tamara Lenard and Christine Straehle, 117–138. Montreal: McGill-Queen's University Press.

Hennebry, Jenna, and Kerry Preibisch. 2010. "A Model for Managed Migration? Re-Examining Best Practices in Canada's Seasonal Agricultural Worker Program." *International Migration* 50, no. 1: e19–e40.

Hesse-Biber, Sharlene. 2007. "Feminist Approaches to Mixed-Methods Research." In *Feminist Research Practice: A Primer*, edited by Sharlene Hesse-Biber, 249–291. Thousand Oaks, CA: Sage.

Hindess, Barry. 2000. "Citizenship in the International Management of Populations." *American Behavioral Scientist* 43, no. 9: 1486–1497.

Hugo, Graeme. 2009. "Best Practice in Temporary Labour Migration for Development: A Perspective from Asia and the Pacific." *International Migration* 47, no. 5: 23–74.

Hunt, Jo. 2014. "Making the CAP Fit: Responding to the Exploitation of Migrant Agricultural Workers in the EU." *International Journal of Comparative Labour Law and Industrial Relations* 30, no. 2: 131–152.

Jackson, Patrick T. 2011. *The Conduct of Inquiry in International Relations: Philosophy of Science and Its Implications for the Study of World Politics.* London: Routledge.

Jensen, Heather. 2013. "Unionization of Agricultural Workers in British Columbia." LL.M. thesis, University of Victoria.

———. 2014. "A History of Legal Exclusion: Labour Relations Laws and British Columbia's Agricultural Workers, 1937–1975." *Labour/Le Travail* 73, no. 1: 67–95.

Kalir, Barak. 2013. "Moving Subjects, Stagnant Paradigms: Can the 'Mobilities Paradigm' Transcend Methodological Nationalism?" *Journal of Ethnic and Migration Studies* 39, no. 2: 311–327.

Kelley, Ninette, and M. Trebilcock. 2010. *The Making of the Mosaic: A History of Canadian Immigration Policy.* Toronto: University of Toronto Press.

Kuhn, Annette. 1982. *Women's Pictures: Feminism and Cinema.* London: Routledge & Kegan Paul.

Kuptsch, Christine, and Phillip Martin. 2011. "Low-Skilled Labour Migration." In *Global Migration Governance*, edited by Alexander Betts, 34–59. Oxford: Oxford University Press.

Latham, Robert, Leah F. Vosko, Valerie Preston, and Melisa Bretón. 2014. "Challenges to Liberating Temporariness." In *Liberating Temporariness? Migration, Work, and Citizenship in an Age of Insecurity*, edited by Leah F. Vosko, Valerie Preston, and Robert Latham, 3–33. Montreal: McGill-Queen's University Press.

Law, John. 2007. "Making a Mess with Method." In *The Sage Handbook of Social Science Methodology*, edited by William Outhwaite and Stephen P. Turner, 595–606. London: Sage.

Lemaitre, Georges, Thomas Liebig, Cécil Thoreau, and Pauline Fron. 2007. *Standardised Statistics on Immigrant Inflows: Results, Sources and Methods.* Paris: OECD Publishing.

Lenard, Patti T., and Christine Straehle. 2012. *Legislated Inequality: Temporary Labour Migration in Canada.* Montreal: McGill-Queen's University Press.

Lutz, Helma. 2018. "Care Migration: The Connectivity between Care Chains, Care Circulation and Transnational Social Inequality." *Current Sociology* 66, no. 4: 577–589.

MacDonald, Diane. 1997. "Sectoral Certification: A Case Study of British Columbia." *Canadian Labour and Employment Law Journal* 5: 243–286.

Marsden, Sarah. 2012. "The New Precariousness: Temporary Migrants and the Law in Canada." *Canadian Journal of Law and Society* 27, no. 2: 209–229.

———. 2014. "Silence Means Yes Here in Canada: Precarious Migrants, Work and the Law." *Canadian Labour & Employment Law Journal* 18: 1–38.

Martin, Phillip. 2007. "Guest Workers: New Solution or New Problem." *University of Chicago Legal Forum* 2007: 289–315.

Maynes, Mary J., Jennifer L. Pierce, and Laslett, Barbara. 2008. *Telling Stories: The Use of Personal Narratives in the Social Sciences*. Ithaca, NY: Cornell University Press.

McLaughlin, Janet, Jenna Hennebry, and Ted Haines. 2014. "Paper versus Practice: Occupational Health and Safety Protections and Realities for Temporary Foreign Agricultural Workers in Ontario." *Perspectives interdisciplinaires sur le travail et la santé* 16, no. 2: 2–17.

McNally, David. 2011. *Global Slump: The Economics and Politics of Crisis and Resistance*. Black Point, Nova Scotia: Fernwood Publishing.

McNevin, Anne. 2009. "Contesting Citizenship: Irregular Migrants and Strategic Possibilities for Political Belonging." *New Political Science* 31, no. 2: 163–181.

Mezzadra, Sandro, and Brett Neilson. 2013. *Border as Method, or, the Multiplication of Labor*. Durham, NC: Duke University Press.

Mirchandani, Kiran, Leah F. Vosko, Urvashi Soni-Sinha, Adam J. Perry, Andrea M. Noack, Rebecca Jane Hall, and Mary Gellatly. 2018. "Methodological K/nots: Designing Research on the Enforcement of Labor Standards." *Journal of Mixed Methods Research* 12, no. 2: 133–147.

Mundlak, Guy. 2009. "De-Territorializing Labor Law." *Journal of Law and Ethics of Human Rights* 3, no. 2: 188–222.

Ness, Immanuel. 2005. *Immigrants, Unions, and the New U.S. Labor Market*. Philadelphia: Temple University Press.

——. 2011. *Guest Workers and Resistance to U.S. Corporate Despotism*. Champaign: University of Illinois Press.

Nyers, Peter. 2018. *Irregular Citizenship, Immigration, and Deportation*. New York: Routledge.

Oxford Dictionary of English. 2010. 3rd ed. Oxford: Oxford University Press.

Pécoud, Antoine. 2010. "Informing Migrants to Manage Migration? An Analysis of IOM's Information Campaigns." In *The Politics of International Migration Management: Migration, Minorities and Citizenship*, edited by Martin Geiger and Antoine Pécoud, 184–201. London: Palgrave Macmillan.

——. 2013. "Introduction." In *Disciplining the Transnational Mobility of People*, edited by Martin Geiger and Antoine Pécoud, 1–14. London: Palgrave Macmillan.

Piché, Victor. 2012. "In and out the Back Door: Canada's Temporary Worker Programs in a Global Perspective." In *The New Politics of International Mobility: Migration Management and its Discontents*, edited by Martin Geiger and Antoine Pécoud, 113–122. Osnabrück, Germany: Institute for Migration Research and Intercultural Studies, University of Osnabrück.

Plascencia, Luis F. B. 2009. "The 'Undocumented' Mexican Migrant Question: Re-Examining the Framing of Law and Illegalization in the United States." *Urban Anthropology* 38, no. 2: 375–434.

Plewa, Piotr, and Mark J. Miller. 2005. "Postwar and Post–Cold War Generations of European Temporary Foreign Worker Policies: Implications from Spain." *Migraciones Internacionales* 3, no. 2: 58–83.

Preibisch, Kerry. 2010. "Pick-Your-Own Labor: Migrant Workers and Flexibility in Canadian Agriculture." *International Migration Review* 44, no. 2: 404–441.

——. 2012. "Development as Remittances or Development as Freedom? Exploring Canada's Temporary Migration Programs from a Rights-Based Approach." In *Constitutional Labour Rights in Canada: Farm Workers and the Fraser Case*, edited by Fay Faraday, Judy Fudge, and Eric Tucker, 81–108. Toronto: Irwin Law.

Rajkumar, Deepa, Laurel Berkowitz, Leah F. Vosko, Valerie Preston, and Robert Latham. 2012. "At the Temporary-Permanent Divide: How Canada Produces Temporariness and Makes Citizens through Its Security, Work, and Settlement Policies." *Citizenship Studies* 16: 483–510.

Rolland, Anne-Julie. 2017. "Recent Developments in Unionizing the Precarious Workforce: The Exemption Regimes of Care Workers and Farm Workers in Quebec." *Canadian Labour & Employment Law Journal* 20: 107–140.

Russo, Robert. 2011. "Case Comment: Temporarily Unchained: The Drive to Unionize Foreign Seasonal Agricultural Workers in Canada—A Comment on Greenway Farms and UFCW." *BC Studies* 169: 131–141.

——. 2012. "Solidarity Forever, Canadians Never: SAWP Workers in Canada." PhD diss., University of British Columbia.

Salter, Mark B. 2003. *Rights of Passage: The Passport in International Relations.* Boulder, CO: Lynne Rienner.

Sassen-Koob, Saskia. 1978. "The International Circulation of Resources and Development: The Case of Migrant Labour." *Development and Change* 9, no. 4: 509–545.

——. 1981. "Towards a Conceptualization of Immigrant Labor." *Social Problems* 29, no. 1: 65–85.

Satzewich, Vic. 1988. "The Canadian State and the Racialization of Caribbean Migrant Farm Labour." *Ethnic and Racial Studies* 11, no. 3: 282–304.

——. 1989a. "Racism and Canadian Immigration Policy: The Government's View of Caribbean Migration, 1962–66." *Canadian Ethnic Studies* 21, no. 1: 77–97.

——. 1989b. "Unfree Labour and Canadian Capitalism." *Studies in Political Economy* 28: 89–110.

——. 1991. *Racism and the Incorporation of Foreign Labor: Farm Labor Migration to Canada since 1945.* New York: Routledge.

——. 2007. "Business or Bureaucratic Dominance in Immigration Policymaking in Canada: Why Was Mexico Included in the Caribbean Seasonal Agricultural Workers Program in 1974?" *International Migration and Integration* 8: 255–275.

Sayad, Abdelmalek. 2004. *The Suffering of the Immigrant.* Malden, MA: Polity Press.

Schmidt, Verena. 2006. "Temporary Migrant Workers: Organizing and Protection Strategies by Trade Unions." In *Merchants of Labour*, edited by Christiane Kuptsch, 191–206. Geneva, Switzerland: International Institute for Labour Studies.

Segal, Naomi. 2009. "Anti-Union or Pro-Property? Worker Surveillance and Gold Theft in Western Australian Gold Mines, 1899–1920." *Labour History* 97: 37–52.

Sharma, Nandita. 2006. *Home Economics: Nationalism and the Making of "Migrant Workers" in Canada.* Toronto: University of Toronto Press.

Simmons, Alan B. 2010. *Immigration and Canada: Global and Transnational Perspectives.* Toronto: Canadian Scholars' Press.

Spaulding, Stacy. 2009. "Off the Blacklist, but Still a Target: The Anti-Communist Attacks on Lisa Sergio." *Journalism Studies* 10, no. 6: 789–804.

Talavera, Victor, Guillermina Gina Núñez, and Josiah Heyman. 2005. "Deportation in the U.S.-Mexico Borderlands: Anticipation, Experience, and Memory." In *The Deportation Regime: Sovereignty, Space, and the Freedom of Movement*, edited by Nicholas De Genova and Nathalie Peutz, 166–195. Durham, NC: Duke University Press.

Thomas, Mark. 2016. "Producing and Contesting 'Unfree Labour' through the Seasonal Agricultural Worker Program." In *Unfree Labour? Struggles of Migrant and Immigrant Workers in Canada*, edited by Aziz Choudry and Adrian Smith, 21–36. Oakland, CA: PM Press.

Torpey, John. 2000. *The Invention of the Passport: Surveillance, Citizenship and the State.* Cambridge: Cambridge University Press.

Trachtman, Joel. 2009. *The International Law of Economic Migration: Toward the Fourth Freedom.* Kalamazoo, MI: W. E. Upjohn Institute for Employment Research.

Tucker, Eric. 2012. "Farm Worker Exceptionalism: Past, Present, and the Post-Fraser Future." In *Constitutional Labour Rights in Canada: Farm Workers and the Fraser*

Case, edited by Fay Faraday, Judy Fudge, and Eric Tucker, 30–56. Toronto: Irwin Law.

——. 2014. "Shall Wagnerism Have No Dominion?" *Just Labour: A Canadian Journal of Law and Society* 21: 1–27.

Valiani, Salimah. 2012. *Rethinking Unequal Exchange: The Global Integration of Nursing Labour Markets*. Toronto: University of Toronto Press.

Van den Broek, Diane. 2003. "Recruitment Strategies and Union Exclusion in Two Australian Call Centres." *Industrial Relations* 58, no. 3: 515–536.

Vertovec, Steven. 2008. "Circular Migration: The Way Forward in Global Policy?" *Canadian Diversity* 6, no. 3: 36–40.

Vosko, Leah F. 2000. *Temporary Work: The Gendered Rise of a Precarious Employment Relationship*. Toronto: University of Toronto Press.

——. 2010. *Managing the Margins: Gender, Citizenship, and the International Regulation of Precarious Employment*. New York: Oxford University Press.

——. 2011. "Out of the Shadows? The Non-Binding Multilateral Framework on Migration (2006) and Prospects for Forging Global Labour Market Membership through International Labour Regulation." In *The Idea of Labour Law*, edited by Guy Davidov and Brian Langille, 365–384. London: Hart Publishing.

——. 2014. "Tenuously Unionised: Temporary Migrant Workers and the Limits of Formal Mechanisms Designed to Promote Collective Bargaining in British Columbia." *Industrial Law Journal* 43, no. 4: 451–484.

——. 2015. "Blacklisting as a Modality of Deportability: Mexico's Response to Circular Migrant Agricultural Workers' Pursuit of Collective Bargaining Rights in British Columbia, Canada." *Journal of Ethnic and Migration Studies* 42, no. 8: 1371–1387.

——. 2018. "Legal but Deportable: Institutionalized Deportability and the Limits of Collective Bargaining among Participants in Canada's Seasonal Agricultural Workers Program." *ILR Review* 71, no. 4: 882–907.

Vosko, Leah F., Valerie Preston, and Robert Latham. 2014. *Liberating Temporariness? Migration, Work, and Citizenship in an Age of Insecurity*. Montreal: McGill-Queen's University Press.

Walters, William. 2010a. "Imagined Migration World: The European Union's Anti-Illegal Immigration Discourse." In *The Politics of International Migration Management*, edited by Martin Geiger and Antoine Pécoud, 73–95. London: Palgrave Macmillan.

——. 2010b. "Deportation, Expulsion, and the International Police of Aliens." In *The Deportation Regime: Sovereignty, Space, and the Freedom of Movement*, edited by Nicholas De Genova and Nathalie Peutz, 69–100. Durham, NC: Duke University Press.

Wells, Don, André Lyn, Janet McLaughlin, and Aaraón Díaz Mendiburo. 2014. "Sustaining Precarious Transnational Families: The Significance of Remittances from Canada's Seasonal Agricultural Workers Program." *Just Labour: A Journal of Work & Society* 22 Autumn: 144–167.

Wickramasekara, Piyasiri. 2011. *Circular Migration: A Triple Win or a Dead End*. Global Union Research Network Discussion Paper No. 15. Geneva: International Labour Office.

Wimmer, Andreas, and Nina Glick Schiller. 2002. "Methodological Nationalism and Beyond: Nation-State Building, Migration and the Social Sciences." *Global Networks* 2, no. 4: 301–334.

Wishnie, Michael J. 2007. "Labor Law after Legalization." *Minnesota Law Review* 92: 1446–1461.

Wong, Lloyd. 1984. "Canada's Guest Workers: Some Comparisons of Temporary Workers in Europe and North America." *International Migration Review* 18, no. 1: 85–98.

Yin, Robert K. 2006. "Mixed Methods Research: Are the Methods Genuinely Integrated or Merely Parallel?" *Research in the Schools* 13, no. 1: 41–47.

Index

threat wielded by, 32; interviews with, 65; responsibilities under SAWP, 24, 68–69, 75–77, 75f; testimony of, in LRB hearing, 72, 74, 75–77, 79; unionization discouraged by, 57, 67, 70, 74, 76; Vienna Convention on Consular Relations (VCCR) and, 69

continuity in employment: CA provisions and, 63. *See also* recall

contractor system, farm labor, 125n28, 129n1

control: blacklisting as mode of, 39; deportability as means of, 6, 29, 33, 37, 111; migration management and new modes of, 12, 14, 15, 33; SAWP and modes of, 27, 28, 43, 44–45, 113

Cornelisse, Galina, 31

corporate sector, and emigration and exploitation of workers, 14, 122n2

critical mixed-methods, engagement of, 36–37

cross-classification bargaining units: employer arguments against, 52, 56; Local 1518's flexibility regarding, 59; LRB's reluctance to certify, 53–54, 55, 56, 130n10

decertification campaign(s): at Floralia, 9, 65, 70, 71, 83, 85, 90, 91–93, 133n14; at Greenway Farms, 27; improper interference with, 79–80; at Mayfair Farms, 58; at Sidhu, 3, 8, 65–66, 67, 70, 71, 74, 79–81, 83

De Genova, Nicholas, 29–30, 31, 68, 126nn32–34

deportability: attrition as modality of, 4, 9, 10, 40–41, 85, 87, 88, 110, 119; blacklisting as modality of, 4, 39–40, 66, 69, 80–82, 110; CAs aiming to address challenges related to, 11, 58, 63, 65, 117; employer evaluations and, 4, 38, 47, 88; as essential condition of possibility for migration management, 4, 5–6, 10, 11, 28–29, 66, 106, 110; *how* of, focus on, 5, 6, 35, 37; interventions aimed at curbing, 5, 10, 112, 115–16, 118, 119–20; and labor rights, impact on exercise of, 3–4, 7; legal and administrative processes giving rise to, 33; as means of control, 6, 29, 33, 37, 111; modalities of, 4, 8–10, 13, 38–41, 66, 83, 110; operation among TMWP participants, 4; origins of concept, 29–30, 126n32; SAWP and, 35, 64, 111; among SAWP employees, study of, 30–32, 34–37; scholarship on, 29–33, 126n36; subtle processes and practices of, 13; termination as modality of, 4, 38–39, 110, 113–14; among undocumented migrant workers, 29–30, 121n7; unionization aiming to circumvent, 2, 4, 11, 47

deportation: vs. deportability, 29; increased use of, 28–29, 126n31; nonrenewal of SAWP employees compared to, 31; "unmaking of citizenship" through, 126n35

dignity and respect concerns: AWA and, 56, 57; Local 1518's emphasis on, 56, 60, 114; of SAWP employees, CA provisions addressing, 61–62

disciplinary power: employer evaluation process and, 47; insecurity and, 31–32, 126n34

dissonances, between immigration and labor laws, 111; and attrition, 119; and blacklisting, 116–17; and constraints on LRB, 106; institutional design of TMWPs and, 33; proposed measures to reduce, 5, 10, 112, 115–16, 118, 119–20; and termination prompting repatriation, 113–16; in U.S., 121n7

docility, deportability used to encourage, 31–32, 126n34

documentary analysis, 36–37

domestic workers (Canadian citizens/permanent residents): "Canadians first" approach to hiring and, 40, 88, 119; efforts to recruit, documenting in LMIA, 89; SAWP employees distinguished from, 42, 51, 53, 55–56; at Sidhu, reluctance to support unionization, 129n1; use of term, 133n6

Dunmore case, 51, 53, 125n29, 129n7

employer(s): and attrition, 40; as beneficiaries of migration management/TMWPs, 2, 15, 34, 111, 115, 137n1; and blacklisting, 39; on CA as secondary to TMWP terms, 61; collusion with bargaining unit members, 96–97; collusion with Mexican officials, 73, 74, 80, 82, 96, 97–98; flexibility in adjusting size and composition of temporary migrant workforce, 3, 4, 9, 28, 44, 86, 87, 88–89, 98, 119; LMIA applications by, 89, 90, 94, 133n8; manipulation of recall process by, 9, 92, 93, 94–99, 104; modes of control granted to, 44–45; need for greater accountability of, 94; power asymmetries with SAWP employees, 28, 31, 113; resort to different (deregulated) streams of TMWPs, 84–85, 107, 108, 118, 119; resort to non-unionized employees, 9, 85, 86, 99–103, 104, 105; sending states seeking to appease, 8; temporary migration for employment and benefits for, 16; and termination without just cause, 38, 45–46

employer associations, and SAWP administration/oversight, 23, 24, 27
employer evaluations, under TMWP, 38–39, 46–47; and blacklisting, 39, 47, 116–17; and deportability, 4, 38, 47, 88; as means of flagging troublemakers, 39, 47, 116–17; and online system (SIMOL), 46; publication of, recommendation for, 118; and recall, 39, 47, 68, 88
employer surveillance: and blacklisting, 128n47; and difficulty organizing, 85, 108
Employment and Social Development Canada (ESDC): HRSDC and, 123n13; LMIAs issued by, 24, 123n13, 123n14
Employment Standards Act (ESA), British Columbia, 25
ethnographic approaches, to study of deportability, 126n36
EU countries, seasonal migrant workers in, 17, 123n11
European Migrant Workers' Union, 138n5
evaluation process. See employer evaluations
exploitation of migrant workers: in agriculture, 22, 124n17; corporate sector and, 14, 122n2; TMWPs' contribution to, 22
extra-economic coercion, 32

farm labor contractor system, in BC, 125n28, 129n1
FARMS, and operation/oversight of SAWP, 23, 24, 113, 124n20
federal government, Canadian, and oversight of SAWP, 23, 124n19
feminist objectivity, 6, 13, 35–36; and reflexivity, 35, 127n40
FERME, and operation/oversight of SAWP, 23, 24, 113, 124n20
field, notion of, 127n38
Floralia Plant Growers Ltd.: attrition strategies used by, 3, 9, 64, 94–99, 107; decertification attempt at, 9, 65, 70, 71, 83, 85, 90, 91–93, 133n14; facility-sharing agreement with S&G, 133n15; interruption in operations at, 107, 136n37; LMIA applications submitted by, 90, 103–4; Local 1518's bid to represent all-employee bargaining unit at, 86, 91; manipulation of recall process by, 94–99, 96t; ownership structure at, 101t; resort to non-unionized employees by, 99–103, 119; and S&G, as common employers, 85, 92, 93, 99–103, 104–5, 106, 134n16; termination of SAWP employees at, 46, 48, 91, 129n2, 131n20;

unfair labor practices complaint against, 9, 86–87, 93–105, 129n2
Fondation des Entreprises en Recrutement de la Main-d'oeuvre. See FERME
Foreign Agricultural Resource Management Service. See FARMS
Foucault, Michel, 127n38
Fraser, Nancy, 23, 31
Fraser decision, 125n29
Frontex, 122n3
Fudge, Judy, 33, 34, 125n29
functional integration: as criterion of bargaining-unit determination, 48; as principal concern for LRB, 60

Gabriel, Christina, 18, 21, 28, 34, 127n37
Geiger, Martin, 14, 15, 22
gender: of immigrant agricultural workers in Canada, 125n28, 129n1; and migration management, 16; in SAWP, 23, 123n7, 127n39; and Wagnerian orientation of BC's LRC, 7
geography, as criterion for bargaining-unit determination, 48, 49, 52, 129n8
Ghosh, Bimal, 13–14
global capitalism: deterritorialized, vs. territory-based labor laws, 27, 112, 120; and migration management, 111; and race to the bottom, 83; racialized character of, 23; and TMWPs, literature on, 23, 34–35
Goldring, Luin, 34
Gordon, Jennifer, 137n5
Greenway Farms Ltd.: certification of bargaining unit at, 26–27, 126n30; LRB decision on (2009), 48, 61
grievance and arbitration procedures, for SAWP employees: CA and, 61–62, 65; need for, 5, 60; repatriation before, 64
Guatemala, participation in TMWPs, 22, 108, 136n40

H2-A program (U.S.), 28
Hanley, Jill, 124n16
Haraway, Donna, 13, 33, 35–36, 37, 127n41
Harvey, David, 23
Heery, Edmund, 128n47
Hennebry, Jenna, 18, 21, 23, 24, 27, 28, 31, 34, 57, 68, 128n48
high-skilled positions: in agriculture, trends in Canada, 20t; in migration for employment, 15
hiring hall model, 116, 137n5
Hoffman Plastic Compounds, 121n7